Continuum Renaissance Drama

Series Editors: Andrew Hiscock, University of Wales Bangor, UK and Lisa Hopkins, Sheffield Hallam University, UK

Continuum Renaissance Drama offers practical and accessible introductions to the critical and performative contexts of key Elizabethan and Jacobean plays. Each guide introduces the text's critical and performance history but also provides students with an invaluable insight into the landscape of current scholarly research through a keynote essay on the state of the art and newly commissioned essays of fresh research from different critical perspectives.

KING LEAR

A Critical Guide

Edited by Andrew Hiscock and Lisa Hopkins

continuum

Continuum International Publishing Group

The Tower Building	80 Maiden Lane, Suite 704
11 York Road	New York
London SE1 7NX	NY 10038

www.continuumbooks.com

British Library Cataloguing-in-Publication Data
A catalogue record for this book is available from the British Library.

ISBN: 978-1-4411-5896-3 (Paperback)
       978-1-4411-3041-9 (Hardback)

Library of Congress Cataloguing-in-Publication Data
A catalog record for this book is available from the Library of Congress.

Typeset by Newgen Imaging Systems Pvt Ltd, Chennai, India
Printed and bound in Great Britain

Contents

Series Introduction

The drama of Shakespeare and his contemporaries has remained at the very heart of English curricula internationally and the pedagogic needs surrounding this body of literature have grown increasingly complex as more sophisticated resources become available to scholars, tutors and students. This series aims to offer a clear picture of the critical and performative contexts of a range of chosen texts. In addition, each volume furnishes readers with invaluable insights into the landscape of current scholarly research as well as including new pieces of research by leading critics.

This series is designed to respond to the clearly identified needs of scholars, tutors and students for volumes which will bridge the gap between accounts of previous critical developments and performance history and an acquaintance with new research initiatives related to the chosen plays. Thus, our ambition is to offer innovative and challenging Guides which will provide practical, accessible and thought-provoking analyses of Renaissance drama. Each volume is organised according to a progressive reading strategy involving introductory discussion, critical review and cutting-edge scholarly debate. It has been an enormous pleasure to work with so many dedicated scholars of Renaissance drama and we are sure that this series will encourage to you read 400-year old playtexts with fresh eyes.

Andrew Hiscock and Lisa Hopkins

Preface

King Lear has seen some dramatic changes in its critical fortunes since it was first composed circa 1605–6. In preparing a tragedy for the stage, Shakespeare took not one but two stories which were already familiar to his audience. The first concerned the pseudo-historical King Leir, mentioned in Geoffrey of Monmouth's *History of the Kings of Britain*, whose story would have been familiar to Shakespeare's audience because it had recently been retold in the anonymous play *The Chronicle History of King Leir*. The second was related in Sir Philip Sidney's epic (and unfinished) romance *The Countess of Pembroke's Arcadia* as the story of the blind king of Paphlagonia and his two sons: one good and loyal, like Edgar; the other ambitious and treacherous, like Edmund. Shakespeare would make significant changes to the original narratives themselves but, in bringing them together, he also forced the narratives to speak to each other, just as the main plot and the sub-plot of the play mirror and cast light upon each other.

Recent scholarship has continued to be exercised by the complex relationship between Shakespeare's tragic narratives and his sources, and indeed between the differing versions of the play which have survived into the modern period in the shape of the Quarto and Folio versions published during the Jacobean period. Time and space now have to be made for these thorny issues, alongside more abiding interests in the Shakespearean dramatizations of: temporal power and social order; multifarious human investments in cosmology, theology and morality; the status and functions of the nation and political violence; and the performance and reception of this celebrated tragedy down the centuries, across continents and via increasingly diverse media. This volume is designed to extend reader interest in all of these areas, and to establish newer angles of vision on the tragedy by raising questions about seventeenth-century Britishness, early modern understandings of landscape, the changing interpretations of 'self-murder' in this period and the implications of the insatiable appetite for Shakespearean adaptation.

The 1608 text of the play describes itself as a history and in the 1623 text we are presented with a 'tragedy': indeed, it is because of the continuing and vigorous editorial debates surrounding the relationships between, and the integrity of, these two different texts that the contributors to this volume have of necessity made choices from the variety of modern editions of *King Lear* in their own analyses which follow. René Weis's introduction maps out the reception of the play from 1606 to the present day, ranging widely across engagements with it over the centuries in the forms of editions, performances, critical debates and adaptations, and he focuses particularly on the long struggle of critics and audiences alike to come to terms with the chaos and apparent nihilism which has so often been perceived as lying at the very heart of this tragedy. In the chapter devoted to the 'Critical Backstory', Joan Fitzpatrick reviews in detail the reception of *King Lear* by attending to the seventeenth-century desire to shine a light on the tragedy's 'faults' and to 'amend' it through 'refining' its (perceived) narrative excesses and its distressing dénouement. The development of *King Lear* as a reading, rather than a theatrical, experience is considered, as well as the manner in which the tragedy has responded to critical appetites for psychological interest and the interrogation of early modern social theories. With regard to the contemporary period, Fitzpatrick demonstrates how *King Lear* emerged as a primary text upon which to test a succession of different critical procedures which might involve the study of thematic continuities in figurative language, early modern 'world pictures', constructions of heroism, interrogations of ideology and history, or dilemmas of performativity.

The next chapter by Ramona Wray extends these emphases by exploring the ways in which performance itself is a critical undertaking. Of particular relevance here is Wray's insistence that *King Lear* has presented film and stage directors (and novelists) with particular and abiding problems concerning the communication of communal life, political heroism, distinctions of rank and race, and the evocation of familial identity and human loss. Her decision to attend to the internationalization of the Lear narrative during the twentieth century contributes importantly to this volume's more general interest in the global appropriation of Shakespeare's writing. Philippa Kelly's discussion of the state of the (critical) art concerning *King Lear* may be firmly linked with the preceding discussions. Kelly initially focuses upon scholars' consuming interests in the play, its potential engagement with early modern theological debates, and latterly how it has been seen by critics to speak to audiences who often belong to non-Christian or post-Christian cultural environments. She then considers the evolving debates surrounding (self-)government, familial allegiance, criminal violation and economic marginality in contemporary scholarship concerning *King Lear*. Her discussion is brought to an impressive close by reviewing not only the proliferation of *King Lears* for international consumption in the twenty-first century in terms of multi-medial performance, but also the enormous diversity of texts now available for what has been perceived as a fiendishly intractable playtext by generations of editors.

Lori Anne Ferrell opens the *New Directions* section focusing upon the intriguing, and often competing, cultural inflections associated with suicide in the early modern period. What Ferrell views as 'the suicide-trick' may be seen to have wide-ranging effects upon the play's generic affiliations, our understanding of its relations with its sources, and seventeenth-century formulations of subjectivity. However, Ferrell's treatment of 'self-murder' expands equally interestingly beyond the consideration of the single subject to embrace a consideration of the threat it poses to familial and political union in this Jacobean dramatic narrative. In the next chapter, Anthony Parr not only attends to the enduring critical formulation of *King Lear* as Shakespeare's 'central achievement', he reflects upon the ways in which the well-established critical interest in Shakespeare's representation of 'Nature' may negotiate the twenty-first-century preoccupation with the ecological implications of human habitat. Beginning with an exploration of the Christian promotion of a divinely created environment which awaits human husbandry, Parr discusses at length early modern anxieties concerning the tractability, scrutability and senescence of the natural environment. He unveils a *King Lear* which acts as a fulcrum for the working out of these widely held attitudes to the landscape at the turn of the seventeenth century and encourages us to ponder how these concerns may link with vigorous cultural debate, then and now, relating to the decay of both natural orders of existence and human codes of ethical obligation. John J. Norton brings the *New Directions* section to a close by re-inscribing Shakespeare's tragedy tightly within early modern theological debate concerning spiritual discipline. Examining Reformation doctrines of human fallen-ness, 'plain dealing' and spiritual witness, Norton analyses how *King Lear* stages scenes of human failing in order to urge audiences to reflect upon how 'prideful men are brought into a right relationship with themselves, with others, and ultimately with God'.

In the final chapters of this volume, Willy Maley offers an ambitious critical review of the ways in which *King Lear* is increasingly being perceived as a play which engages with and problematizes Britishness in the early years of James VI/I's rule, when the new king was aggressively promulgating an idea of a united Britain to which many of his subjects were very strongly resistant. Teasing out the many and complicated strands of *King Lear*'s topicality, Maley also traces the growing critical emergence of a British perspective on the play and maps the fissures and disagreements in the resulting body of work. In his examination of the resources now available to readers, students and scholars, Peter Sillitoe showcases the continuing richness and diversity of the critical and editorial discussions surrounding the tragedy and the ways in which this tragedy may be analysed in the university classroom. His chapter concludes with an invaluable annotated bibliography detailing many of the most recent publications linked to *King Lear*.

Sir Philip Sidney had declared poetry – by which he essentially meant fiction – to be more ennobling than history because truth was often sordid, whereas poetry could attain to the ideal rather than the merely real, and thus inspire high thoughts and good behaviour in its readers. If *King Lear* were a tragedy, it would belong to the realm categorized by Sidney as poetic, and would also be expected to effect an Aristotelian catharsis in its readers; if it were a history, it would belong to a very different realm, and would be expected by its Jacobean readers to reflect on contemporary political issues, as indeed it does with a story of a 'British' king with two sons-in-law whose titles echoed those of James VI/I's sons. The continuing failure of this text to be shoe-horned convincingly within any critical categories (history play, heroic tragedy, tragedy of state, tragedy of love, the list goes on) has inevitably excited continuing debate and this critical collection bears witness to the endlessly perplexing and stimulating character of Shakespeare's great work – and to the fact that Shakespeare's tragedy continues to challenge audiences in the twenty-first century just as much as it did in the seventeenth.

Andrew Hiscock and Lisa Hopkins

Acknowledgements

It has been an enormous pleasure to work with so many committed scholars in the preparation of this volume. As editors, our main difficulty has been to ensure that all the many and various perspectives which the contributors proposed might be contained within the page allocation for the volume. Our thanks go out to all the contributors for the enormously stimulating scholarship which has been invested in the chapters which follow, but especially to Linda Jones, research administrator at Bangor University, who oversaw the preparation of this volume. Her contribution has proved invaluable, and the collection could not have been completed without her input. We would also like to take this opportunity to thank once again our long-suffering families, Chris and Sam Hopkins, Siân, Bronwen and Huw Hiscock. We could not have done it without your support.

Timeline

c. 1136: Likely date of composition of Geoffrey of Monmouth, *Historia Regum Britanniae*, which contains the earliest known version of the story of King Lear

1534: Polydore Vergil's *Historia Anglica* casts doubt on the veracity of the 'British History'

1577: Raphael Holinshed's *Chronicles of England, Scotland and Ireland* include the story of Lear and his daughters

6 and 8 April 1594: Only known performances of the anonymous play *The Chronicle History of King Leir* at the Rose (there may well have been others)

14 May 1594: *The Chronicle History of King Leir* entered in the Stationers' Register

8 May 1605: *The Chronicle History of King Leir* entered again in the Stationers' Register and published later that year

27 September and 2 October 1605: a solar eclipse followed a few days later by a lunar eclipse which may well lie behind the play's reference to eclipses of the sun and moon

5 November 1605: Gunpowder Plot

16 December 1606: *King Lear* acted at court – this is the first known performance

1608: Publication of the Quarto version (Q1)

1619: Publication of Q2

1623: Publication of the First Folio (F1)

1681: Nahum Tate publishes a version of the play in which the good characters survive and Cordelia marries Edgar

1725: Pope's edition of Shakespeare offers the first conflated text of the play

1765: Dr Johnson's edition of *King Lear* in which he mentions that he had in his younger years been so shocked by the death of Cordelia that he had never reread the play before editing it

1838: William Charles Macready restores Shakespeare's text to the stage

1875: Edward Dowden, *Shakspere: A Critical Study of his Mind and Art*

1904: A. C. Bradley, *Shakespearean Tragedy*

1906: Tolstoy castigates *Lear* as 'absurd'

1930: G. Wilson Knight, *The Wheel of Fire*

1931: Madeleine Doran, *The Text of 'King Lear'*

1940: W. W. Greg, *The variants in the first quarto of 'King Lear'*

1948: Robert B. Heilman, *This Great Stage: Image and Structure in 'King Lear'*

1950: George Orwell, 'Lear, Tolstoy and the Fool'

1952: The second Arden edition, edited by Kenneth Muir

1960: Barbara Everett, 'The New *King Lear*'

1964: Jan Kott's '*King Lear* or *Endgame*', in *Shakespeare Our Contemporary*

1966: William Elton, *King Lear and the Gods*

1971: Grigori Kozintsev's film *Korol Lir*; Peter Brook's film *King Lear*; Edward Bond, *Lear*

1983: Gary Taylor and Michael Warren, *The Division of the Kingdoms: Shakespeare's Two Versions of 'King Lear'*

1985: Akira Kurosawa's film *Ran* adapts the Lear story

1986: The Oxford University Press edition of the Complete Works prints both Q and F

1987: Jean-Luc Godard's film *King Lear*

1991: Jane Smiley's novel *A Thousand Acres*

1993: René Weis's parallel-text edition of the play and R. A. Foakes, *Hamlet versus Lear*

1997: The third Arden edition, edited by R. A. Foakes

2000: Stanley Wells's Oxford edition prints only Q1. Kristian Levring's film *The King is Alive*

2001: Uli Edel's film *King of Texas*; Don Boyd's film *My Kingdom*

2007: Rituparno Ghosh's film *The Last Lear*

9 October 2010: Alexander Goehr's *Promised End*, an opera based on *King Lear*, premieres at the Royal Opera House, Covent Garden

Introduction: *King Lear* 1606–2009

René Weis

The reception of *King Lear* from 1606 to the present day is one of coming to terms with the play's desolation and its stubborn refusal to offer solace. This tension is reflected even in the different ways in which the two early printed texts present the death of Cordelia and Lear's response to it. In the 1608 Quarto, Lear's last speech reads:

> *Lear*: And my poor fool is hanged. No, no life.
> Why should a dog, a horse, a rat have life,
> And thou no breath at all? O, thou wilt come no more.
> Never, never, never. Pray you, undo
> This button. Thank you, sir. O, O, O, O!
> *Edgar*: He faints. My lord, my lord.
> *[Kent / (Lear?)]: Break, heart, I prithee break. [Lear dies]*
> *Edgar*: Look up, my lord.
> *Kent*: Vex not his ghost. O, let him pass. He hates him
> That would upon the rack of this tough world
> Stretch him out longer. (Q1, 5.3.297–307)[1]

In the 1623 Folio this becomes:

> *Lear*: And my poor fool is hanged. No, no, no life.
> Why should a dog, a horse, a rat have life,
> And thou no breath at all? Thou'lt come no more.
> Never, never, never, never, never.
> Pray you, undo this button. Thank you, sir.
> Do you see this? Look on her, look, her lips,
> Look there, look there. *He dies*

| *Edgar*: | He faints. My lord, my lord. |
| *Kent*: | Break, heart, I prithee break. (F1, 5.3.279–87) |

In Shakespeare's original draft of the play – the 1608 Quarto is based on foul papers – Lear dies in a paroxysm of grief. His last sounds are not human speech at all, but the wailing lament 'O, O, O, O!' He is reduced to nothing, that very 'O without a figure' prophesied earlier by the Fool. Repeatedly language in the play contracts to the barest phonetic minimum, whether in 'Off, off', 'Now, now, now, now', or 'kill, kill, kill, kill, kill, kill'. Lear is suffocating from despair and his heart breaks. It is a moot point whether or not he revives for a fleeting moment to speak the apostrophic 'Break, heart, I prithee break', which is given to Kent in F1 but to Lear in Q1. It should probably be Kent's in Q1 as well, the more so since 'Kt' and 'Lr' are easily confused, especially in lower case, which may be the preferred form of Hand D (Shakespeare's longhand) of *Sir Thomas More*. In Folio 'O, O, O, O!' becomes 'Do you see this? Look on her, look, her lips, / Look there, look there. *He dies*' (F1, 5.3.308–9). An aura of ambiguity now surrounds Lear's death. Perhaps he, too, is after all allowed to die like Gloucester whose 'flawed heart, / Alack too weak the conflict to support, / Twixt two extremes of passion, joy and grief, / Burst smilingly' (Q1, 5.3.90–93).

Up to this point the construction of the two betrayed fathers has served above all to underline the contrasts between them. Would they really be joined by Shakespeare in Lear's death? In a play obsessed with the metaphors and reality of sight and blindness, Lear's final invitation in the Folio to the others to join him in *looking*, reiterated four times, carries a strong emotional charge. Does it chime though with the play's wider imaginative patterning in which rare moments of hope are flagged up only to be shot down? Just this is what happens in 5.2, when Edgar enters with Gloucester and instructs him 'Here, father, take the shadow of this bush [. . .] If ever I return to you again / I'll bring you comfort' (Q1, 5.2.1–4). Edgar exits. Gloucester has just enough time to shout 'Grace go with you, sir' before Edgar rushes back in again with 'Away, old man [. . .] away! / King Lear hath lost' (Q1, 5.2.5–7). So much for his promise to bring his father salvation. He is barely off-stage for more than two or three seconds. Glimpses of hope in the play last no longer.

The centre cannot hold in *Lear*, which is now commonly acclaimed as Shakespeare's greatest play. Although it is not possible to be absolutely certain, the most likely date of composition is 1605–6, following the lunar and solar eclipses of September and October 1605. Gloucester appears to allude to these when he remarks that

These late eclipses in the sun and moon portend no good to us. Though the wisdom of nature can reason thus and thus, yet nature finds itself scourged by the sequent effects. Love cools, friendship falls off, brothers divide; in cities mutinies, in countries discords, palaces treason, the bond cracked between son and father. (Q1, 1.2.97–102)

Barely three weeks after the solar eclipse the Gunpowder Plot happened on 5 November 1605. It was a non-event, as it turned out, but one which nevertheless rocked the nation to the core by showing up severe fault lines in the flimsy fabric of the Stuart attempts to reconcile Catholics and Protestants. Yeats's phrasing from the first stanza of his poem 'The Second Coming' could be the epigraph of Shakespeare's apocalyptic *Lear*: 'Things fall apart; the centre cannot hold [. . .] The ceremony of innocence is drowned; / The best lack all conviction, while the worst / Are full of passionate intensity.'[2] To paraphrase a further line from Yeats's poem 'Easter, 1916', in *Lear* a terrible beauty is born: it is a work about nothing, maybe even signifying nothing, since in it good, if not saintly, characters like Cordelia die unrewarded. In the eighteenth century, Samuel Johnson struggled with this radical aspect of the play while Jan Kott, writing after the horrors of the Second World War, saw in it the clearest proof of Shakespeare's visionary, if not transcendent, greatness. In his essay '*King Lear*, or *Endgame*', in a book suggestively entitled *Shakespeare our Contemporary* (1964), Kott writes about *Lear* that

> this new *Book of Job*, or a new Dantean *Inferno*, was written towards the close of the Renaissance. In Shakespeare's play there is neither Christian heaven, nor the heaven predicted and believed in by humanists. *King Lear* makes a tragic mockery of all eschatologies: of the heaven promised on earth, and the heaven promised after death; in fact – of both Christian and secular theodicies; of cosmogony and of the rational view of history; of the gods and natural goodness, of man made in the 'image and likeness'. In *King Lear*, both the medieval and the renaissance orders of established values disintegrate. All that remains at the end of this gigantic pantomime is the earth – empty and bleeding.[3]

The fact that *Lear* exists in two discrete early versions curiously consolidates its defining relationship with instability. At least since the publication in 1986 by Oxford University Press of *The Complete Works*, a number of influential scholars have argued that some years after first writing *Lear* Shakespeare revised it extensively so that the two distinct early versions of the play, one preserved in a Quarto of 1608 and the other in the First Folio of 1623, may in fact both be authentic Shakespearean versions.

   Lear was probably completed in time for the resumption of playing after Lent in 1606 and was performed at court on Boxing Day that year.

It is likely that it was put on at the Globe Theatre on Bankside shortly after it was finished. Shakespeare, it seems, also wrote *Macbeth* and *Antony and Cleopatra* in 1606, his creativity aided and abetted by the fact that the theatres closed in July 1606. The fact that *Lear* was picked over its two successors for the Court performance suggests that it enjoyed a certain popularity, notwithstanding the demands it makes of its audience. Not the least of the play's many attractions is its searing indictment of political power not grounded in compassion and empathy, as in Lear's 'O, I have ta'en / Too little care of this. Take physic, pomp, / Expose thyself to feel what wretches feel, / That thou mayst shake the superflux to them / And show the heavens more just' (Q1, 3.4.28–32). To see the world feelingly, one of the core imaginative concerns of the play, it is first required to suffer on an equal footing in the abyss with starving beggars and madmen, among others 'eating cow-dung for sallets' and slurping the algae ('green mantle') of standing pools for sustenance.

The death of Cordelia has divided later generations more than any other aspect of Shakespeare's play, which is why in 1681 Nahum Tate rewrote Shakespeare's tragedy as a melodrama called *The History of King Lear*, ending with the marriage of Edgar and Cordelia. The two of them, Tate admits in his dedication and prologue, 'never chang'd a Word with each other in the Original'. In the recast version Cordelia's love for Edgar renders, he notes, her 'Indifference, and her Father's Passion' in the opening scene of the play 'probable' (that is, plausible) and would likewise account satisfactorily for Edgar's disguise, 'making that a generous Design that was before a poor Shift to save his Life', thus concluding 'in a Success to the innocent distrest Persons'.[4]

Tate's tragicomedy held sway until 1838 when William Charles Macready at last reverted to Shakespeare's text. By the time Tate was writing his version of *Lear*, the third seventeenth-century one after 1608 Q1 and 1623 F1, the English theatre had changed. From the rough and tumble of a lawless Elizabethan–Jacobean idiom, one which tolerated clowns and madmen in the primal creative soup of *Lear* (Tate called it 'a Heap of Jewels, unstrung, and unpolisht' though 'dazling in their Disorder'[5]), it now became impregnated by the neoclassicism to which the Court had become exposed during its French exile. Decorum, Tate claimed, played a part in his decision to end his *Lear* in marriage because, 'Otherwise I must have incumbred the Stage with dead Bodies, which Conduct makes many Tragedies conclude with unseasonable Jests.'[6]

Such dread of unseemly raucousness at live performances was not uppermost in Samuel Johnson's mind when in the 1765 preface to his edition of Shakespeare he rallied behind Tate's melodrama, at the expense of Shakespeare's play. For Johnson the death of Cordelia showed up the distance Shakespeare's play had strayed from what Johnson considered to be the true function of a work of literature: 'Shakespeare has suffered the virtue of Cordelia to perish in a just cause, contrary to the natural ideas of justice, to the hope of the reader and, what is yet more strange, to the faith of chronicles.' Johnson concedes that 'a play in which the wicked prosper and the virtuous miscarry may doubtless be good, because it is a just representation of the common events of human life; but since all reasonable beings naturally love justice, I cannot easily be persuaded that the observation of justice makes a play worse.'[7] Underpinning Johnson's response to Shakespeare's *Lear* is a polemical sense of the proper purpose of literature. In his view, audiences relish the vindication of goodness and the punishment of evil even though, or perhaps especially because, life is hardly fair: poetic justice is there to provide a panacea for the sorrows of the real world's injustices.

Shakespeare's play pulls towards chaos at every juncture, notably in its apparently random plotting and in the cruelty of the blinding of Gloucester. The fact that he chose to let Cordelia die in the teeth of the authority of his sources (cf. Bullough's *Narrative and Dramatic Sources*)[8] constitutes clear intent on Shakespeare's part with regard to the darkness of the final scene. At the end of *Lear* the play's three women, sisters and daughters of the king, are all dead. Over their untimely, violent demise there hovers the shadow of their dead mother. When Lear meets Regan in 2.4 after his caustic encounter earlier with Goneril, he replies to her disingenuous welcome, 'I am glad to see your highness', with, 'Regan, I think you are. I know what reason / I have to think so. If thou shouldst not be glad / I would divorce me from thy mother's tomb, / Sepulchring an adult'ress' (Q1, 2.4.102–7). This is the only reference in the play to the daughters' mother. She is missing too in the source play *King Leir* (1594; printed 1605), but is there prominently present by her absence because the earlier play begins with a long tribute by the bereaved king to her: 'Thus to our griefe the obsequies performd / Of our (too late) deceast and dearest Queen' he starts, and then notes that he intends to marry off his daughters 'For wanting [lacking] now their mothers good advice, / Under whose government they have receyved / A perfit patterne of a virtuous life' (*King Leir* 1.1.1–14).[9] The memory of the sisters' mother from *Leir* lingered in Shakespeare's mind and imagination as far-flung materials from his sources often do, breaking through the texture of his play sooner or later, and often unexpectedly so.

A dead mother and all her daughters, too – what is left is a sterile masculine world without the prospect of renewal. When in the Young Vic production of *Lear* in 2009 Rupert Goold cast Caroline Faber as a heavily pregnant Goneril (Lear was played by Pete Postlethwaite), he was responding creatively to a powerful prompt from Act 1 scene 4, when Lear evokes a curse of childlessness on his eldest daughter:

> *Lear.* It may be so, my lord. Hark, nature; hear,
> Dear goddess. Suspend thy purpose if
> Thou didst intend to make this creature fruitful.
> Into her womb convey sterility;
> Dry up in her the organs of increase,
> And from her derogate body never spring
> A babe to honour her. If she must teem,
> Create her child of spleen, that it may live
> And be a thwart disnatured torment to her.
> Let it stamp wrinkles in her brow of youth,
> With cadent tears fret channels in her cheeks,
> Turn all her mother's pains and benefits
> To laughter and contempt; that she may feel
> How sharper than a serpent's tooth it is
> To have a thankless child. (Q1, 1.4.261–75)

Goneril with child gives pause for thought, but it forms an integral part of the play's obsessive concerns with sexuality, particularly the female organs of generation, which are excoriated by Lear in 4.6 in a monomaniacal invective against the bogus coyness of women:

> Down from the waist
> They are centaurs, though women all above;
> But to the girdle do the gods inherit,
> Beneath is all the fiend's: there's hell, there's darkness,
> There's the sulphurous pit, burning, scalding,
> Stench, consumption. Fie, fie, fie; pah, pah. (Q1, 4.5[6].119–24)

We are at a long remove here from the romantic worlds of Shakespearean comedy. The nuptial conclusions of his comedies paradigmatically associate the sexual union of men and women with a future of children born beyond the conclusion of the plays; *Lear* instead equates with emptiness and death. It dramatizes a story of humankind tearing itself apart inside the most universally recognized space of natural bonding, the family, a microcosm of society based on instinct and blood rather than social and legal contract. Albany's anguished cry in 4.2, 'If that the heavens do not their visible spirits / Send quickly down to tame these vile offences, / It will come / Humanity must perforce prey on itself / Like monsters of the deep' (Q1, 4.2.44–48), carries the same charge as Salvador Dali's 1936 painting *Premonition of Civil War*.

Some of the theological and political burden of Albany's words may be lost on modern audiences who, unlike Shakespeare and his contemporaries, are not exposed to Scripture in the home or at compulsory church attendance, obliged to listen to countless homilies from the pulpit.[10] As it is, Shakespeare's *Lear* coincides with a time of unparalleled questioning of old orthodoxies, including the rejection of Ptolemaic astronomy and physics by Johannes Kepler (1571–1630), whose revolutionary thinking about the laws of gravitation vindicated Galileo. Shakespeare was born in the same year as Galileo, who proved that the earth revolved around the sun, and twenty-one years after the death of Nicolaus Copernicus (1473–1543), who first proposed supplanting the ancient theocentric model of the universe with a heliocentric one. The science that would change the world and cause religion to tumble was just emerging, and Shakespeare bears witness to it in the profound theological scepticism of *Hamlet* and in the secular *aporia* of *Lear*. The inquisitive and religiously self-divided John Donne responded to the *Zeitgeist* by writing in 'The Anatomy of the World' that 'new philosophy calls all in doubt, / The element of fire is quite put out, / The sun is lost, and th' earth, and no man's wit / Can well direct him where to look for it.'[11]

The grim closures at the end of *Lear* are that much more final as there is no resurrection envisaged beyond the grave, no walking together in paradise of king and daughter of the kind granted by Christ on the cross to one of the two thieves who shared his fate on Golgotha: 'And Jesus said unto him, Verily I say unto thee, Today shalt thou be with me in paradise' (Luke 23. 43). The play may be an imaginative crucifixion in post-1945 readings, but that is where its links with the metaphors of Christianity stop; resurrection there is none in *Lear*.

Johnson was editing Shakespeare four years before David Garrick's Stratford Jubilee in 1769, which helped enshrine Shakespeare in the national consciousness as a font of essential wisdom about life. What George Bernard Shaw would later call 'bardolatry', the worshipping of Shakespeare as a uniquely privileged mind and imagination, a guide for living, torch rather than mirror, was born then even if the word itself only dates from 1901. The poetic use of 'bard' applied to Shakespeare seems first to enter the language with Garrick who wrote 'For the bard of all bards was a Warwickshire Bard' (*OED* 'bard' n^1.4). In the course of the eighteenth century, from Nicholas Rowe's first edition and biography of 1709 to Johnson's 1765 edition and preface, the plays moved to the forefront of the national culture, no longer bound to performance in the capital's theatres but now there to be read as well as seen. Through print Shakespeare's reputation spread nationally and internationally.

If a broad sweep of moral and socially responsible views of the function of literature underlies Johnson's responses to *Lear*, the next movement in English literature, the so-called Romantics, produced readers who treated the plays as dramatic poetry above all. Foremost among them was Keats. In a letter of December 1817, best known for its definition of the genius of Shakespeare as 'Negative Capability, that is when man is capable of being in uncertainties, Mysteries, doubts, without any irritable reaching after fact & reason', he homed in on *Lear* as the epitome of great art claiming that the

> excellence of every art is its intensity, capable of making all disagreeables evaporate from their being in close relationship with Beauty & Truth – Examine King Lear & you will find this exemplified throughout.[12]

Keats's use of capital letters for Beauty and Truth is significant here. For him these are the cardinal virtues of great art; compared to them nothing else matters. *Lear* is undoubtedly full of 'disagreeables', but its language, passion or 'intensity' and its time in history raise it above specific moral concerns. Keats's framing of his praise of *Lear* in terms of the wider 'excellence of every art' shows that his sense of this play's greatness is just as bound up with implicit views on the nature of art as Johnson's; only his is a broader understanding of art from the one proposed in the eighteenth century. Keats's lines about the play's intensity were triggered by his seeing the 1796 picture *Death on the Pale Horse* by Benjamin West. What brought to mind the idea that *Lear* above all others constituted the highest form of artistic achievement, through transforming moral chaos into great art, was evidently the apocalyptic motif of West's painting.

Keats's text of *Lear* was that of the First Folio of 1623, of which he owned an 1808 facsimile. It is into this that he wrote out his poem about the play, which he had originally inserted into a letter to his brothers. Keats's sonnet 'On sitting down to King Lear once Again' (thus in his letter, but later in his Shakespeare Folio the title of the revised poem – used here for citing – is 'On Sitting Down to Read King Lear Once Again') is redolent of Aristotle's biochemical interpretation of the impact on us of great tragedy. In his letter of 23, 24 January 1818, Keats remarked about *Lear* that 'the thing appeared to demand the prologue of a Sonnet',[13] which he then provided. He knew of course from his Folio facsimile that *Romeo and Juliet* was prefaced by a sonnet, which in fourteen short lines charts the whole plot of the play. Keats's sonnet does nothing of the kind. Rather, it is a subjective expression of the impact of Shakespeare's play on him.

The quintessence of *Lear* for Keats is 'the fierce dispute, / betwixt damnation and impassioned clay'.[14] Reading the play is to 'burn through', to be 'consumed' in its fire before finally rising on phoenix wings. His vision of the play is Dantesque, including the metaphor of wandering through the old oak forest of life before dying into a new imaginative life through the experience of *Lear*. Keats did not just 'read' the tragedy but ingested it, hence the aptness of 'the bitter-sweet of this Shakespearian fruit'. There is nothing passive about Keats's response to the play. For him *Lear* is not a product, a text read in a study, but an active, life-transforming experience which engenders a spiritual renewal of the self. In the famous sixth chapter of *Poetics*, Aristotle noted that tragedy is an imitative art, a relentless turning of the screws of plot until such time that the resolution, when it comes, is inevitable, final, and curiously satisfying. The main *raison d'être* of such an art that hurts or is disagreeable is the purging it induces in the audience. Tragedy for Aristotle is a form of therapy, if not exorcism. He was thinking primarily of *Oedipus Rex* when he described the psychosomatic impact of tragedy, an idiom in which human responsibility hardly features: try as he might Oedipus cannot escape his fate and whatever he did wrong – kill his father, marry his mother, beget his own brothers and sisters – he did so without intent or knowledge. Lear, on the other hand, bears a heavy burden of responsibility, even if he may be more sinned against than sinning.

Keats's *Lear* and Johnson's are quite different plays: a strong censor controls and guides the responses of the older man while Keats surrenders himself to the enchantment of Shakespeare's drama, sinking 'lethewards' without feeling the need to probe the play's implications as a social act. Keats's exceptional poetic gifts equipped him superbly as a reader of Shakespeare. Not a word here about what Johnson might have deemed to be the moral irresponsibility of an art that contemplates the slaughter of the innocent without proper counterbalance. The young cockney poet asserted the fundamental good faith of Shakespeare's play that its terrible beauty resides precisely in its being a true representation of life. He was not likely to be tempted by what would become the distinctive categories of the century of the novel, realism and character.

Keats's pronouncements on *Lear* coincide with the publication in 1818 of Dr Thomas Bowdler's *The Family Shakespeare, in Ten Volumes; in which nothing is added to the original text; but those words and expressions are omitted which cannot with propriety be read aloud in a family.* With the 'Family Shakespeare', Bowdler uncannily anticipated the anxieties of the dawning new age, a squeamishness about the sometimes raw sexuality of Shakespeare's plays rather than their ideological content. The Victorians could hardly have Juliet yearn for sex with Romeo, as she undoubtedly does in 3.2 which opens with her longing for night to approach, 'Gallop apace, you fiery-footed steeds'. Bowdler drastically excised lines from this speech for their alleged unseemliness, notably Juliet's desire for Romeo to 'leap' in her arms. He deleted her wanting to play 'a winning match' for 'a pair of stainless maidenhoods' and could not abide the thought of her 'unmanned blood'. The worlds of innocent child brides like Little Nell would not be the most hospitable breeding ground for the sexual passions that flow so freely in Shakespeare.

Accordingly, Bowdler emasculates (if that is the right word) Lear's twenty-line invective to Gloucester against female sexuality. Shakespeare's 'Adultery? / Thou shalt not die for adultery' (Q1, 4.6.108), which escalates into a furious cheering on of unchecked copulation since simpering women are in truth sex-crazed polecats, in Bowdler blandly becomes

> Adultery. – Thou shalt not die: for Gloucester's bastard son
> Was kinder to his father than my daughters
> Born in the lawful bed[15]

even substituting a chaster version for Shakespeare's part-line 'Got 'tween the lawful sheets.'

Not all Victorian authors shied away from the exposed passions in *Lear*. Arguably the most Shakespearean work of the age for drama, pain and poetic verve, *Wuthering Heights* (1847), was poorly received by its contemporaries because of its explicitness about sex and violence. In her tempest-tossed narrative, Emily Brontë alludes to *Lear* on several occasions. As early as Chapter 2 the link is made when the ineffectual Lockwood, brought down by Heathcliff's dogs, utters 'several incoherent threats of retaliation that, in their indefinite depth of virulency, smacked of King Lear', proof of quite how much the play was in Brontë's mind at the time.[16]

While the novel held sway, theatre took a back seat, at least until the advent of Henrik Ibsen during the second half of the nineteenth century. After *A Doll's House* (1879) and particularly *Ghosts* (1881), Shakespeare's plays lost whatever sting and power to embarrass they possessed, because Ibsen's characters were simultaneously men and women of the day and sexual beings; indeed, creatures ruled and destroyed for following their instincts (Nora) and also for not doing so (Mrs Alving). The most powerful form of drama throughout the nineteenth century though was drama in its pristine original form of melodrama or opera. No composer ever engaged more deeply with Shakespeare than did Giuseppe Verdi. Over a period of more than forty years he wrestled with Shakespeare, from *Macbeth* in 1847 to his last two great music dramas, *Otello* (1887) and *Falstaff* (1893, based on *The Merry Wives of Windsor*), works deemed by many to be among his greatest operas. He had considered *Lear*, too, as could be expected from the author of the great storm scene in *Rigoletto* (1851), a poignant tragedy in which a father, a hunchbacked court jester and a daughter are bound on a course of destruction. Shortly before composing *Rigoletto* (based on Victor Hugo's play *Le roi s'amuse*) and fired up by the success of *Luisa Miller* (1849), Verdi once more reverted to his pet project *Il Re Lear* in 1850, instructing Salvatore Cammarano to prepare a libretto: '*Il Re Lear* si presenta a prima vista così vasto, così intrecciato che sembra impossibile cavarne un melodrama. [. . .]' [*King Lear* at first sight appears so vast, so interwoven that it seems impossible to quarry a melodrama out of it].[17]

The script did not materialize and Cammarano died in 1852. In 1853, the year of *La Traviata*, Verdi, more than ever convinced that an opera *Il Re Lear* would be his crowning achievement, tried again. This time he commissioned a libretto from the Italian playwright Antonio Somma, which duly came about (two versions, of 1853 and 1855, are extant), although in the end Verdi never used either. In 1896, three years after his last opera *Falstaff*, Verdi confessed to Pietro Mascagni that he could not set *Lear* to music because 'the scene in which King Lear finds himself on the heath scared me'.[18] By then, Verdi was eighty-three years old, the age of Shakespeare's Lear who describes himself as 'fourscore and upward'. Goethe had famously remarked '*Ein alter Mann ist stets ein König Lear*' which translates as 'every old man is always a King Lear figure'. Perhaps the ageing Verdi was so, too, old and bowed, so that the scale of the play became ever more daunting.

Not long after Verdi's tribute to the overwhelming power of *Lear*, Leo Tolstoy, at the age of seventy-five the foremost novelist of his age, also pronounced on Shakespeare. The year was 1903. Tolstoy records that, as an old man in his seventies, he once more read the whole of Shakespeare, only to be hugely disappointed. Instead of finding Shakespeare's reputation as 'a great genius' confirmed, he discovered that his influence was pernicious, 'a great evil', just like every untruth that is imitated as an example by others who fail to recognize its shallowness. Shakespeare is a fake, Tolstoy alleges, 'not an artist' at all, and *Lear* is marred by, among others, the fact that the Fool keeps uttering 'senseless words'.[19]

How could Tolstoy get it so wrong? In his rebuttal of Tolstoy's critique, George Orwell points out that the Russian writer failed conspicuously to respond to the genius of Shakespeare's language:

> Tolstoy criticises Shakespeare not as a poet, but as a thinker and a teacher, and along those lines he has no difficulty in demolishing him. And yet all that he says is irrelevant; Shakespeare is completely unaffected. Not only his reputation but the pleasure we take in him remain just the same as before. Evidently a poet is

more than a thinker and a teacher, though he has to be that as well. [. . .] Within certain limits, bad thought and bad morals can be good literature.[20]

Shakespeare's plays without words are Mozart sans notes, mere skeletal structures that explore moral and other issues. Tolstoy writes of 'aesthetic and ethical understanding'[21] but that hardly forms the lifeblood of Shakespeare's dramas to the exclusion of all else. Richard III and Falstaff are moral pariahs to varying degrees, but they are above all brilliant dramatic stage figures, inventive, entertaining, momentary in time, rather than evolving over hundreds of pages in a realist novel. They exist in lines of verse; theirs is primarily an oral and auditory presence. If Tolstoy failed the litmus test of rhetoric, he similarly failed to understand drama as a genre with its own rules. The fulcrum of his attack was a repudiation of the alleged plot absurdities of *Lear* and its perceived plagiarism of an earlier play called *King Leir*. The misconceptions here are legion, with regard to the peripatetic nature of Elizabethan drama and also to the fact that creative or inventive *imitatio* was itself a part of originality at the time, with Shakespeare excelling at his use of sources.

Within a year of Tolstoy's swipe at Shakespeare, A. C. Bradley published his famous essay on Lear in *Shakespearean Tragedy* (1904), a collection that covered the four iconic tragedies, *Hamlet*, *King Lear*, *Othello* and *Macbeth*, since then frequently referred to as the Bradleian tragedies. Bradley's essays were written by a trained classicist at a time when English, as a discrete academic discipline, had not yet become part of the canonical syllabus in England (unlike Scotland). They rank among the most influential pieces of criticism ever written about Shakespeare. Bradley's approach, like Tolstoy's, was ethical and attempted to distil the essence of each of Shakespeare's tragic protagonists in a particular 'flaw': indecisiveness in Hamlet, jealousy in Othello, ambition in Macbeth and *hubris* (presumption, pride, arrogance) in Lear. Bradley, too, sharing Tolstoy's application of novelistic categories to drama, believed that *Lear* was chaotically plotted:

> The improbabilities in *King Lear* surely far surpass those of the other tragedies in number and in grossness. And they are particularly noticeable in the secondary plot.[22]

Bradley viewed the play's 'double action', that is its unique use among the tragedies of a subplot, as a structural weakness, while taking exception to the improbabilities of the detailed aspects of the plot of the play: why, for example, should Edgar write a letter to Edmund when they live in the same house? The reader's mind in *King Lear*, alleges Bradley, is confused repeatedly by its erratic plotting. It is 'the most faultily constructed of all the tragedies', but the fact that it is 'imperfectly dramatic' makes it cry out for 'a purely imaginative realisation'. 'It is therefore Shakespeare's greatest work, but it is not what William Hazlitt called it, "the best of his plays" '.[23]

Hazlitt (1778–1830) was less to Bradley's liking in this than Hazlitt's contemporary Charles Lamb (1775–1834) whom Bradley saluted with 'there is no higher authority'. According to Lamb,

> the Lear of Shakespeare cannot be acted [...] On the stage we see nothing but corporal infirmities and weakness, the impotence of rage; while we read it, we see not Lear, but we are Lear, we are in his mind [...] the play is beyond all art, as the tamperings with it shew [...] Tate has put his hook in the nostrils of this Leviathan, for Garrick and his followers, the showmen of the scene, to draw the mighty beast about more easily. [...] *Lear* is essentially impossible to be represented on a stage.[24]

Although Bradley and Keats would seem to come to the play from very different angles, Bradley, in turn, intuitively responded to the range and imaginative power of *Lear*. He might have borrowed Keats's famous phrase of 'soul-making' when he wrote, somewhat sanguinely perhaps, that

> There is nothing more noble and beautiful in literature than Shakespeare's exposition of the effect of suffering in reviving the greatness and eliciting the sweetness of Lear's nature [...] Should we not be at least as near the truth if we called this poem *The Redemption of King Lear*, and declared that the business of 'the gods' with him was neither to torment him, nor to teach him 'a noble anger', but to lead him to attain through apparently hopeless failure the very end and aim of life?[25]

At his best Bradley's responses to the play combine close attention to detail and acute literary flair, as in his reading of Cordelia whom he calls 'not a masterpiece of invention or subtlety like that of Cleopatra; yet in its own way it is a creation as wonderful'. Cordelia, he notes, 'appears in only four of the twenty-six scenes of *King Lear*; she speaks – it is hard to believe it – scarcely more than a hundred lines'.[26] Like Lamb, Bradley too delved into the girlhood of Shakespeare's heroines, notably this one who had to endure the indignity of growing up 'with Goneril and Regan for sisters'. Such burrowing away inside the hidden, inner recesses of Shakespeare's characters' lives owes much to Lamb and, conceivably, to Freud, as well, whose *Interpretation of Dreams* had appeared in 1900.

Writing in the wake of the New Critics and the Chicago School, which championed the integrity of the text over context, Robert B. Heilman in *This Great Stage: Image and Structure in King Lear* (1948) studied unifying patterns of interconnected imagery and rhetoric in *Lear*. He subjected the play's iterative image patterns to the minutest scrutiny, consciously reflecting the pioneering work on just this topic by Caroline Spurgeon's *Shakespeare's Imagery and What It Tells Us*, published in 1935, the same year as Enid Welsford's groundbreaking study of the Fool in *King Lear*. For Heilman, the play itself was one 'large metaphor'. Whereas critics like Hazlitt and Bradley responded to the play's epic scale, taking for granted its artistic achievement, Heilman analysed its metaphors and similes to tease out submerged meanings from the play. His study encompassed the two plots of *Lear* and he found significant common rhetorical ground in them. By teasing out the minutiae of the verbal layers of the play, Heilman's book scored a number of notable successes as, for example, in his powerful readings of the haggling scene in 2.4 when Goneril and Regan barter with their father over the number of knights he could safely be allowed, culminating in Regan's 'What needs one?' And yet the *Lear* book, which was followed by a similar study on *Othello*, *Magic in the Web* (1956), seemed at times curiously flat when compared to Bradley's essays on the play, or indeed when measured against Barbara Everett's influential study 'The New *King Lear*' (1960), one which shared Heilman's close attention to the words on the page but moved forward the discussion to an entirely different plane.

Everett was keen to test the sometimes-cosy assumptions of orthodox criticism of the play, particularly the notion that the portrayal of suffering in *Lear* in the end served to vindicate the emergence of a purged, better world. According to Everett

> Pascal's image of man – perhaps one learned from Montaigne – is of a creature bewilderingly made 'un milieu entre rien et tout', perpetually conditioned and limited by his senses, and yet able to comprehend 'all and nothing'. It is such an image that Lear presents in the closing scene of the play.[27]

This is a far cry from Bradley's reading of the quintessentially noble aspirations of the play, a dramatic 'poem' that ought by rights to be called 'the redemption of King Lear'.[28] From Everett's demolition of *Lear's* Christian consolations to Jan Kott's famous comparison of it to Samuel Beckett's *Endgame* was only a short step, much though Kott's readings offered a broader, more philosophical sweep, with Gloucester's fall from the cliffs of Dover turning him into a symbol of Everyman, the flat boards of the stage assuming the character of 'the medieval *Theatrum Mundi*': 'A biblical parable is now enacted: the one about the rich man who became a beggar, and the blind man who recovered his inner sight when he lost his eyes. Everyman begins his wanderings through the world.'[29]

The range and power of *Lear* to move is unique even among Shakespeare's plays. Moreover, its appeal to natural justice, in the teeth of all the injustices in it that cannot be set right, at times affords a tantalizing glimpse, perhaps, of a belief deep inside the play that it may after all be better to be Fool than Machiavel, to do the right thing than to be opportunistically evil.[30] In *Lear*, good characters may not be rewarded, but in that very absence may rest a belief in the unshakeable nature of human kindness, in residual goodness that exists for its own sake. When Edgar is asked by Albany, 'How have you known the miseries of your father?', he replies, 'By nursing them, my lord' (Q1, 5.3.174–75). Edgar's gain from his selfless devotion to his father is hardly material. The fact that such behaviour is not acknowledged in the formulaic ways of poetic justice bears witness further to the play's standalone imaginative greatness, being of its day as well as visionary and transcendent.

In '*King Lear*: A retrospect, 1939–79' G. R. Hibbard remarked, 'Throughout the period under review there has been a wide measure of agreement that *King Lear* is the greatest of all the plays' and that consequently the play's language has been analysed with unparalleled thoroughness. Under those circumstances it is therefore, he notes, somewhat paradoxical that 'there is no general consensus among editors as to what Shakespeare actually wrote'.[31] The reason for this is, of course, the existence of two substantially different source texts, the Quarto of 1608 and the Folio of 1623. Hibbard cites G. K. Hunter's listing more than one hundred readings, where his Q1/F1 conflated edition (New Penguin) differed from similar Q1/F1 ones by Peter Alexander, Kenneth Muir, Dover Wilson and G. I. Duthie. Of these, the most influential text was the Arden *Lear*, first edited by Muir in 1952.

Muir sensibly based his text on Folio but accepted into it readings of 1608 Quarto in cases where Folio was corrupt and the readings of Q1 'palpably superior'.[32] Muir defended his attitude to Q1 by pointing out that it was printed not long after Shakespeare wrote the play and that, moreover, there were clear links between Q1 and F1, even if their exact nature could not be determined. Muir chose the Folio as his copy-text because he took it to be the prompt-book used by the King's Men, even though it missed 300 lines that feature in Quarto, some of them among the most famous in the play, concerning Cordelia, Albany and Goneril, and the mad trial scene in Act 3. There could be no question of leaving out these lines in a modern edition of *Lear*. According to Muir, Folio was set from a copy of 1608 Quarto which

> had been substantially altered, to bring it into line with the prompt-book [. . .] This involved the deletion of some 300 lines of the Q text, the addition of some 100 lines which had been omitted from Q, and a very large number of verbal alterations. A modern editor will, of course, restore these omitted lines, whether his text is based mainly on the Quarto or on the Folio.[33]

Underpinning Muir's desire not to rule out the contribution of Q1 is his recognition of its importance and a determination not to jettison a precious 300 lines, inexplicably missing from 1623 Folio. In 1952, Muir was well aware of the editorial debates surrounding the respective pedigrees of Q1 and F1, particularly the theories advanced by Madeleine Doran (*The Text of King Lear*, 1931) and W. W. Greg in his short *The Variants in the First Quarto of 'King Lear': A Bibliographical and Critical Inquiry* (1940).[34] Doran and Greg both compared readings and textual problems in Q1 and F1, and demonstrated by palaeographic analyses that, in a number of key instances, the Q1/F1 variant readings constituted guesses at the same manuscript copy. In other words, the first two printed versions of *Lear*, 1608 Q1 and 1623 F1, may originate in the same manuscript. Doran had argued that behind Q1 lie Shakespeare's foul papers, thereby conferring considerable authority on a text that was in many ways self-evidently corrupt. But not so much that it ought ever to have been mistaken for a memorial reconstruction, a now largely discredited view of the *First Quarto of Lear* but one which held sway when Muir was editing the play and one of the reasons why he was wary of drawing too freely on Q1. That Doran was right about the close links between Q1 and foul papers is now widely accepted. It is the reason why one of the boldest editions of the play to date, Stanley Wells's Oxford *King Lear* (2000), prints the text of Q1 as *the* text of the play, notwithstanding the claim by the *Complete Oxford Shakespeare* (1986) that Folio *Lear* was Shakespeare's own revised version.

In retrospect one may want to be grateful that Muir and other editors of so-called conflated texts (editions which include the 300 Q1-only lines as well as the 100 lines unique to F1) had the courage not to let editorial theories of the day override their sense that the Quarto lines were unmistakably by Shakespeare and, therefore, earned their place in editions of the play. Muir's text and the ones which followed offered inclusive or integrated texts of *Lear*, whatever their readings of the editorial debates over Quarto and Folio.

In 1986–7, Oxford University Press published the most iconoclastic edition of Shakespeare's plays since Dr Bowdler. The edition appeared in three volumes, a flagship core text, without notes, accompanied by a *Textual Companion* and an old spelling text. The core text modernized spelling radically and abandoned the prevailing editorial consensus about the proper balance between bibliographical theories and their implementation in a standard edition. Othello's nefarious commander was no longer 'Ancient Iago' but 'Ensign Iago', and the Falstaff of *Henry IV* reverted to his original name of Oldcastle in *Henry IV Part I*. The change from Oldcastle had been forced on Shakespeare by the Lord Chamberlain (or by the Queen herself, according to Nicholas Rowe, Shakespeare's first biographer), a descendant of the historical Oldcastle, a Protestant martyr; whence the Epilogue of the second part of *Henry IV* telling us that 'Oldcastle died martyr, and this is not the man.' Most strikingly of all though, the edition featured two versions of *Lear*, *The History of 'King Lear'* (1608 Q1) and *The Tragedy of 'King Lear'* (1623).

It seems that Shakespeare's most restless play would not settle, rising up divisively even in its bibliographical features. From being textually unified, albeit uneasily, *Lear* now split into two under the impulse of the Oxford editors' well-honed theories about Shakespeare, revision and the plays as scripts for the theatre. By moving the plays' theatrical dimensions to the fore, Oxford turned them from books for readers into fluid, dynamic verbal structures whose primary reason for being was their intrinsic theatricality. They were thus restored to a more unstable state, with Folio becoming Shakespeare's rewritten version of the play while Q1 was his original foul paper play. While there were other plays in which early printed texts competed for editorial attention, notably *Hamlet* and *Othello*, none cast the spell of *Lear*. Would Shakespeare really have rewritten his greatest tragedy a mere three or four years after first writing it? And why, if he did rewrite it, would he leave so much of the original text in place, at best only tinkering with passages locally while seeming above all to focus on cuts?

The Achilles heel of the revisionist school was that, by definition, the bulk of the differences between Q1 and F1 became willed ones by Shakespeare. Almost each and every one of the major changes to the roles of Albany, the curtailing of the French war in the play and, of course, the thousand or so micro-differences between the texts now formed part of a reshaping of the play, intended by Shakespeare. While the general thesis of the Oxford editors and subsequent editors working in their slipstream won widespread admiration, for restoring Shakespeare back to the theatre where he belonged, the closer application of their thinking to the texts themselves engendered much scepticism. Why, to quote just a handful of instances, would he have wanted to invert so many of the readings from Q1 in F1 when nothing could conceivably be gained from this, as in 'you to this / this to you', 'would not, could not / could not, would not' or in 'food and fire / fire and food' and

'You do climb it up now / You do climb up it now', to mention only a few from a much longer list? Moreover, Doran and Greg had proved conclusively that Q1 and F1 were repeatedly guessing at the same manuscript, a characteristic of the two texts that tended to be played down by the Oxford editors.

The Oxford Shakespeare made a huge impact on the study of Shakespeare globally. It did not, however, establish itself as the standard Shakespeare text. For that it was too daring while nevertheless informing, if not reshaping, the editorial debate for nearly a generation. It revitalized Shakespeare studies through the unlikely medium of debates over editing. In its immediate wake Michael Warren published a facsimile Q1/F1 parallel text of *Lear, William Shakespeare: The Parallel King Lear 1608–1623* (1989), which presented students of the play with all the materials needed for comparing, contrasting, collating and assessing the case for and against revision. A further parallel text by the author of this essay followed in 1993, the same year as Jay L. Halio published an F1-only edition of the play for Cambridge University Press, to be followed by a Q1-only one in 1994 and then, in 2000, Stanley Wells's Oxford edition of *Lear* appeared, based on Quarto/foul papers, Shakespeare's greatest play as he first wrote it.[35] Even before Wells's Quarto *Lear* appeared, The Arden Shakespeare had reissued the play in 1997 under the expert hand of R. A. Foakes, an edition that carried the typographical stigmata of the Oxford Shakespeare in a plethora of superscripts that served to identify words, phrases and passages unique to either Q1 or F1. Arden had decided not to follow the Oxford thesis of seeing Q1 and F1 as discrete texts but had instead remerged them as Muir had done forty-five years earlier, while acknowledging the impact of the Oxford edition.

All along, the Oxford push was led by theatre and performance. If its greatest contribution was to reinstate and consolidate our sense of the plays as scripts while simultaneously prompting a whole generation to think again about the textual foundations of the plays, the theatre could not always follow where editors led, even those who desired to do so. Thus Nicholas Hytner discovered that in his 1990 RSC *Lear* with John Wood (Lear), David Troughton (Kent), Linus Roache (Edgar) and Ralph Fiennes (Edmond), he could not forego the famous trial scene in 3.6, missing from Folio, while otherwise enthusiastically supporting the concept of a revised Folio text. Literary judgements in editorial matters are rarely the best option though, in truth, they are always present even when not directly acknowledged. As yet there is no pre-eminent production of *Lear* that owes its fame to being based on Quarto rather than Folio or vice-versa. Indeed, the signs are, if anything, that there will be no more Quarto or Folio *Lear*s in the theatre and that conflated, or integral *Lear* texts may be coming back into fashion (see below, Trevor Nunn in conversation with James Shapiro). Gary Taylor's assertion, that the most radical editorial theories generate their own obsolescence, applies to the Oxford Shakespeare, too.

Because of Tate's rewriting of *Lear* and the success on stage of his version, the theatrical history proper of Shakespeare's play effectively only starts towards the middle of the nineteenth century. It was really Harley Granville-Barker's 1930 *Preface to King Lear* which put the play back on the theatrical map, rescuing it from the dramatic oblivion into which the Romantics and the paeans of Bradley had consigned it.[36] Granville-Barker was adamant that Shakespeare meant the play to be acted, because its 'grandeur and simplicity, this setting of vision in terms of actuality, this inarticulate passion which breaks now and again into memorable phrases [. . .] all the magnificent art of this is directed to one end; the play's acting in a theatre'.[37] In 1940, Granville-Barker turned theory into practice when he directed John Gielgud as Lear at the Old Vic, using 'an almost complete text, in Elizabethan costume, with great theatrical success'. Recalling the experience later, Gielgud remarked

> I remember doing the death scene of Lear with him [Granville-Barker], and he began stopping me on every word and I thought every moment he'd say 'Now stop, don't act any more, we'll just work it out for technical effects'. Not at all. He didn't say stop; so I went on acting and crying and carrying on, and trying to make the corrections as he gave them to me. And when I looked at my watch, we had been working on this short scene for 40 minutes. [. . .] He could give you more than any person I ever met in my life.[38]

Gielgud's Lear was followed, though not eclipsed, by Paul Scofield's Lear in Peter Brook's bleak Stratford-upon-Avon Beckettian production of 1962, with a young Diana Rigg as Cordelia and Alec McCowen playing the Fool. Scofield reprised the role in the 1971 film of the play, once again directed by Brook, riding the crest of his iconic *Midsummer Night's Dream*, arguably the most inventively stark twentieth-century production ever of this comic masterpiece. According to the reviewer of Brook's *Lear* in the *Times* of 7 November 1962, 'What Mr Brook and his cast brought out of the play shone before us like something they had polished with love. You could see your face in it, so clean and bright it was.' Reflected in it was, he noted, 'clarity', 'mellowness' the 'image of humanity' itself.

An egalitarian ethos resonates in Lear's 'Take physic, pomp, / Expose thyself to feel what wretches feel, / That thou mayst shake the superflux to them / And show the heavens more just' (Q1, 3.4.29–32). A socialist solecism from 1606 maybe, but it fuelled Grigori Kozintsev's film *Korol Lir* of 1971, based on a translation by Boris Pasternak and a score by Dmitri Shostakovitch, with Yuri Yarvet as Lear. The film foregrounded the cold, storm-swept landscapes of the play, a populace of beggars who, in Shakespeare's text, haunt the countryside. As Edgar disguises himself as Poor Tom, he remarks

> The country gives me proof and precedent
> Of Bedlam beggars who, with roaring voices,
> Strike in their numbed and mortified bare arms
> Pins, wooden pricks, nails, sprigs of rosemary,
> And with this horrible object from low service,
> Poor pelting villages, sheepcotes and mills
> Sometime with lunatic bans, sometime with prayers
> Enforce their charity. 'Poor Turlygod! poor Tom!'
> That's something yet. Edgar I nothing am. (Q1, 2.3.13–21)

These lines lie behind Kozintsev's opening shot, a panorama of the suffering masses, ragged and pathetic, gathering on a hillside, biblical in its convergence on a mount. And yet the film ends on a less bleak note than Brook's *Lear*. The king is surrounded by friends even as he is calling out 'Nyet! Nyet! Nyet!' [No!, No!, No!], echoing the 'nothing' spoken by Cordelia which launched the tragedy in the first instance. As Kenneth Rothwell notes, the final cortège at the play, with the Fool playing his flute, 'winds through the ruined villages, where there are signs of restoration as a man attempts to raise the joist on a ruined house'.[39]

In 1982, Michael Gambon, directed by Adrian Noble, played Lear in a star-studded cast, which included Antony Sher as the Fool, Pete Postlethwaite as the Duke of Cornwall, Malcolm Storry as Kent and Jenny Agutter as Regan. The production, shaggy and bleak, was structured around the relationship of the King and Fool, who is accidentally stabbed by his master as he cowers in a barrel in the hovel during the storm. In the words of one reviewer, Sher's Fool 'was a clown – a Charlie from the late Victorian circus with Dan Leno boots, a Grock violin and a red button nose on a length of elastic'.[40] When his lines could not make us laugh he entertained us instead by miming and fooling, thus making the audience understand 'why he was tolerated'. Gambon commented that the play's sheer majesty made him feel insignificant in measuring himself against it: 'It's a part that makes you want to play it again – you can never grasp all of it'.[41]

Three years later, Akira Kurosawa loosely adapted the play in his film *Ran*. The daughters have become sons, with the youngest son, loyal Saburo, corresponding to Cordelia. He will suffer her fate and die in the arms of his warlord father Hidetora. The work by the then-veteran director (he had filmed *Macbeth* as *Throne of Blood* in 1957) sits alongside the Kozintsev film as one of the most admired adaptations of Shakespeare's play. Although it departs from Shakespeare's script, the original echoes beneath the surface of the film. When in the opening sequence of the boar hunt the king takes aim, the image dissolves into the title 'Ran', the drawing of the bow a visual quotation of Lear's angry response to Kent's urging him not to cast out Cordelia: 'The bow is bent and drawn, make from the shaft'; to which Kent replies defiantly 'Let it fall rather, though the fork invade / The region of my heart.' (Q1, 1.1.133–35).

Japanese and English cultures merged again in the 1999 production of the play by Yukio Ninagawa, with Nigel Hawthorne as Lear and Hiroyuki Sanada playing the Fool as a capering kabuki entertainer. The *Sunday Times* reviewer described it as 'a hauntingly but savagely beautiful production'. Its set was 'dominated by a huge black wooden walkway sloping gently towards you and widening into an immense platform', evoking the Noh stage, while the production as a whole reinforced 'the uncomfortable Shakespearian vision of a world where you are left without the consolation or guidance of a moral order. The great achievement of director and designer is to have created a world that is both fifteenth-century Japanese and pre-Christian English.'[42]

In 2007–8, Ian McKellen and Trevor Nunn, who years earlier had collaborated on a legendary *Macbeth* in 1976–8 (the RSC at the Warehouse and Young Vic, with Judi Dench as Lady Macbeth) teamed up for *Lear*, the role of the king being superbly executed by McKellen who bestrode the play and cast like a giant. The production interpreted the play's appeal to strip naked, to experience the full blast of cold and poverty, with singular literalism when McKellen bared all. The greatest actor in the country did what Laurence Olivier had long ago also offered to do for this part. McKellen gave visual substance to the obsession with nakedness and human fragility in the play: 'And with presented nakedness outface / The winds and persecutions of the sky', Edgar notes when he decides that henceforth his only refuge will be a life of beggary (2.3.11–12).

So which text of *Lear* would this RSC production use? A complete QF *Lear*, according to Trevor Nunn. In conversation with James Shapiro, author of the celebrated *1599: A Year in the Life of William Shakespeare* (2005), Nunn noted that in the 1960s and 1970s he had directed *Lear* using conflated texts, citing John Barton's claim that by doing so he would get the 'best of both worlds'. Even now, Nunn stated, 'I found myself unwilling to lose rich and evocative material from either version, and so I am working with a conflation again.' Shapiro replied that, if he were directing the play, he would follow suit, stressing that he was not a textual purist, that Shakespeare must have 'tinkered with his plays and that he handed over a script he knew would be changed in theatrical practice'.[43] For now it seems the wheel has come full circle, with the two texts of *Lear* merging once again in performance just as they are doing too in editorial debates where the pendulum may have swung back to conflation or integration a mere twenty years after the publication of the 1986 Oxford Shakespeare.

The textual fortunes of *Lear* never featured prominently in the wider debates about the play over the centuries, because engaging with the two-texts issue required specialist knowledge of concepts such as foul papers, promptbooks and palaeography. Historically, the fortunes of *Lear* have been determined above all by its radical imaginative demands, its apocalyptic scope, its deep sense of engaging with some of the profoundest human concerns. Perhaps all along the play's search for moral and philosophical meanings through plot and character accounts for some of the resistance to seeing it as a script for performance. The track record of *Lear* in the theatre is impressive. If it does not boast an even more prestigious stage history, this is down to Tate's rewriting of the play as a melodrama. That for 150 years the 'real *Lear*', as Lukas Erne punningly put it with reference to the texts' multiplicity,[44] could only be read rather than seen may partly account for its rising to the national consciousness as primarily a script to be played out in the mind, imagined and ultimately idealized.

More than any other play, *Lear* has spoken to posterity at different times. It is a secular eschatological text, insistent on our shared humanity, socially and morally radical in its refusal to accept authority as legitimate unless it is grounded in compassion and fellow-feeling. Just occasionally, even modern students of the play feel the need to remind themselves of the fact that *Lear* was written more than four centuries ago and for audiences who enjoyed none of the freedoms that we take for granted. Its scope is that much bolder for being written in a period when there was no concept of free speech. Yet this did not inhibit Shakespeare from writing a play in which the legitimacy of kingship is grounded in ethical awareness and inclusion, the king being the sum total of all his subjects rather than the figurehead of a few. How, one wonders, did such ideas sit with his Stuart sovereign on Boxing Day 1606, since the Scots king held strong views on the divine right of kings and liked to lecture his subjects on that topic? Though not effectively enough, it seems, since in 1649 the subjects of England rose and killed the king; his refusal to enter a plea at his trial, on the grounds that no court in the land could try an anointed sovereign, received short shrift.

As a keen admirer of Shakespeare, Charles I might have learnt from reading the royal history plays that no one was untouchable, at least not in Shakespeare's view, that kingship had to reinvent itself again and again if it was to survive. Richard II notoriously failed this test, no matter how eloquently he appealed to loyal poisonous spiders, patriotic 'heavy-gaited' toads and to God's angels in heaven to fight on his side. No amount of empty ritual could save the Plantagenet king from the machinations of the wronged son of John of Gaunt, Henry Bolingbroke.[45]

Unlike his predecessor Queen Elizabeth I, James I could, it seems, contemplate the printing of the deposition scene of *Richard II* in the Fourth Quarto of the play in 1608, the same year as *The First quarto of King Lear*, not quite two years after the king and court had watched *Lear* in Whitehall. There may be no more to this than a fortuitous coinciding in time. On the other hand, we ought not entirely to discount the possibility that the performing and printing of *Lear* and the textual history of *Richard II* are linked. Did *Lear*, sanctioned *de facto* by the crown after the December 1606 staging, clear the way to the first printing of the previously censored deposition scene? What renders this a tempting hypothesis is that *Lear* would become mould-breaking from the start; in this instance by, perhaps, a long-range undermining of the case for censoring the deposition of Richard II. Frank Kermode has remarked that

> We can accept *Hamlet* as the fulcrum of Shakespeare's career [...] The works that followed are very different, but in their various ways equally adventurous', with *Lear* 'the craftiest as well as the most tremendous of Shakespeare's tragedies [...] There is a finality about *Lear*; it even instructs us to think that.[46]

The metaphoric peeling back in *Lear* of layers of clothes and pretence, to expose the fragile inner core of essential humanity, renders the play stark, abstract, and timeless. It is as contemporary with Elizabethan fools, beggars and madmen as it is with Beckett's tramps and vaudeville clowns. To that extent, *Lear* is Shakespeare's most permeable play, capable of absorbing countless projections mapped on to it at different times. Questions about life, love, duty and death run as eternally in the human breast as hope. The striking immediacy of the language of *Lear* flows directly from its deep and global concerns; indeed, it is its vehicle.[47] So does the absence of soliloquies by the main character, those often long and intimate two-handed sparring matches between protagonist and audience, working in collusion between the inner play and the outside, illusion and reality. But Lear is too preoccupied for such indulgences: he has after all taken too little care of his country hitherto. *Lear* is not only democratically populated, like the English histories and particularly the *Henry IV* plays, but the king blends into the social and rhetorical texture of the play to the point where he can no longer be extricated from it, becoming king only in as much as he is also Everyman. In that sense, Lear is as much our contemporary as he is Everyman in a Morality play; the tragedy looks back as much as forward, fittingly so for a drama about universal themes.

Notes

1   Unless otherwise stated all references to *King Lear* in this chapter are to *King Lear: A Parallel Text Edition*, ed. René Weis, 2nd edn (London and New York: Longman, 2010).

2   W. B Yeats, *Michael Robartes and the Dancer* (Dundrum: Cuala Press, 1921).

3   Jan Kott, *Shakespeare our Contemporary*, trans. Boleslaw Taborski (London: Methuen, 1964), p. 116.

4   Tate, quoted in Frank Kermode, ed., *Shakespeare: King Lear: A Casebook* (London: Macmillan, [1969] 1973), p. 25.

5   Ibid.

6   Ibid.

7   Samuel Johnson, 'Preface to the Edition of Shakespeare's Plays (1765)', in *Samuel Johnson on Shakespeare*, ed. by H. R. Woudhuysen (London: Penguin, 1989).

8   Geoffrey Bullough, *Narrative and Dramatic Sources of Shakespeare's Plays*, 8 vols (London: Routledge and Kegan Paul, 1973), VII, pp. 269–420 (*King Lear*).

9   Bullough, *Narrative and Dramatic Sources*, pp. 337–402.

10 See E. M. W. Tillyard, *Shakespeare's History Plays* (London: Chatto & Windus, 1974), 64. ff.

11 'The Anatomy of the World', in *John Donne: The Complete English Poems*, ed. by A. J. Smith (London: Penguin Classics, 1986).

12 *Letters of John Keats: A New Selection*, ed. by Robert Gittings (London and Oxford: Oxford University Press, 1975), pp. 42–43.

13 *Letters of John Keats*, ed. by Gittings, p. 57.

14 *The Poems of John Keats*, ed. Miriam Allott (London: Longman, 1970).

15 *The Family Shakespeare, in Ten Volumes*, ed. by Thomas Bowdler (London: Longman, 1855), p. 809.

16 Emily Brontë, *Wuthering Heights* (London: Everyman, 1975), p. 14.

17 See Julian Budden, *Verdi* (New York: Oxford University Press, 2008), p. 55.

18 Budden, *Verdi*, pp. 77–78.

19 George Orwell, 'Lear, Tolstoy and the Fool', in *King Lear: A Casebook*, pp. 150–52.

20 George Orwell, *The Collected Essays, Journalism and Letters of George Orwell: 'My country right or left', 1940-1943*, II, ed. by Sonia Orwell and Ian Angus (New York: Harcourt, Brace & World, 1968), p. 130.

21 Orwell, 'Lear, Tolstoy and the Fool', p. 150.

22 In his *Shakespearean Tragedy: Lectures on Hamlet, Othello, King Lear, Macbeth* (London: Macmillan, 1904), pp. 210–11. A. C. Bradley lists a whole range of such 'inconsistencies'.

23 Bradley, *Shakespearean Tragedy*, pp. 202, 213.

24 Charles Lamb, 'On the tragedies of Shakespeare', *The Reflector* (1810–11).

25 Bradley, *Shakespearean Tragedy*, pp. 234–35.

26 Bradley, *Shakespearean Tragedy*, p. 263.

27   Barbara Everett, 'The New King Lear', *Critical Quarterly*, 2 (1960).

28   Bradley, *Shakespearean Tragedy*, p. 235.

29   Kott, *Shakespeare Our Contemporary*, p. 116.

30   Thus the Fool in 2.4: 'We'll set thee to school to an ant [. . .] The fool no knave, perdy.'

31   G. R. Hibbard, '*King Lear*: A retrospect, 1939–79', *Shakespeare Survey*, 30 (1980), 1–12.

32   *King Lear*, ed. by Kenneth Muir, Arden Shakespeare, rev. edn (London: Methuen, 1972), p. xvii.

33   Kenneth Muir (ed.), in *Lear*, Arden Shakespeare (London: Methuen, 1952), p. xiv.

34   Madeleine Doran, *The Text of King Lear* (Stanford, CA: Stanford University Press; London: Oxford University Press, 1931) and W. W. Greg, *The Variants in the First Quarto of 'King Lear': A Bibliographical and Critical Inquiry* (London: Bibliographical Society, 1940).

35   René Weis, *King Lear: A Parallel Text Edition*, Longman Annotated Texts (London and New York: Longman, 1993; 2nd rev. edn, 2010); Jay L. Halio, *The Tragedy of King Lear* (Cambridge: Cambridge University Press, 1992); *The First Quarto of King Lear*, ed. by Jay L. Halio, New Cambridge Shakespeare (Cambridge: Cambridge University Press, 1994); *The History of King Lear*, ed. by Stanley Wells (Oxford: Oxford University Press, 2000).

36   It is worth noting that Harley Granville-Barker firmly believed that Folio was the true performance text of the play: *Prefaces to Shakespeare*, 2 vols (London: Batsford, 1930), I, p. 78.

37   Granville-Barker, *Prefaces to Shakespeare*, I, p. 29.

38   National Theatre programme note on King Lear 1986.

39   Kenneth Rothwell, *A History of Shakespeare on Screen* (Cambridge: Cambridge University Press, 2004), p. 182.

40   Nicholas Shrimpton, 'Shakespeare Performances in Stratford-upon-Avon and London, 1981–2', *Shakespeare Survey*, 36 (1983), 149–55 (p. 152).

41   Shrimpton, 'Shakespeare Performances', p. 152.

42   John Peter, *The Sunday Times*, 1999.

43   The Royal Shakespeare Company, *King Lear* 2007–8.

44   Lukas Erne, 'Editing the Real Lear', in Shakespeare's Modern Collaborators (London: Continuum, 2008), pp. 87–102.

45   Cf. Richard's deluded claim in 3.2 that 'Not all the water in the rough rude sea / Can wash the balm off from an anointed king [. . .]'.

46   Frank Kermode, *Shakespeare's Language* (London: Allen Lane, 2000), pp. 126–200.

47   Kermode, *Shakespeare's Language*, p. 184, notes how curious it is that Lear affords 'few of the local excitements to be found, say, in the narrower context of "Measure for Measure"', concluding that the reason for this is that 'the subjects of King Lear reflect a much more general, indeed a universal tragedy'.

CHAPTER ONE

The Critical Backstory

Joan Fitzpatrick

Shakespeare's *King Lear* was probably written in 1605 and performed shortly after, probably in 1606, by the King's Men at the Globe Theatre in London. Unfortunately, we have no eyewitness account of this or any other performances of *King Lear* during Shakespeare's lifetime, although such records do exist for other early modern performances of Shakespeare's plays.[1] The play was first printed in 1608 and referred to on its title page as *The True Chronicle History of the life and death of King Lear and his three daughters. With the unfortunate life of Edgar, sonne and heire to the Earle of Gloster, and his sullen and assumed humor of Tom of Bedlam.*[2] Those playgoers who went to see Shakespeare's *King Lear*, or who read the play, would have been surprised by his version of the story if they had read or seen other versions of it, such as the anonymous play *The True Chronicle History of King Leir and his three daughters, Gonorill, Ragan, and Cordella*, probably performed twice at the Rose in 1594 and first published in 1605.[3] This was the main source from which Shakespeare worked when writing his play. As Geoffrey Bullough indicated in his book on Shakespeare's sources, he was also clearly indebted to the English history available via Holinshed's *Chronicles* (1577) and John Higgins's *Mirror for Magistrates* (1574). He also used Samuel Harsnett's *Declaration of Egregious Popish Impostures* (1603) and Geoffrey of Monmouth's twelfth-century history *Historia regum Britanniae*, which features the story of Leir and which Shakespeare probably knew from the version in Edmund Spenser's epic poem *The Faerie Queene* (Book 2, canto 10), where the youngest daughter is named Cordelia, rather than 'Cordella' as in *Leir*. The subplot featuring Gloucester and his two sons comes from Sidney's *Arcadia* (specifically Book 2 Chapter 10), which features the story of a Paphlagonian king who is mistreated by his illegitimate son but saved from suicide by his good and legitimate son.[4] As with most of his source material, Shakespeare reshaped the original in significant ways: for example, in the anonymous play, Leir initially wants Cordella to marry the King of Ireland not France, who turns up only after the division of the kingdom, but the most significant change Shakespeare made is that Leir and his youngest daughter die. Where the anonymous play ended in victory for the French army, Leir in power, and the reconciliation of Leir and Cordella, Shakespeare's play ends in tragedy.

A second edition of the play, also in Quarto form, was printed in 1619 with only minor differences that were accidentally introduced by the printer; the next printing, in the First Folio of 1623, incorporated a number of important changes that constitute deliberate revision by Shakespeare several years after his original composition. According to the *Textual Companion* to the Oxford Shakespeare

> The Folio text contains about 100 lines not printed in Q; it does not contain about 300 lines (including one whole scene) which are present in Q; it also differs from Q in hundreds of substantive readings, and divides the play into acts and scenes.[5]

As the *Textual Companion* pointed out, several scholars 'have argued at great length the case for the artistic integrity and independence of the two early versions', so that what we have, in effect, are 'two different "versions" of the play'.[6] The differences between the versions are set out in considerable detail in Gary Taylor and Michael Warren's 1983 study[7] but, to summarize, it is usually thought that Q1 is more historical in scope and the Folio presents a more theatrical text, focusing less on France as an invading force and presumably reflecting changes Shakespeare made in order to make the play work better on stage. Those who encountered Shakespeare's play throughout the early to mid-seventeenth century would have experienced it much as playgoers did during Shakespeare's lifetime, that is, in the form of two distinct texts: the Quarto and Folio. It was later generations of readers who understood a conflated *King Lear* to be one play, a perception that lasted until 1986 with the publication of two distinct versions in the Oxford Shakespeare. But not all critics agree that the Q1 and F1 should be printed as two distinct 'King Lears'. R. A. Foakes, for example, acknowledges the differences between the 'versions', but argues that 'the reworking of *King Lear* is not so thorough as to mean that we have to think of two plays'.[8] In his recent Arden edition of *King Lear*, Foakes explains these differences in detail but presents the reader with only one text.[9]

The later seventeenth century saw an important development, with the production on stage of Nahum Tate's adaptation of *King Lear* in 1681. The play was printed in the same year with a title page that did not mention Shakespeare but announced the text as *The History of King Lear. Acted at the Duke's Theatre. Reviv'd with Alterations. By N. TATE.* In a foreword to his edition, Tate explains his reasons for making a major change to Shakespeare's original play by presenting a love affair between Cordelia and Edgar:

> 'Twas my good Fortune to light on one Expedient to rectifie what was wanting in the Regularity and Probability of the Tale, which was to run through the whole A Love betwixt Edgar and Cordelia, that never chang'd word with each other in the Original. This renders Cordelia's Indifference and her Father's Passion in the first Scene probable. It likewise gives Countenance to Edgar's Disguise, making that a generous Design that was before a poor Shift to save his Life. The Distress of the Story is evidently heightned by it; and it particularly gave Occasion of a New Scene or Two, of more Success (perhaps) than Merit.[10]

Tate makes a connection between this major alteration and his revision of the play's ending:

> This Method necessarily threw me on making the Tale conclude in a Success to the innocent distrest Persons: Otherwise I must have incumbred the Stage with dead Bodies, which Conduct makes many Tragedies conclude with unseasonable Jests. Yet was I Rackt with no small Fears for so bold a Change, till I found it well receiv'd by my Audience . . . [11]

Tate also cut the character of the fool, a decision that Sonia Massai noted was 'prompted by matters of ideological rather than dramatic concern': the main source of criticism of the king had to go.[12]

Tate has been much maligned for daring to rewrite Shakespeare but, as Stanley Wells pointed out

> What Tate did to Shakespeare was not essentially different to what Shakespeare had done to *King Leir*: Shakespeare had turned an old tragicomedy into a tragedy, Tate reversed the process. In doing so he created a new, different play which, critics have increasingly argued, has its own artistic validity.[13]

Wells went on to acknowledge that by retaining so much of Shakespeare, Tate exposed himself to unflattering comparisons between Shakespeare's verse and his own, but added that when Tate was writing, 'Shakespeare was not thought of as an immortal classic' and it was considered acceptable to adapt his works to suit 'the new theatrical and social circumstances of the time, as well as to changes in taste'.[14] Tate saw himself as a collaborator with Shakespeare, one who could correct the faults in *King Lear*, which he termed 'a Heap of Jewels, unstrung and unpolisht'.[15]

Tate's adaptation of *King Lear*, like Dryden's adaptation of a number of Shakespeare plays, including *Antony and Cleopatra* as *All for Love*, signalled a desire for fresh material in the period that followed the reopening of the theatres upon the Restoration of the monarchy. As Shakespeare's handling of the anonymous *King Leir* indicates, the tradition of reviving and altering old plays was well established. Like the early moderns who adapted source material for their playhouses, upon the Restoration, dramatists wanted something of their own. They also needed to adapt to new theatrical circumstances, namely more elaborate stage scenery and the presence of women for the first time on the public stage in the history of the English theatre. As Massai pointed out, the introduction of a love affair between Edgar and Cordelia and Tate's expansion of other female roles 'are clearly a tribute to the new practice' of women taking female roles.[16]

In 'The Grounds of Criticism in Tragedy' (1679) John Dryden put forward the view that drama ought to be didactic. Dryden admired Shakespeare, and thought him superior to the playwright John Fletcher (whose work he thought to be derivative of Shakespeare's),[17] but he criticized Shakespeare's 'defective' plots – most obviously, he thought, when compared to Jonson's, that adhered to the unities of time, place and action. Dryden also criticized Shakespeare's 'manner of expression' by which 'he often obscures his meaning by words, and sometimes makes it unintelligible'.[18] Thomas Rymer, admired by Dryden for his criticism of Shakespeare's plots,[19] also offered his views on what worked best in tragedy. In the essay, 'A Short View of Tragedy', he presented a lengthy criticism of Shakespeare's *Othello* in which he criticized Shakespeare's diction and was also perturbed by the play's 'moral', asking what crime Desdemona or her parents had committed to bring about her murder by Othello:

> What instruction can we make out of this Catastrophe? Or whither must our reflection lead us? Is not this to envenome and sour our spirits, to make us repine and grumble at Providence; and the government of the World? If this be our end, what boots it to be Vertuous?[20]

Rymer did not write about *King Lear* but if he had then, presumably, he would have held a similar view about its dénouement.

Eighteenth-Century Editions and the Critics

A conflated *King Lear* has its origins in the early eighteenth century with Alexander Pope's new edition of Shakespeare's *Complete Works*, based largely on Nicholas Rowe's revised edition of 1714. Rowe had made some changes to the text, which he based on the Fourth Folio of 1685, but Pope went further by adding passages from the Quarto to the Folio text and deleting passages elsewhere from the Folio. He thus produced a conflation of the two texts, and one of the characteristics of Pope's edition was that he relegated to footnotes those passages from Shakespeare of which he disapproved. Lewis Theobald also produced a collected edition of Shakespeare's works in 1733 and in the preface was strongly critical of Pope, denouncing what he termed Pope's 'injury' to Shakespeare with his 'pompous' edition.[21] Eight years earlier, Theobald had attacked Pope's scholarship in *Shakespeare Restored: A Specimen of the Many Errors, as well committed, as Unamended, by Mr Pope in his Late Edition of this Poet*. Crucially, Theobald supported any changes made in his edition with evidence rather than the subjectivity that had governed Pope's edition, as Jean I. Marsden underlines, 'For Theobald, only evidence from Shakespeare's text, not an editor's faulty judgment, can authorize corrections and amendments.'[22] And so the serious job of editing Shakespeare had begun in earnest, although Theobald, too, presented a conflated text of *King Lear*, as was the editorial norm until the 1986 Oxford edition.

So eighteenth-century readers would have experienced a conflated *King Lear* and, since Tate's adaptation still held the stage, those watching the play in performance would have experienced a happy ending. What then did critics make of the play they knew as *King Lear* during this century? The project of eighteenth-century criticism was to aid discrimination of Shakespeare's writing so that its perceived faults would not be imitated by young writers. Shakespeare's deviations from Augustan neo-classicism, such as the unities of time, place and action, were considered errors but excusable ones because Shakespeare was thought to lack a classical education. The rise of the notion of intellectual property made it important to show that Shakespeare's plays were original, in the sense of new-made, rather than based on classical analogues – an unlearned Shakespeare was deemed more honourable than a learned one. And so emerged the notion of a writer who could be considered a 'poet of Nature': one who did not need learning in order to represent life.

In Samuel Johnson's 1765 edition of the *Complete Works*, his notes on *King Lear* praised the play as 'deservedly celebrated', remarking that 'The artful involutions of distinct interests, the striking opposition of contrary characters, the sudden changes of fortune, and the quick succession of events, fill the mind with a perpetual tumult of indignation, pity, and hope.'[23] Regarding what he termed 'the seeming improbability of Lear's conduct', Johnson observed that it 'would be yet credible, if told of a petty prince of Guinea or Madagascar', in other words, an eighteenth-century reader or playgoer might encounter just such a king, in some far-flung corner of the known world. Crucially, Johnson contends that Shakespeare 'so minutely describes the characters of men, he commonly neglects and confounds the characters of ages, by mingling customs ancient and modern, English and foreign.'[24] This is typical of the Augustan tendency to read Shakespeare's characters as universal, not specific to a certain time or place. The stressing of such universality was partly a literary taste for the general but also served to explain Shakespeare's longevity since it also suggested that the general cannot go out of fashion.

Johnson cited his fellow critic Joseph Warton, who attacked *King Lear* as a savage and shocking play, but defended Shakespeare's depiction of the aggression shown towards Lear by his daughters: 'These objections may, I think, be answered, by repeating, that the cruelty of the daughters is an historical fact, to which the poet has added little, having only drawn it into a series by dialogue and action.'[25] So Shakespeare based his play on historical material and cannot be faulted for that. But Johnson is more critical of the most violent scene in the play: the blinding of Gloucester, which he describes as 'an act too horrid to be endured in dramatick exhibition, and such as must always compel the mind to relieve its distress by incredulity.'[26] For Johnson, this action was artistically indecorous. Johnson was not impressed, either, by the character of Edmund, and believed he inflicted 'injury' upon what he termed 'the simplicity of the action' but thought this 'abundantly recompensed' by the manner in which Shakespeare combined 'perfidy with perfidy [. . .] connecting the wicked son with the wicked daughters, to impress this important moral, that villany is never at a stop, that crimes lead to crimes, and at last terminate in ruin.'[27] The key word here is 'moral': the reader or playgoer can, indeed should, learn from Shakespeare that evil deeds will meet their due reward. Johnson was most perturbed by Shakespeare's treatment of Cordelia: 'Shakespeare has suffered the virtue of Cordelia to perish in a just cause contrary to the natural ideas of justice, to the hope of the reader, and, what is yet more strange, to the faith of chronicles.'[28] He disagrees with Joseph Addison, who condemned Tate's happy ending for destroying some of the beauty of Shakespeare's original, observing that natural justice dictates that the wicked perish and the good be rewarded. Moreover, the public liked Tate's version:

> In the present case the publick has decided. Cordelia, from the time of Tate, has always retired with victory and felicity. And, if my sensations could add any thing to the general suffrage, I might

relate, that I was many years ago so shocked by Cordelia's death, that I know not whether I ever endured to read again the last scenes of the play till I undertook to revise them as an editor.[29]

Tate's *Lear* continued to play in the London theatres, although other voices were added to Addison's view that his version was unpalatable. Among them was Frances Brooke who, commenting on a performance of *Lear* with Spranger Barry in the lead (a rival to David Garrick's Lear), wondered why Garrick, and by implication those who follow him, 'should yet prefer the adulterated cup of *Tate* to the pure genuine draught offered him by the master he avows to serve with such fervency of devotion'.[30] Similarly, Thomas Wilkes, who (like Johnson) noted that the happy conclusion 'sends away all the spectators exulting with gladness', objected that Tate 'has left out some of the finest speeches in the character of Lear'.[31] This was not entirely fair on Garrick since, as Jean Marsden has indicated, it seems likely that by the 1750s he had begun replacing large segments of Tate's adaptations with passages from Shakespeare.[32] In his edition of the play, published in 1773, Garrick cut Tate's depiction of the subplot featuring Gloucester and his sons and other Tate-authored scenes such as Cordelia's explanation for her apparently heartless answer. Yet Garrick retained many of the scenes from Tate that emphasized Cordelia's concern for her father so that 'scenes of daughterly love become the background for Lear's suffering and for the play's emotional impact'.[33] Nevertheless, the emphasis was still very much on Lear as a father who has been mistreated by his daughters, a domestic tragedy rather than the history of a king who has given away his crown.

The Romantics

Given the interest that the Romantic poets took in the natural world, it is not surprising that Samuel Coleridge's analysis of *King Lear* should begin with a focus on what he perceived to be a sense of physical movement in Shakespeare:

> Of all Shakespeare's plays *Macbeth* is the most rapid, *Hamlet* the slowest, in movement. *Lear* combines length with rapidity – like the hurricane and the whirlpool absorbing while it advances. It begins as a stormy day in summer, with brightness; but that brightness is lurid, and anticipates the tempest.[34]

The use of natural imagery, specifically violent movements of water, to describe the play is also invoked to describe the state of Lear's mind when Coleridge compares Lear's sufferings to those endured by Edgar: 'In Edgar's ravings Shakspeare all the while lets you see a fixed purpose, a practical end in view; – in Lear's, there is only the brooding of the one anguish, an eddy without progression.'[35] This description of Lear's madness as an eddy, water that runs contrary to the direction of the tide or current, with the sense of a lack of forward movement, is further developed in Coleridge's analysis of Act 3, Scene 4, which features Lear's exposure to the storm. Here, Coleridge invokes pathetic fallacy in drawing parallels between the natural world and the psychological pain endured by Lear and those around him:

> What a world's *convention* of agonies! Surely, never was such a scene conceived before or since. Take it but as a picture for the eye only, it is more terrific than any which a Michelangelo inspired by a Dante could have conceived, and which none but a Michelangelo could have executed. Or let it have been uttered to the blind, the howlings of convulsed nature would seem converted into the voice of conscious humanity.[36]

In his *Characters of Shakespeare's Plays*, Hazlitt would also consider 'the mind of Lear' in terms of the natural world, specifically its violence:

> [it is] a tall ship driven about by the winds, buffetted by the furious waves, but that still rides above the storm, having its anchor fixed in the bottom of the sea; or it is like the sharp rock circled by the eddying whirlpool that foams and beats against it, or like the solid promontory pushed from its basis by the force of an earthquake.[37]

That Coleridge and Hazlitt share a vocabulary when describing Lear's madness is perhaps inevitable, given that they came from the same philosophical tradition; it is perhaps unconsciously that they echo the natural language and imagery that refers to the storm and violent waters in the play itself, as when Lear calls upon nature: 'Blow, winds, and crack your cheeks! Rage, blow, / You cataracts and hurricanoes, spout / Till you have drenched our steeples, drowned the cocks!' (3.2.1–3).[38]

The Romantics were keenly sensitive to the workings of the mind and mental disturbance so it is understandable that they should focus on a mind in appalling turmoil. However, their sensibilities balked at what they considered too much pain: Coleridge quickly passes over the most violent scene in the play, the blinding of Gloucester, stating only 'What can I say of this scene? – There is my reluctance to think Shakspeare wrong, and yet it is necessary to harmonize their [Goneril's and Regan's] cruelty to their father.[39] Hazlitt says even less about it, referring only to Gloucester's generosity in suffering alongside Lear.[40]

Coleridge observes that Lear's division of his kingdom is a thing already decided by him before he asks for protestations of love from his daughters, thus 'the trial is but a trick' and 'the grossness of the old king's rage is in part the natural result of a silly trick suddenly and most unexpectedly baffled and disappointed'.[41] These references to Lear as a king make way for a focus on Lear the man, specifically Lear the father. Coleridge asserts that we might cut the scene where Lear divides his kingdom 'without any of the *effects* of improbability', something that could not happen in the plays of Francis Beaumont and John Fletcher, since what occurs early in their plays is 'perpetually recurring as the cause and *sine qua non* of the incidents and emotions'.[42] Like Dryden, Coleridge thought Beaumont and Fletcher's drama to be derivative of Shakespeare's.[43] Coleridge concentrates upon

> [that] which in all ages has been, and ever will be, close and native to the heart of man, – parental anguish from filial ingratitude, the genuineness of worth, though confined in bluntness, and the execrable vileness of a smooth iniquity.[44]

Indeed, for Hazlitt also, Lear's sufferings were universal:

> The passion which he [Shakespeare] has taken as his subject is that which strikes its root deepest into the human heart; of which the bond is the hardest to be unloosed; and the cancelling and tearing to pieces of which gives the greatest revulsion to the frame.[45]

Describing the other characters in the play, Coleridge considers Edmund's wickedness excusable since he is exposed to 'his own dishonour and his mother's infamy related by his father with an excusing shrug of the shoulders, and in a tone betwixt waggery and shame'; he admires Kent as 'the nearest to perfect goodness of all Shakspeare's characters', and the Fool as 'as wonderful a creation as Caliban – an inspired idiot'.[46] He also notes 'Something of disgust at the ruthless hypocrisy of her sisters, some little faulty admixture of pride and sullenness in Cordelia's "Nothing"',[47] while the criticism directed towards Goneril and Regan concentrates on their unnaturalness:

> The monster Goneril prepares what is *necessary*, while the character of Albany renders a still more maddening grievance possible; viz., Regan and Cornwall in perfect sympathy of monstrosity. Not a sentiment, not an image, which can give pleasure on its own

account, is admitted. Pure horror when they are introduced, and they are brought forward as little as possible.[48]

Although Lear is described as selfish in his desire to hear that his daughters love him, it is 'the selfishness of a loving and kindly nature', the actions of a father who needs to hear that he is loved and so who displays an understandable 'anxiety . . . distrust [and] . . . jealousy' out of 'mere fondness from love'.[49] For Coleridge 'All Lear's faults increase our pity. We refuse to know them otherwise than as means and aggravations of his sufferings and his daughter's ingratitude'.[50] Yet Goneril and Regan are not afforded any sympathy: Lear's eldest daughters are considered depraved creatures, with Coleridge referring specifically to 'the unfeminine violence' of Regan.[51]

Hazlitt also expresses pity for Lear, noting that it is 'his violent impetuosity, his blindness to every thing but the dictates of his passions or affections, that produces all his misfortunes, that aggravates his impatience of them, that enforces our pity for him'.[52] He similarly admires Kent and the Fool and offers an excuse for Edmund, noting that his honesty in his villainy is 'admirable' and that his character is one of 'careless, light-hearted villainy, contrasted with the sullen, rancorous malignity of Regan and Gonerill'.[53] He is more sympathetic towards Cordelia than Coleridge, claiming that she 'desires them [her sisters] to treat their father well' but portrays the same attitude towards Goneril and Regan, who reveal 'petrifying indifference' and 'cold, calculating, obdurate selfishness'.[54] At one point Hazlitt exclaims that 'they are so thoroughly hateful that we do not even like to repeat their names'.[55]

The sympathy for Lear and condemnation of Goneril and Regan evident in Coleridge and Hazlitt's criticism of the play highlights how reading King Lear can be a very different experience from seeing it performed. For example, it may be difficult for a reader to remember that Lear has one hundred knights in his retinue, a number that Goneril and Regan complain about and ask him to reduce, something Lear finds objectionable. A production might choose to show Lear's knights, even a smaller number of them for practical reasons, behaving badly, as when Goneril claims 'this our court, infected with their manners, / Shows like a riotous inn' and that is 'more like a tavern or a brothel / Than a graced palace' (1.4.221–24). As Foakes pointed out, Peter Brook in his 1962 production of the play 'brought on enough knights to cause something like a riot in Goneril's house when Lear overturned a table and his knights followed his example'.[56] Such a production would presumably increase audience sympathy for the exasperated daughters of an aged parent who hangs out with a loutish gang. Alternatively, a production that showed the knights being no trouble at all would presumably provoke the opposite view, but the point is that productions tend to make decisions about the kind of indeterminacies that need not bother the reader.

Hazlitt was typical of the Romantics in preferring to read *King Lear*, as his opinion of a production with Edmund Kean as Lear, in Tate's version of the play, demonstrates. Hazlitt had heard reports of the fabulous performances given by the actors David Garrick and John Kemble as Lear, but was disappointed in Kean whom he blamed for 'the deficiency and desultoriness of the interest excited'.[57] Hazlitt admired Kean in the part of Othello, but considered Lear too magnificent for his abilities: 'there is something (we don't know how) in the gigantic, outspread sorrows of Lear, that seems to elude his grasp, and baffle his attempts at comprehension'. Where Othello is 'like a river', Lear is 'more like a sea, swelling, chafing, raging, without bound, without hope, without beacon, or anchor'.[58] Quite a challenge for any actor and one suspects that even Garrick or Kemble would have fallen short of Hazlitt's expectations.

In addition, in an essay entitled 'On the Tragedies of Shakespeare', Charles Lamb notoriously proclaimed that 'the Lear of Shakespeare cannot be acted', denouncing the 'old man tottering about the stage with a walking stick' and his mistreatment that 'has nothing in it but what is painful and disgusting'.[59] Lamb specifically criticized efforts to stage the storm against which Lear rages: 'The contemptible machinery by which they mimic the storm which he goes out in, is not more inadequate to represent the horrors of the real elements, than any actor can be to represent Lear'.[60] Like the other Romantics, he expressed his views of the play via the imagery of the natural world, noting, 'The greatness of Lear is not in corporal dimension, but in intellectual: the explosions of his passion are terrible as a volcano: they are storms turning up and disclosing to the bottom that sea, his mind, with all its vast riches'.[61] The point is that, for the Romantics, no one could capture the essence of such a play. Although Hazlitt was more generous in his reviews of Kean playing Richard III and Hamlet,[62] he was generally critical of the efforts to stage Shakespeare, which could not hope to capture all the complexity only a reader could fully grasp. It would be easy to sneer at Lamb's anti-theatrical views, but we ought to bear in mind that, like the other Romantic critics, he was seeing Tate's Lear, of which he was highly critical: 'Tate has put his hook in the nostrils of this Leviathan, for Garrick and his followers, the showmen of the scene, to draw the mighty beast about more easily.' He is especially scathing of the happy ending: 'as if the living martyrdom that Lear had gone through, – the flaying of his feelings alive, did not make a fair dismissal from the stage of life the only decorous thing for him',[63] a point with which most modern readers or playgoers would arguably concur.

Another Romantic reader of Shakespeare, John Keats, wrote the famous poem 'On Sitting Down to Read King Lear Once Again'. Here, Keats states that he must leave to one side a Romance he is either reading or writing since 'once again, the fierce dispute / Betwixt damnation and impassioned clay / Must I burn through, once more humbly assay / The bitter-sweet of this Shakespearian fruit' (lines 5–8). Keats's characterization of *King Lear* as a distinctly violent work is in keeping with the views of other Romantic critics. His praise of Shakespeare as 'Chief Poet!' (line 9, note Shakespeare is a 'poet' rather than a 'dramatist') is also typical, and marks a distinct departure from earlier critics such as Rymer, who were mostly critical of Shakespeare's writing. His reference to 'ye clouds of Albion, / Begetters of our deep eternal theme!' (lines 9–10) is Romantic in its emphasis on the universality of Shakespeare that we have encountered so far: England has produced Shakespeare and his works, but they speak of the wider world and universal themes. Keats describes the action of reading as going 'through the old oak forest' (line 10), again a typical Romantic reference to nature and the final lines of the poem feature a plea: 'Let me not wander in a barren dream, / But, when I am consumèd in the fire / Give me new Phoenix wings to fly at my desire' (lines 12–14).[64] This indicates the extreme emotions reading provoked for the Romantics; Keats does not approach the play as a critic or playgoer might but is absorbed by it, using the imagery of fire to evoke the intensity of his experience. Keats did go to the theatre, indeed he wrote in praise of Kean's performance as Othello and Richard III[65] but, similar to Hazlitt, his review is of the actor rather than the production. When he says of Kean, 'He feels his being as deeply as Wordsworth, or any other of our intellectual monopolists'[66] we know that he values reading poetry above all.

Later Nineteenth-Century Critics

Tate's adaptation of *King Lear* dominated the English stage until 1838 when the first performance of Shakespeare's text (albeit a shortened and modified version) was staged, with William Charles Macready in the role of Lear.[67] The Romantic critics had made an impact in their view of the play as unperformable, although Victorian stage spectacle made every effort to prove them wrong. Among the critics, the focus on character criticism continued with Lear considered the personification of suffering and, above all, a father whose daughters had wronged him.

Charles Dickens saw Macready playing Lear and praised the production: it reintroduced the character of the Fool, who Dickens considered 'one of the most wonderful creations of Shakespeare's genius'.[68] Dickens imagines Shakespeare writing the play and 'feeling suddenly, with an

instinct of divinest genius, that its gigantic sorrows could never be presented on the stage' since, without the 'quiet pathos' of the fool, we
would experience 'a suffering too frightful, a sublimity too remote, a
grandeur too terrible'.[69] Dickens says little about the other characters in
the play, and does not mention the blinding of Gloucester, but claims
that Lear's 'love for the Fool is associated with Cordelia, who had been
kind to the poor boy, and for the loss of whom he pines away'. His view
of the elder sisters is in keeping with that of earlier critics when he refers
to 'the wolf Goneril'.[70] He also regards the play as a domestic tragedy,
never mentioning that Lear is a king but, rather, characterizing him as
'the father [. . .] broken down to his last despairing struggle, his heart
swelling gradually upwards till it bursts in its closing sigh'.[71]

The Victorians tried to match the grandeur of a play many thought
unperformable by using every technical innovation at their disposal, as
is clear from an anonymous review of Charles Kean's production in
1858, with Kean in the role of Lear. The production was set in ancient
Britain and the reviewer praised the marvellous scenery provided by
'the mechanist's and scene-painter's department' in the second scene of
the third act when Lear contends with the storm:

> The clouds and electric fluid travelling rapidly across the sky in
> the distance, and with a lurid gloom investing the entire land-
> scape, were grandly terrific; and, when associated by the mind
> with the animated figures in the foreground – the raving Lear, the
> exhausted Fool, and the provident Kent – composed a picture
> that was truly sublime.[72]

But many remained unconvinced that Lear's mental turmoil could be
realized and for them the best *Lear* was in the imagination. Writing in
1883, Henry James echoes the opinion of Charles Lamb when he asserts
'*King Lear* is not to be acted', adding '*Lear* is a great and terrible poem, –
the most sublime, possibly, of all dramatic poems; but it is not to my
conception, a play'.[73] When Henry Irving presented a production of
King Lear in 1892, he cut 46 per cent of the lines, six of the original
twenty-six scenes, including the blinding of Gloucester, and made a
number of other modifications, but still reviews of the play were mixed.[74]
George Bernard Shaw proclaimed that Irving 'murdered Shakespear's
Lear so horribly in cutting it down that he made it unintelligible'.[75]

The leading critic of the later nineteenth century was Edward
Dowden, whose *Shakspere: A Critical Study of his Mind and Art*, the first
critical book on Shakespeare by a professional academic, was published
in 1875 and went through twelve British editions before 1901.[76] In the

preface, Dowden explained that his aim was to inquire into the mind of Shakespeare, 'to observe, as far as possible, in its several stages the growth of his intellect and character from youth to full maturity'.[77] Where earlier critics had focused on the minds of Shakespeare's characters, Dowden's objective was to explore what kind of mind it was that had created the plays, in order to better understand them:

> The stupendous mass of Lear's agony, and the spasms of anguish which make Othello writhe in body as in mind, fell within the compass of the same imagination that included at the other extremity the trembling expectation of Troilus, before the entrance of Cressida [. . .][78]

Yet Dowden resembled earlier critics in his conception of *King Lear* as almost unbearably magnificent in scale: he echoes Coleridge and Hazlitt when he describes it as a play where 'Everything [. . .] is in motion, and the motion is that of a tempest' so that 'All that we see around us is tempestuously whirling and heaving'.[79] Dowden emphasized 'the moral mystery, the grand inexplicableness of the play', observing that it has 'some vast impersonal significance, like the Prometheus bound of Æschylus, and like Goethe's Faust'.[80] Although Dowden noted that 'ethical principles radiate through the play', he maintained that its 'chief function is not, even indirectly, to teach or inculcate moral truth' but, rather, to 'free, arouse, dilate' in a manner similar to music.[81] Nonetheless, the play presented the reader with a sense that 'evil is abnormal' and 'good is normal'.[82] Like previous critics, Dowden admired the Fool and Kent and, like them, he found Edmund's behaviour explicable: 'His birth is shameful, and the brand burns into his heart and brain'.[83] He also accepted as a given Edgar's harsh moralizing of Gloucester's sin in begetting Edmund ('The dark and vicious place where thee he got / Cost him his eyes', 5.3.163–64), noting that 'Gloucester's sufferings do not appear to us inexplicably mysterious'.[84] Like those before him, he saw Goneril and Regan as monstrous, although he found Goneril the more abnormal and monstrous of the two and described Cordelia as possessing 'unmingled tenderness and strength, a pure redeeming ardour'.[85] He characterized Lear as 'grandly passive – played upon by all the manifold forces of nature and of society'.[86]

A few years after Dowden's *Shakespeare: His Mind and Art*, the poet and critic Algernon Charles Swinburne published *A Study of Shakespeare* (1880). Where Dowden found much of the play inexplicable, Swinburne considered it unrelentingly grim. Like Dowden, he found the play magnificent and made the same comparisons with classical writing: 'It is by far the most Æschylean of his works; the most elemental and primeval, the most oceanic and Titanic in conception.'[87] But Swinburne also thought it the least optimistic of Shakespeare's plays:

> in one main point it differs radically from the work and the spirit of Æschylus. Its fatalism is of a darker and harder nature. To Prometheus the fetters of the lord and enemy of mankind were bitter [. . .] yet in the not utterly infinite or everlasting distance we see beyond them the promise of the morning on which mystery and justice shall be made one; when righteousness and omnipotence at last shall kiss each other. But on the horizon of Shakespeare's tragic fatalism we see no such twilight of atonement, such pledge of reconciliation as this.[88]

Swinburne thought Gloucester's view of the world ('As flies to wanton boys are we to th' gods; / They kill us for their sport', 4.1.37–38) served to 'strike the keynote of the whole poem'.[89] As for the characters, Regan is 'devilish', Goneril is 'hellish' and even Cordelia is imperfect, revealing 'one passing touch of intolerance for what her sister was afterwards to brand as indiscretion and dotage in their father'.[90] Although Kent is referred to as 'the exception' to the evil we witness in Regan, the play offers no hope. George Bernard Shaw concurred, noting that in other plays Shakespeare mixed comedy with tragedy, but 'Lear may pass for pure tragedy; for even the fool in Lear is tragic'[91] and observing what he termed 'the blasphemous despair of Lear'.[92]

Swinburne did not connect *King Lear* with early modern political realities and nor did Dowden. As Foakes pointed out, Denton Snider's *The Shakespearian Drama* was the first work to recognize that the play engaged with contemporary political issues: corruption, the abuse of power and, specifically, an absolutist monarchy. Unfortunately, as Foakes noted, Snider's work would be entirely eclipsed by A. C. Bradley's famous book *Shakespearean Tragedy*,[93] which will be considered below.

The Twentieth Century

In an essay first published in 1906, 'Shakespeare and the Drama', Leo Tolstoy objected to Shakespeare's *King Lear* as 'absurd', complaining that its reputation was ill-deserved, since 'far from being the height of perfection it is a very poor, carelessly constructed work'.[94] Tolstoy objected that Shakespeare's play was unrealistic, noting that 'the characters all talk as no people ever talked or could talk'[95] and that he preferred the anonymous *King Leir*. His views on the play were challenged in an essay by George Orwell, 'Lear, Tolstoy and the Fool', first published in 1950, yet even Orwell thought that Shakespeare's play would have been more appealing if some characters and scenes did not exist – if there had been only one wicked daughter and if the Dover Cliff scene and Edgar himself had been omitted.[96] More insightful criticism was forthcoming in A. C. Bradley's *Shakespearean Tragedy*, first published in 1904 and based on a series of lectures Bradley delivered as Professor of poetry at Oxford. Bradley presents what is essentially an Aristotelian view of Shakespeare's *Hamlet, Othello, King Lear* and *Macbeth* with each tragedy containing, as Ruth Nevo put it, 'an idealized noble hero marred by a fatal flaw, which, after causing a convulsion in nature, is expiated by his death'.[97] Bradley considers Lear's flaw to be his self-indulgence: 'Lear follows an old man's whim, half generous, half selfish; and in a moment it looses all the powers of darkness upon him'.[98] Unlike Swinburne, Bradley views the world in which Lear is set as one that appears to be guided by 'a rational and a moral order' and one where consequences are important,[99] something he detected in all Shakespeare's tragedies. He claims that the play offers not a pointlessly cruel universe where suffering has no meaning, but one in which Lear is finally redeemed and suggests that the play might be more truthfully entitled 'The Redemption of King Lear'.

Following Charles Lamb in considering *King Lear* 'too huge for the stage',[100] Bradley embarks upon a critical analysis of the play as literature, dividing most of the characters in *King Lear* into two categories: good or evil. Among the latter, he finds Oswald 'the most contemptible of them'[101] but notes that we do feel some sympathy toward him because of the loyalty he shows towards Goneril, his mistress. Bradley is typical in his assessment of Goneril and Regan as monstrous, noting that Regan 'is the most hideous human being (if she is one) that Shakespeare ever drew' and he finds Cornwall a coward with 'no redeeming trait'.[102] He considers Edmund 'an adventurer pure and simple' and, like critics before him, has some sympathy for his behaviour, noting that his illegitimacy makes him 'the product of Nature', which thus explains why he rejects social order and moral codes.[103]

Among the good characters, he placed Cordelia, Kent, Edgar and the Fool, yet he recognizes their failings: Kent is 'hot and rash' and although he considers Cordelia in positive terms as 'a thing enskyed and sainted', he is also critical of her, noting that, 'At a moment where terrible issues join, Fate makes on her the one demand which she is unable to meet.'[104] Similarly, Edgar is considered good, and his determination admired, but he is too judgmental to be much liked.[105] For Bradley neither Gloucester nor Albany fit neatly into the categories of good or evil. He finds Gloucester 'weak though good-hearted' and thinks his character neither interesting nor distinct, while Albany's 'is merely sketched' and, having just married Goneril, 'the idea is, I think, that he has been bewitched by her fiery beauty not less than by her dowry'.[106] Bradley's consideration of what might have attracted Albany to Goneril, something Shakespeare does not mention, is one example of his tendency to imagine the characters' lives outside the play. For example, he wonders what it must have been like for Cordelia when growing up:

Of all Shakespeare's heroines she knew least of joy. She grew up with Goneril and Regan for sisters. Even her love for her father must have been mingled with pain and anxiety. She must early have learned to school and repress emotion. She never knew the bliss of young love: there is no trace of such love for the King of France.[107]

Bradley has been much criticized for this approach to the plays, most famously in a 1933 essay by L. C. Knights, 'How Many Children Had Lady Macbeth?',[108] the title based on her announcement, 'I have given suck, and know / How tender 'tis to love the babe that milks me' (1.7.54–55). The question posed by Knights is rhetorical; Macbeth and his wife have no children and Knights's purpose is to denounce speculation about the lives of characters outside of what the fiction tells us.

Like the Romantic critics before him, A. C. Bradley did not concern himself with the generic distinction between drama, written for the stage, and poetry, written for private reading. The notion that Shakespeare's plays should be read as poems is no longer accepted and, although outright dismissal of the view has been challenged by Lukas Erne,[109] it is fair to say that the critical consensus is currently for a stage-centred view of Shakespeare. This development emerged in the first half of the twentieth century. In 1927, Harley Granville-Barker, a theatre director and playwright, published his *Prefaces to Shakespeare*, the first of a number of essays on Shakespeare's plays, including *King Lear*. Although Granville-Barker's influence would not make itself fully felt until the 1950s, this was the beginning of a move toward regarding Shakespeare primarily as a playwright and his plays as scripts for performance.

In his essay on *King Lear*, Granville-Barker's retort to Charles Lamb and A. C. Bradley, who both thought *King Lear* should not be performed, was that 'Shakespeare meant it to be acted, and he was a very practical playwright'.[110] Granville-Barker interprets *King Lear* from the actor's point of view, claiming that any good performance emerges from synergy between the actor and the text: 'the matured actor [. . .] must comprehend the character, identify himself with it, and then – forget himself in it'.[111] Crucially, a production should not aim at realism by presenting the storm on stage (something earlier critics had scorned) because 'the storm is not in itself [. . .] dramatically important, only its effect upon Lear'.[112] Granville-Barker provides a fascinating analysis of the play's language (for example Shakespeare's use of repetition) and notes that it is anchored in a simplicity that prevents the characters from ranging so wide that 'interpretation could hardly compass them'.[113] He describes Edgar's 'imaginary tale of Dover' as consisting of 'the clearest-cut actualities of description' and, focusing on the play's final scene, points out that it is the 'contrast and reconciliation of grandeur and simplicity, this setting of vision in terms of actuality, this inarticulate passion which breaks now and again into memorable phrases' that makes the play 'directed to one end', and that end is its performance in a theatre.[114] In his section analysing 'the characters and their interplay', Granville-Barker focuses on Lear, specifically on what an actor should make of Lear's development as the play progresses and, throughout, he displays an actor's sensitivities to how a particular scene could most effectively come alive on stage.

It was precisely because Granville-Barker was an actor and playwright that his stage-centred views on Shakespeare, initially at least, did not penetrate the academy that still venerated Bradley. It was a book by a professional academic that triggered the rise in stage-centred thinking among professional academic critics and helped establish Shakespeare primarily as a dramatist rather than a poet. M. C. Bradbrook's *Elizabethan Stage Conditions*, first published in 1932, claimed that the key to understanding Shakespeare was to understand the theatre industry within which he worked. Commenting on *King Lear*, Bradbrook notes, 'It was only the bareness of the stage that allowed Shakespeare to introduce the heath scenes in *Lear*, where "the actor impersonates the storm and Lear together", or rather the poetry provides them both'.[115] For Bradbrook, to privilege the reading of Shakespeare's plays over their performance was to ignore the creative conditions which gave rise to them and, in effect, to misread drama as poetry.

Bradbrook's work was hugely influential and encouraged the performance of Shakespeare's plays as a serious subject for academic study. Another kind of criticism that was emerging in the 1930s, and one that took less time to make its impact felt, was 'New Criticism'. Character criticism, of the kind offered by Bradley, was still read, but a new generation of critics was becoming more interested in the language of the plays and how it impacted upon their structure. Soon character study was demoted, and symbols, metaphors and images, the minutiae within the whole, became more important. In 1930, G. Wilson Knight published his influential study *Wheel of Fire: Interpretation of Shakespeare's Tragedy*, in which he remarked that each of Shakespeare's plays should be understood as an 'expanded metaphor'.[116] The title of the book is taken from an exchange between Lear and Cordelia when they meet for the first time since her return from France:

> Cordelia (to Lear) How does my royal lord? How fares your
>   majesty?
> Lear   You do me wrong to take me out o' th' grave.
>   Thou art a soul in bliss, but I am bound
>   Upon a wheel of fire, that mine own tears
>   Do scald like molten lead. (4.6.37–41)

Knight was influenced by new particle physics, the process of splitting into smaller parts a larger whole, and thus conceived the play in those terms. For Knight, the image of 'a wheel of fire' indicates a larger meaning (the pain of mortal life), and his focus is on the symbolic function of character, whereby a Christ-like Cordelia is 'bright with an angel brightness'.[117] In his analysis of Goneril and Regan, Knight concentrates on the animalistic imagery and metaphors used to describe them, concluding that such language 'show[s] how firmly based on thoughts of nature is the philosophy of *King Lear*'.[118] The Fool becomes a 'symbol of humour' and Gloucester's physical torments are symbolic of the mental anguish suffered by Lear, whereby 'the Gloucester-theme throughout reflects and emphasizes and exaggerates all the percurrent qualities of the Lear theme'.[119]

In the preface to the fourth edition of the book, first published in 1949, Knight defended his work against accusations that he had been too critical of the work of his predecessors, specifically the character analysis of Bradley and the stage-centred approach to the plays promoted by Granville-Barker. Although he praises Bradley's approach, albeit less than effusively, he argues that 'the literary analysis of great drama in terms of theatrical technique accomplishes singularly little', adding that although a critic ought to be 'dramatically aware' his criticism of the play must attend to 'the penetration of its deeper meanings'.[120]

Consideration of metaphor and imagery in Shakespeare plays developed further in the work of Image Critics, the most important being Caroline Spurgeon, whose book *Shakespeare's Imagery: And What It Tells Us* was first published in 1935. Although she did not use the term 'unconscious' and did not announce herself as a psychoanalytical critic, Spurgeon was clearly doing such work when she identified conscious and unconscious images in Shakespeare's plays, noting patterns and repetitions in specific plays and comparing Shakespeare's use of imagery with that of his contemporaries such as Christopher Marlowe and Ben Jonson. Spurgeon argued that the dominating image in *King Lear* is that of a body subjected to immense violence:

> In the play we are conscious all through of the atmosphere of buf-
> feting, strain and strife, and, at moments, of bodily tension to the
> point of agony [. . .] of a human body in anguished movement,
> tugged, wrenched, beaten, pierced, stung, scourged, dislocated,
> flayed, gashed, scalded, tortured, and finally broken on the
> rack.[121]

Spurgeon's work was hugely influential and her book was reprinted five times by 1968, and although she had her detractors such as Stanley Edgar Hyman, even he had to admit that Spurgeon's study 'does a good many things of real value' and that later critics were indebted to her work: he noted that, 'Almost all critical writing on Shakespeare since 1935 has taken advantage of Miss Spurgeon's researches' and 'the ser-ious imaginative constructions it demands'.[122] One of the critics indebted to Spurgeon's work was Wolfgang Clemen who, in *The Development of Shakespeare's Imagery*, considered *King Lear* as the play most able to withstand an interpretation wholly on the basis of its imagery because its imagery 'seems to be more fully integrated into the structure of the drama'.[123] Clemen provides a detailed analysis of language used through-out the play, observing that many of the images in the first scene are prophetic and he attends to the play's focus on natural imagery, specific-ally references to the animal world. He considers figurative language a characteristic form of expression for Lear and the Fool: Lear's inability to understand others makes him speak 'to the elements, to nature to the heavens' and the Fool communicates to him 'in simile, proverb and image'.[124] Clemen argues that the 'bad' characters do not exploit the resources of poetic language and considers Goneril, Regan and Edmund 'calculating, cool and unimaginative people who are incapable of "cre-ative" imagery'.[125] For Clemen, the middle acts of the play are the richest in imagery, since 'the outer drama has become an inner drama', plot is less important and the focus becomes 'not what Lear does, but what he suffers, feels and envisions with his inner eye',[126] his personal suffering symbolizing the suffering that is going on in the world around him.

We have seen that in the 1930s stage-centred criticism had begun to emerge and the study of language became more important than charac-ter study but still under-developed was an historicizing of the drama, an awareness of the plays as products of their time and thus specific to the world that had created them. An interest in historicism emerged again with Lily B. Campbell's *Shakespeare's Tragic Heroes: Slaves of Passion*, first published in 1930. Campbell incorporates early modern views about the body and philosophy. So, too, E. M. W. Tillyard's *The Elizabethan World Picture*, first published in 1943, also presents the view that Shakespeare's plays reflected and endorsed the social and political realities of his time. These critics, later described as Old Historicists, structured their books innovatively by delaying a discussion of Shakespeare until after the reader had received what they termed 'background', their reconstruction of what they considered to be Shakespeare's thought-system. Old Historicism was very influential in the 1940s and 1950s, and incompatible with New Criticism that ignored the play's political context in order to focus on the metaphors and images that the New Critics thought explained the larger structure of the play. Campbell saw Shakespeare's plays as 'mirrors' of early modern ideology, while Tillyard considered the Elizabethans' outlook to be structured by what he termed 'the chain of being', a concept which described Shakespeare's world, and his understanding of it, as providential and ordered. Indeed, Nicholas Grene underlines that Tillyard read Shakespeare's history plays as

> the grandly consistent embodiment of the orthodox political and social morality of the Elizabethan period, preaching order and hierarchy, condemning factious power-seeking and the anarchy of civil war to which it led, commending the divinely sanctioned centralised monarchy of the Tudors.[127]

Tillyard's view of what most Elizabethans believed about social order and providence was that God or his agents would punish those who violated God's order. Tillyard did not comment at great length on *King Lear*, but his re-creation of the Elizabethan mind-set encouraged the view that the play should be understood in terms of a violation against order and hierarchy and its conclusion as the putting right of that violation by divine providence. Campbell's *Shakespeare's Tragic Heroes* included chapters on what were now known as 'the big four' Shakespeare plays, those that had been focused on by Bradley: *Hamlet, Othello, King Lear* and *Macbeth*. In the chapter on *King Lear*, Campbell shows that in the Renaissance, intemperate anger was condemned and thought invariably to bring shame upon those who gave way to it. Shakespeare, and his audience, would have believed the old especially prone to anger; it was also believed that old men used their age as an excuse for sloth, which makes Lear's decision to give up his kingdom a selfish desire to release himself from his duties. A contemporary audience would also have recognized Goneril and Regan as flatterers, something Lear cannot spot because he is guilty of self-love. These philosophical themes in the main plot are repeated in the Gloucester subplot, where, 'Again a father is moved by the flattery of an undeserving child to cast off the loyal child and prefer the flatterer in his place'.[128] Campbell also considers other Renaissance ideas such as the relationship between the elements and the mind of man.

Later critics, the so-called New Historicists and Cultural Materialists, objected to what they saw as the totalizing models of ideology used by Old Historicism. What these later critics particularly disliked about their predecessors was what they perceived as the lack of space for dissent: they believed that the view of Elizabethan culture presented by critics such as Tillyard and Campbell suggested that no Elizabethan could think the unthinkable or could imagine a radically different ordering of the world. This is not quite fair on the Old Historicists, who would likely have acknowledged that their focus was on the culture's dominant beliefs and who had, after, all made important inroads into contextualizing Shakespeare studies, but all that tended to get lost in the new emphasis on the marginal and subversion that would emerge in the 1980s. New Historicism and Cultural Materialism did not develop until that decade and will be considered below, but first it is important to mention a significant development regarding critical consensus about the kind of play Shakespeare presented in *King Lear*.

In 1960, an essay by Barbara Everett, entitled 'The New *King Lear*' and published in the academic journal *Critical Quarterly*, questioned the established view that Shakespeare's play was primarily Christian in outlook and dealt with Lear's redemption. Everett noted that this view, expressed by Kenneth Muir in his recent Arden edition of the play, originated with A. C. Bradley, but misrepresented Bradley's suggestions as clear opinion. She traced the shift from a focus on plot to a focus on poetry so that, from the Romantics onwards, what actually happens in the play became less important than its poetry and what happens to Lear's body became less important than what might happen to his soul. The notion that Lear dies in an agony of ecstasy, suggested by Bradley, had become a commonplace, argued Everett, but critics tended to overlook what she termed Bradley's 'honest doubt'[129] about Lear's redemption and the complexity of his argument – for example his depiction of Cordelia as not entirely ideal.

Everett's essay was an important corrective to a view of the play that had long become orthodox and was taken up by William Elton in his book-length study of the play, *King Lear and the Gods*, first published in 1966. Elton challenged the still widespread view 'that Lear is an optimistically Christian drama' in the sense that Lear is redeemed by his suffering and that it indicates 'a cosmically derived plan, which somehow gives providential significance to the events of the tragedy'.[130] Elton pointed out that in the period in which Shakespeare was writing, the concept of providence came increasingly into question and there emerged a view of God as apparently arbitrary and capricious. Moreover, the Christian reading of the play took little account of the heathen landscape in which it is set and of the role given to superstition; while Shakespeare's source, the anonymous play *King Leir*, is full of Christian emphases, these were clearly avoided by Shakespeare.[131] Crucially, Elton asserts that 'no evidence exists to show that Lear arrives finally at "salvation", "regeneration" or "redemption"', and 'the purported benevolent, just or special providence cannot be shown to be operative'.[132] According to Elton, 'those interpretations which see the tragedy as a traditional morality and those which see it as following the sin-suffering-redemption pattern are a result of unhistorical, a priori misreading of the work's significance'.[133] These critics seem to be on the right track but only until the end of Act Four because the fifth act destroys any sense of providential redemption.

It should be remembered that Elton, like the critics before him and those who would come after, held views on *King Lear* that did not develop in a vacuum but were influenced by the world around them. In *'Hamlet' versus 'Lear'* (1993), Foakes considered why, since the mid-1950s, *King Lear* had knocked *Hamlet* off the top spot in generally being considered Shakespeare's most profound play. Foakes provided a list of world events that occurred between 1954 and 1965, among them the assassination of President John F. Kennedy and incidents relating to the development of nuclear weapons and noted that although there is no simple explanation for *King Lear* overtaking *Hamlet*, the shift in dominance of each play 'strikingly coincided with a period of political change'.[134] As Foakes indicated, the traditional understanding of *King Lear* as a play about 'Lear's pilgrimage to discover his soul' changed post-1960, whereby the play came to be seen as 'significant in political terms, in a world in which old men have held on to and abused power, often in corrupt or arbitrary ways'.[135] As we saw earlier, Swinburne also viewed the play as bleak, but he was the exception rather than the rule; in 1960s, the consensus had shifted.

Political consciousness was clearly at work in Jan Kott's *Shakespeare Our Contemporary*, a study of Shakespeare's tragedies and comedies, originally written in Polish and first published in English in 1964, with the second edition revised for publication in 1967. In the chapter entitled *'King Lear*, or Endgame' Kott invokes Samuel Beckett's play and throughout draws parallels between Shakespeare and Beckett's *Endgame*, an example of what was termed 'the new theater', with its focus on the grotesque. In his analysis of the *King Lear*, Kott concentrates on the Dover cliff scene and the figure of the Fool. The Dover cliff scene is a 'pantomime', one in which 'a madman leads a blind man and talks him into believing in a non-existing cliff'.[136] In this scene, Gloucester represents Everyman and his struggle in the world and it reveals the wider theme of the play, which is 'an inquiry into the meaning of this journey, into the existence or non-existence of Heaven and Hell'.[137] Gloucester's 'suicide mime' is grotesque and so, too, is the accompanying dialogue with his pleas to the Gods because they do not intervene. As Kott put it 'if the gods, and their moral order in the world, do not exist, Gloster's suicide does not solve or alter anything. It is only a somersault on an empty stage'.[138] *King Lear* is, thus, concerned with 'the decay and fall of the world'[139] and it is a world where no one is healed, where even the good who survive are 'ruined pieces of nature', as Gloucester says to Lear when he meets him in his madness. For Kott, the Fool is a philosopher and the only figure in the play who stands apart from the dominant ideology and 'deprives majesty of its sacredness'.[140] In using 'dialectics, paradox and an absurd kind of humour', the Fool evokes the modern grotesque, exposing the absurdity of the world and taking Lear though 'the school of clown's philosophy'.[141]

Kott was living and writing under Eastern European Communist rule and it is clear that his understanding of *King Lear* was informed by the political realities of a one-party system where there was little free speech and challenging the ruling elite in any significant way was severely punished. He was what we would call a 'Presentist' critic, one for whom the present informs our understanding of the past, who considers Shakespeare's writings not in the context of Renaissance ideology or early modern staging, but in terms of current ideas and concepts and their relevance to his writings.

Campbell and Tillyard had used their synthesis of Elizabethan ideology as a map-grid to provide the bearings for critical interpretation. Where the Old Historicists tended to take the official line coming from centres of authority, like the Church and the Monarchy, and to assume that everyone believed what they were told to believe, the New Historicists wanted to emphasize that people can often see beyond the official line, and can think new thoughts forbidden by the dominant ideology in their culture. The New Historicist critic typically takes an obscure, marginal, non-literary text to read as a parallel text alongside the literary text, and draws common threads. In *Shakespearean Negotiations*, first published in 1988, Stephen Greenblatt's analysis of *King Lear*, 'Shakespeare and the Exorcists', is typically New Historicist in that it does not privilege the literary text but, instead, focuses on the interplay between *King Lear* and one of Shakespeare's sources, Samuel Harsnett's *A Declaration of Egregious Popish Impostures* (1603). Greenblatt considers what Harsnett's attack on Catholic exorcism can tell us about Edgar's feigned madness and how this relates to theatrical performance itself. New Historicists and Cultural Materialists share a rejection of what they perceive as idealism, whether in the alleged totalizing models of ideology of the Old Historicists or the assertion of transcendent meanings in literary texts. This is clear from Jonathan Dollimore's *Radical Tragedy*, first published in 1980, which included a chapter on *King Lear*. Dollimore rejected Humanist readings of tragic protagonists from critics such as Clifford Leech[142] and Wilbur Sanders,[143] both of whom replaced the notion of Christian redemption by privileging humanity rather than God, offering an analysis of tragedy that 'mystifies suffering and invests man with a quasi-transcendent identity'.[144] Dollimore offers instead a materialist reading of *King Lear*, one that reminds us that it is 'above all, a play about power, property and inheritance'.[145]

Power, property and inheritance would also be the concerns of later critics who continued to engage with politics and produce theoretically inflected criticism. Unlike *Othello* and *The Merchant of Venice*, *King Lear* has not much interested critics investigating race and racism but an important area of criticism that emerged from the 1980s onwards was gender-criticism. With the emergence of feminist politics in the 1970s there was a new focus on the manner in which Shakespeare negotiated relationships between men and women. Where previous generations of mostly male critics had condemned the monstrous Goneril and Regan, praised the angelic Cordelia, and presented Lear as a flawed hero, feminist critics considered more carefully the gender dynamics at work in the plays. In her article 'The Patriarchal Bard', Kathleen McLuskie considered the play in terms of the patriarchal family as well as the misogyny of the play and its eponymous hero, arguing that Cordelia's 'saving love' works as 'an example of patriarchy restored'.[146] Another important essay was Coppélia Kahn's 'The Absent Mother in *King Lear*', which also focused on the patriarchal family, one where the figure of the mother has been suppressed. The very absence of a literal mother in the play, argues Kahn, 'points to her hidden presence',[147] such as when Lear describes the hysteria within him as a mother ('O, how this mother swells up toward my heart!', 2.2.231). Kahn proposes that 'Lear's madness is essentially his rage at being deprived of the maternal presence',[148] something he sought in Cordelia. She contends that, 'Despite a lifetime of strenuous defense against admitting feeling and the power of feminine presence into his world [. . .] Lear manages to let them in', learning finally to recognize her as his child and thus 'acknowledging the bond of paternity that he denied in the first act'.[149] Kahn's book was influenced by psychoanalysis, a critical approach also at work in Janet Adelman's 'Suffocating Mothers in *King Lear*', a chapter from her book-length study of masculinity and the maternal body in Shakespeare. Adelman argues that *King Lear* resembles *Hamlet* in dramatizing 'the immense fear and longing of a son's relationship with a mother', the difference being that Lear is both father and son 'collapsed into one figure' and 'here all the traditional guarantees of identity itself dissolve in a terrifying female moisture in which mother and daughter, male and female, inner and outer, self and other, lose their boundaries, threatening a return to the primal chaos'.[150] The politicizing of *King Lear* would continue into the twenty-first century and one important theory to emerge was ecocriticism, an examination of cultural constructions of the natural world via its social and political contexts. Anthony Parr's focus on ecocriticism in the New Directions section of this volume suggests that this way of reading Shakespeare is getting the attention it deserves.

Notes

1. Gāmini Salgādo, *Eyewitnesses of Shakespeare: First Hand Accounts of Performances, 1590–1890* (London: Chatto and Windus, for Sussex University Press, 1975).
2. William Shakespeare, *[King Lear] M. William Shak-speare: His True Chronicle Historie of the Life and Death of King Lear and His Three Daughters*, STC 22292 BEPD 265a (Q1) (London: [Nicholas Okes] for Nathaniel Butter, 1608).
3. William Shakespeare, *The History of King Lear*, ed. by Stanley Wells, The Oxford Shakespeare (Oxford: Oxford University Press, 2000), p. 10.
4. Geoffrey Bullough, ed., *Narrative and Dramatic Sources of Shakespeare*, 8 vols (London: Routledge and Kegan Paul, 1973), VII, pp. 269–420.
5. Stanley Wells, Gary Taylor, John Jowett and William Montgomery, *William Shakespeare: A Textual Companion* (Oxford: Clarendon Press, 1987), p. 509.
6. Wells et al., *William Shakespeare: A Textual Companion*, p. 509.
7. Gary Taylor and Michael Warren, eds, *The Division of the Kingdoms: Shakespeare's Two Versions of King Lear*, Oxford Shakespeare Studies (Oxford: Oxford University Press, 1983).
8. R. A. Foakes, *'Hamlet' Versus 'Lear': Cultural Politics and Shakespeare's Art* (Cambridge: Cambridge University Press, 1993), p. 111.
9. William Shakespeare, *King Lear*, ed. by R. A. Foakes, The Arden Shakespeare, Third series (Walton-on-Thames: Thomas Nelson, 1997).
10. Nahum Tate, *The History of King Lear. Acted at the Duke's Theatre. Reviv'd with Alterations*, WING S2918 (London: E. Flesher, 1681), sig. A2v.
11. Tate, *The History of King Lear. Acted at the Duke's Theatre. Reviv'd with Alterations*, sig. A2v–A3r.
12. Sonia Massai, 'Nahum Tate's Revision of Shakespeare's *King Lear*', *Studies in English Literature*, 40 (2000), 435–50 (p. 436).
13. Shakespeare, *The History of King Lear*, p. 62.
14. Shakespeare, *The History of King Lear*, pp. 62–63.
15. Tate, *The History of King Lear*, sig. A2v.
16. Massai, 'Nahum Tate's Revision', p. 436.
17. John Dryden, *John Dryden: Selected Criticism*, ed. by James Kinsley and George Parfitt, Oxford Paperback English Texts (Oxford: Clarendon Press, 1970), pp. 171, 177.
18. Dryden, *John Dryden: Selected Criticism*, pp. 165, 174.
19. Dryden, *John Dryden: Selected Criticism*, p. 165.
20. Thomas Rymer, *The Critical Works of Thomas Rymer*, ed. by Curt A. Zimansky (Westport, CT: Greenwood, 1971), p. 161.

21 William Shakespeare, *The Works of Shakespeare*, ed. by Lewis Theobald (London: A. Bettesworth and C. Hitch [and] J. Tonson [etc.], 1733), p. xxxi.

22 Jean I. Marsden, *The Re-imagined Text: Shakespeare, Adaptation, and Eighteenth-century Literary Theory* (Lexington: University Press of Kentucky, 1995), p. 70.

23 William Shakespeare, *The Plays of William Shakespeare in Eight Volumes*, ed. by Samuel Johnson (London: J. and R. Tonson et al., 1765), p. 158.

24 Shakespeare, *The Plays in Eight Volumes*, p. 158.

25 Shakespeare, *The Plays in Eight Volumes*, pp. 158–59.

26 Shakespeare, *The Plays in Eight Volumes*, p. 159.

27 Shakespeare, *The Plays in Eight Volumes*, p. 159.

28 Shakespeare, *The Plays in Eight Volumes*, p. 159.

29 Shakespeare, *The Plays in Eight Volumes*, p. 159.

30 Brian Vickers, *Shakespeare: The Critical Heritage*, IV: 1753–1765 (London: Routledge and Kegan Paul, 1976), p. 249.

31 Vickers, *Shakespeare: The Critical Heritage*, IV: 1753–1765, p. 358.

32 Jean Marsden, 'Shakespeare and Sympathy', in *Shakespeare and the Eighteenth Century*, ed. by Peter Sabor and Paul Yachnin (Aldershot: Ashgate, 2008), pp. 29–41 (p. 36).

33 Marsden, 'Shakespeare and Sympathy', p. 37.

34 Samuel Taylor Coleridge, *Coleridge on Shakespeare: A Selection of the Essays, Notes and Lectures of Samuel Taylor Coleridge on the Poems and Plays of Shakespeare*, ed. by Terence Hawkes (Harmondsworth: Penguin, 1969), p. 197.

35 Coleridge, *Coleridge on Shakespeare*, p. 206.

36 Coleridge, *Coleridge on Shakespeare*, p. 207.

37 William Hazlitt, *Characters of Shakespeare's Plays*, Intro. by Sir Arthur Quiller-Couch, World's Classics (Oxford: Oxford University Press, 1916), pp. 125–26.

38 Unless otherwise indicated this and all following references to *King Lear* in this chapter are to *The Complete Works*, prepared by William Montgomery and Lou Burnard, Oxford Electronic Publishing (Oxford: Oxford University Press, 1989).

39 Coleridge, *Coleridge on Shakespeare*, p. 207.

40 Hazlitt, *Characters of Shakespeare's Plays*, p. 140.

41 Coleridge, *Coleridge on Shakespeare*, p. 198.

42 Coleridge, *Coleridge on Shakespeare*, p. 201.

43 Coleridge, *Coleridge on Shakespeare*, p. 202.

44 Coleridge, *Coleridge on Shakespeare*, pp. 201–2.

45 Hazlitt, *Characters of Shakespeare's Plays*, p. 125.

46 Coleridge, *Coleridge on Shakespeare*, pp. 200, 203–4.

47 Coleridge, *Coleridge on Shakespeare*, p. 203

48 Coleridge, *Coleridge on Shakespeare*, p. 204.

49 Coleridge, *Coleridge on Shakespeare*, p. 198.

50 Coleridge, *Coleridge on Shakespeare*, p. 206.

51 Coleridge, *Coleridge on Shakespeare*, p. 205.

52 Hazlitt, *Characters of Shakespeare's Plays*, p. 126.

53 Hazlitt, *Characters of Shakespeare's Plays*, pp. 126, 129.

54 Hazlitt, *Characters of Shakespeare's Plays*, pp. 126–27, 129.

55 Hazlitt, *Characters of Shakespeare's Plays*, p. 126.

56 Shakespeare, *King Lear*, p. 67.

57 Jonathan Bate, ed., *The Romantics on Shakespeare*, New Penguin Shakespeare Library (London: Penguin, 1992), p. 399.

58 Bate, *The Romantics on Shakespeare*, p. 400.

59 Charles Lamb, *Charles Lamb on Shakespeare*, ed. by Joan Coldwell (Gerrards Cross: Smythe, 1978), p. 36.

60   Lamb, *Charles Lamb on Shakespeare*, p. 36.

61   Lamb, *Charles Lamb on Shakespeare*, pp. 36–37.

62   Stanley Wells, *Shakespeare in the Theatre: An Anthology of Criticism* (Oxford: Clarendon Press, 1997), pp. 38–43.

63   Lamb, *Charles Lamb on Shakespeare*, p. 37.

64   John Keats, *John Keats: Selected Poems*, ed. by John Barnard (London: Penguin, 1988), pp. 88–89.

65   Wells, *Shakespeare in the Theatre*, p. 51.

66   Wells, *Shakespeare in the Theatre*, p. 52.

67   Shakespeare, *The History of King Lear*, p. 69.

68   Salgādo, *Eyewitnesses of Shakespeare*, p. 283.

69   Salgādo, *Eyewitnesses of Shakespeare*, p. 284.

70   Salgādo, *Eyewitnesses of Shakespeare*, pp. 285, 284.

71   Salgādo, *Eyewitnesses of Shakespeare: First Hand Accounts of Performances, 1590–1890*, pp. 286–87.

72   Salgado, *Eyewitnesses of Shakespeare*, p. 288.

73   Henry James, *The Scenic Art: Notes on Acting and the Drama, 1872–1901*, ed. by Allan Wade (London: R. Hart-Davis, 1949), p. 178.

74   Alan Hughes, *Henry Irving, Shakespearean* (Cambridge: Cambridge University Press, 1981), pp. 117–19.

75   George Bernard Shaw, *Pen Portraits and Reviews* (London: Constable, 1932), p. 162.

76   Adrian Poole, *Shakespeare and the Victorians*, Arden Critical Companions (London: Arden Shakespeare, 2004), p. 225.

77   Edward Dowden, *Shakspere: A Critical Study of His Mind and Art* (London: Henry S. King, 1875), p. v.

78   Dowden, *Shakspere: A Critical Study*, p. 25.

79   Dowden, *Shakspere: A Critical Study*, p. 257.

80   Dowden, *Shakspere: A Critical Study*, pp. 265, 259.

81   Dowden, *Shakspere: A Critical Study*, p. 260.

82   Dowden, *Shakspere: A Critical Study*, pp. 268–69.

83   Dowden, *Shakspere: A Critical Study*, p. 266.

84   Dowden, *Shakspere: A Critical Study*, p. 266.

85   Dowden, *Shakspere: A Critical Study*, pp. 264, 259.

86   Dowden, *Shakspere: A Critical Study*, p. 272.

87   Algernon Charles Swinburne, *A Study of Shakespeare* (London: Chatto and Windus, 1880), p. 171.

88   Swinburne, *A Study of Shakespeare*, pp. 171–72.

89   Swinburne, *A Study of Shakespeare*, p. 172.

90   Swinburne, *A Study of Shakespeare*, p. 173.

91   Shaw, *Pen Portraits and Reviews*, p. 261.

92   Shaw, *Pen Portraits and Reviews*, p. 117.

93   Foakes, *'Hamlet' Versus 'Lear'*, pp. 48–49.

94   Leo Tolstoy, *Tolstoy on Art*, ed. by Aylmer Maude (London: Oxford University Press, 1924), p. 419.

95   Tolstoy, *Tolstoy on Art*, p. 423.

96   George Orwell, *Collected Essays*, 2nd edn (London: Secker and Warburg, 1961), pp. 415–34.

97   Ruth Nevo, *Tragic Form in Shakespeare* (Princeton, NJ: Princeton University Press, 1972), p. 10.

98   A. C. Bradley, *Shakespearean Tragedy: Lectures on 'Hamlet', 'Othello', 'King Lear', 'Macbeth'* (London: Macmillan, 1904), p. 28.

99   Bradley, *Shakespearean Tragedy*, p. 284.

100 Bradley, *Shakespearean Tragedy*, p. 247.

101 Bradley, *Shakespearean Tragedy*, p. 298.

102 Bradley, *Shakespearean Tragedy*, pp. 300, 299.

103 Bradley, *Shakespearean Tragedy*, pp. 301–2.

104 Bradley, *Shakespearean Tragedy*, pp. 308, 316–18.

105 Bradley, *Shakespearean Tragedy*, pp. 305–6.

106 Bradley, *Shakespearean Tragedy*, p. 297.

107 Bradley, *Shakespearean Tragedy*, p. 317.

108 L. C. Knights, *How Many Children Had Lady Macbeth? An Essay in the Theory and Practice of Shakespeare Criticism* (Cambridge: Minority Press, 1933).

109 Lukas Erne, *Shakespeare as Literary Dramatist* (Cambridge: Cambridge University Press, 2003)

110 Harley Granville-Barker, *Prefaces to Shakespeare*, 2 vols (London: B. T. Batsford, 1958), I: *Hamlet, King Lear, The Merchant of Venice, Antony and Cleopatra, Cymbeline*, p. 261.

111 Granville-Barker, *Prefaces to Shakespeare*, I, p. 269.

112 Granville-Barker, *Prefaces to Shakespeare*, I, p. 266.

113 Granville-Barker, *Prefaces to Shakespeare*, I, p. 280.

114 Granville-Barker, *Prefaces to Shakespeare*, I, pp. 281, 283.

115 M. C. Bradbrook, *Elizabethan Stage Conditions: A Study of Their Place in the Interpretation of Shakespeare's Plays* (Cambridge: Cambridge University Press, 1968), p. 48.

116 G. Wilson Knight, *The Wheel of Fire: Interpretations of Shakespearean Tragedy* (London: Methuen, 1954), p. 15.

117 Knight, *The Wheel of Fire*, p. 200.

118 Knight, *The Wheel of Fire*, p. 185.

119 Knight, *The Wheel of Fire*, pp. 165, 171.

120 Knight, *The Wheel of Fire*, p. vi.

121 Caroline Spurgeon, *Shakespeare's Imagery: And What It Tells Us* (Cambridge: Cambridge University Press, 1935), pp. 338–39.

122 Stanley Edgar Hyman, *The Armed Vision: A Study in the Methods of Modern Literary Criticism* (New York: Alfred A. Knopf, 1948), pp. 215, 221.

123 Wolfgang H. Clemen, *The Development of Shakespeare's Imagery* (London: Methuen, 1951), p. 133.

124 Clemen, *The Development of Shakespeare's Imagery*, p. 141.

125 Clemen, *The Development of Shakespeare's Imagery*, p. 135.

126 Clemen, *The Development of Shakespeare's Imagery*, p. 136.

127 Nicholas Grene, *Shakespeare's Serial History Plays* (Cambridge: Cambridge University Press, 2002), p. 45.

128 Lily B. Campbell, *Shakespeare's Tragic Heroes: Slaves of Passion* (London: Methuen, 1961), p. 189.

129 Barbara Everett, 'The New *King Lear*', in *Shakespeare, 'King Lear': A Casebook*, ed. by Frank Kermode, rev. edn, Casebook Series (Basingstoke: Macmillan, 1992), pp. 159–76 (p. 165).

130 William R. Elton, *'King Lear' and the Gods* (San Marino: Huntington Library, 1966), p. 1.

131 Elton, *'King Lear' and the Gods*, p. 335.

132 Elton, *'King Lear' and the Gods*, p. 336.

133 Elton, *'King Lear' and the Gods*, pp. 336–37.

134 Foakes, *'Hamlet' Versus 'Lear'*, p. 4.

135 Foakes, *'Hamlet' Versus 'Lear'*, p. 6.

136   Jan Kott, *Shakespeare Our Contemporary*, 2nd rev. edn (London: Methuen, 1967), p. 113.

137   Kott, *Shakespeare Our Contemporary*, p. 116.

138   Kott, *Shakespeare Our Contemporary*, pp. 118–19.

139   Kott, *Shakespeare Our Contemporary*, p. 120.

140   Kott, *Shakespeare Our Contemporary*, p. 131.

141   Kott, *Shakespeare Our Contemporary*, pp. 132–33.

142   Clifford Leech, *Shakespeare's Tragedies: And Other Studies in Seventeenth Century Drama* (London: Chatto and Windus, 1950), p. 15.

143   Wilbur Sanders, *The Dramatist and the Received Idea: Studies in the Plays of Marlowe and Shakespeare* (Cambridge: Cambridge University Press, 1968), pp. 336–37.

144   Jonathan Dollimore, *Radical Tragedy: Religion, Ideology and Power in the Drama of Shakespeare and His Contemporaries*, 2nd edn (London: Harvester Wheatsheaf, 1989), p. 190.

145   Dollimore, *Radical Tragedy*, p. 197.

146   Kathleen McLuskie, 'The Patriarchal Bard: Feminist Criticism and Shakespeare: *King Lear* and *Measure for Measure*', in *Political Shakespeare: New Essays in Cultural Materialism*, ed. by Jonathan Dollimore and Alan Sinfield (Manchester: Manchester University Press, 1985), pp. 88–108 (p. 99).

147   Coppélia Kahn, 'The Absent Mother in *King Lear*', in *Rewriting the Renaissance: The Discourses of Sexual Difference in Early Modern Europe*, ed. by Margaret W. Ferguson, Maureen Quilligan and Nancy J. Vickers (Chicago: University of Chicago Press, 1986), pp. 33–49 (p. 36).

148   Kahn, 'The Absent Mother in *King Lear*', p. 41.

149   Kahn, 'The Absent Mother in *King Lear*', pp. 45–46, 48.

150   Janet Adelman, *Suffocating Mothers: Fantasies of Maternal Origin in Shakespeare's Plays, Hamlet to The Tempest* (New York: Routledge, 1992), p. 103.

CHAPTER TWO

King Lear: Performative Traditions / Interpretative Positions

Ramona Wray

King Lear has been multiply understood in performance history, as a celebration of the redemptive impulse, a dystopian reflection on nihilism, a study of fractured family relations and a disquisition on political/territorial authority. This chapter offers three interventions in that history, using 'Classic Approaches', 'Shakespearean Spin-Offs' and 'Intercultural Performances' as shaping structures and interpretative procedures. Within each argumentative unit, both theatrical and cinematic/televisual works are considered, an index of the interpenetration of various media. This is not to suggest, however, that these are mutually exclusive categories. The television productions of *King Lear* discussed, for example, invariably have a theatrical origin and point up the ways in which both the stage and the screen only occasionally function discretely. Similarly, at least one of the cinematic versions of *King Lear* offered for analysis could fall under either a 'Classic Approaches' or an 'Intercultural Performances' rubric; how and why a particular production is characterized is a question of degree, context and 'Shakespearean' connection.

   In the conversations that follow, I argue that how *King Lear* is produced is implicated deeply in the concerns of a particular temporal moment. This may take the form of an engagement with a changing political landscape; alternatively, this may be expressed as developments in the complexion of the screen and theatrical industries. Tendencies in the cultures of representation (embracing modernism and postmodernism), I suggest, have the effect of variously stripping *King Lear* down to a skeletal version of itself or of exposing the play to ironic critique. Different incarnations of *King Lear* illuminate a range of conceptions of

state power at a time of shifting attitudes towards monarchical authority and governance more generally. Competing endings to the play in
film and theatre throw light on institutionalized religion and the continuing – or discontinuing – resonances of its legacy. And representations of Lear's own relation with his larger world are endemic of an
increasing interest in definitions of the human subject in the context of
the environment. Because of the grandeur of its vision and theme, *King
Lear* allows for experiment and adaptation. As I maintain here, the play,
traditionally read and flexibly rewritten, has been used to contemplate
what freedoms, if any, inhere in the margins of gender and class. In
turn, the play in performance has precipitated a linked series of questions. What role is still enjoyed by the rule of the father in the twentieth
and twenty-first centuries? What is the nature of ethical responsibility?
Is Shakespeare really the guarantor of certain kinds of transferable wisdom? And does the play speak the same truths when it is culturally and
geographically relocated? When *King Lear* moves beyond its English-
language borders we find the power inherent in Shakespeare as a world
icon is both vigorously debated and made clearly visible.

Classic Approaches

At an immediate level, five – what might be termed 'classic' – filmic
approaches to *King Lear* are marked by a wide range of prevailing characteristics. That is, in the Russian *Korol Lir* (dir. Grigori Kozintsev, 1971)
and in the *King Lear* film and television productions of 1971, 1983, 1988
and 2008, respectively, we see directors modelling the play according to
a distinctive agenda, which lends a peculiar 'look' or style to the
Shakespearean interpretation. Visually, *Korol Lir*, for instance, invests in
widescreen shots of a vast state hall, replete with glowing fires, as part of
its stress upon social divisions and the segregated lives of the plebeian
and the elite. Such an epic approach can take on tragic proportions – as
when Lear (Yuri Yarvet) is psychologically diminished by the elemental
grandeur of the storm – and heroic associations, not least in the scene
where Cordelia (Valentina Shendrivova) is glimpsed on a cliff-top at her
return: it is a moment that allows her, figuratively, a heightened prominence. Elsewhere in *Korol Lir*, the use of desolate Baltic, Estonian and
Siberian landscapes, including rocky promontories and bleak plains, has
the effect of positioning the key players in relation to larger processes
that seemingly lie beyond human control.[1] Although more modest in
scale, Peter Brook's *King Lear*, also of 1971, corresponds to the Kozintsev
version in a deployment of a landscape that is thematically purposeful
and resonant. The stark black-and-white cinematography is instrumental

in directing audience attention to the unaccommodating nature of the snowy tundra across which the characters traverse, while a concentration on cloudy skies, through which the sun is only occasionally visible, are key contributions to a stylistic reliance on signifiers of oppression and gloom. Indeed, as a whole in this *King Lear*, a sense of an Eliot-like wasteland is highlighted (location shooting was undertaken in northern Jutland), with language and image forming a mutually reinforcing partnership. Lear (Paul Scofield) dies on a stony beach, and his accompanying 'men of stones' lament makes for a telling equation between his place of expiry and his emotional realization (5.3.256).[2]

In the other productions, a characteristic style is again to the forefront. Distinguishing the 1983 Channel 4 television production of *King Lear* directed by Michael Elliott is the prioritization of Laurence Olivier in the title role. This is a star-led Shakespearean statement, as is suggested in the opening on-screen announcement, 'Laurence Olivier Presents': Shakespeare's name is subordinated to second-place on the credits. A studio-set feature that deploys minimal props, the production nevertheless constantly communicates the status of its lead performer: for example, because a prehistoric stone circle dominates, in deference to which the characters prostrate themselves, a powerful impression of obeisance to a cultivated authority is afforded. (The strategy is not an isolated one in approaches to *King Lear*: hence, in the BBC Radio 3 production of the play broadcasted in 1994, ideas of gravitas and venerability were conveyed via the casting of John Gielgud in the central role as part of his ninetieth birthday celebrations.) In terms of minimalist settings, the *King Lear* (1998) broadcast on BBC/PBS, directed by Richard Eyre and based on the successful – intimately oriented – stage production at the Cottesloe Theatre, is also relevant here. Orange-tinted and expressionistically angled, the production eschews furnishings in order to corroborate the play's obsession with 'nothing', while the opening and closing of vast doors in the background bears out Lear's own preoccupation with 'who's in and who's out' (5.3.15). Towards the end, the interiors are increasingly coloured in pale hues, reflecting the casting aside of Lear's (Ian Holm) royalty and the corresponding deathly consequences of his actions: the pallor of the dead Cordelia (Victoria Hamilton) is tragically in keeping with this newly blanched environment.

What this amounts to is a unique vision of the Shakespearean play. Or, to put the point in another way, visuals and aesthetics have an ideological charge. The appearances of the productions carry in their wake readings that are themselves repositories of meaning. In the 2008 Channel 4 television interpretation of *King Lear* directed by Trevor Nunn and Chris Hunt, therefore, which is closely modelled on the RSC production, colour coding (black and red) at the level of costume makes clear internal hierarchies and suggests an approach to Shakespeare that underscores the intricacies of class distinctions. In addition, these gradations of rank are constructed as divinely or supernaturally determined, for, at the moment where Lear (Ian McKellen) appeals to the 'sacred radiance of the sun' (1.1.109), the assembled company falls to its knees in a revealing gesture of worship. As far as its aesthetics are concerned, Brook's *King Lear* is an altogether more sombre and dispassionate experience. The vision of his *King Lear* takes its harsh and barbaric cues from the 1962 RSC production from which the film derives: here, plain walls, exposed thunder-sheets and glaring house-lights were crucial to the creation of an atmosphere marked by austerity, pain and the expression of brute instincts. All of this, and the absurdist echoes of Beckett and Kott, the film retains: typical are the ways in which Oswald (Barry Stanton) squeals like a pig when he is savagely dispatched and the disappearance of the snow towards the end, a false rather than a fruitful spring. Intimations of a better world in the play (such as Edmund's attempt 'Some good [. . .] to do' [5.3.241]) are stripped away, engendering unrelieved despondency, while the predilection for filming characters individually rather than in groups implies isolation and the absence of meaningful dialogue. The whole, in Samuel Crowl's words, is 'short, nasty and grotesque'.[3] Contrasting in tone is the Kozintsev version. In the midst of a concluding tableau of mass destruction, chaos, apocalyptic crowd movements and the effects of battle, hints of reparation are discernible. The fool (Oleg Dal) is not 'hanged' (5.3.304); rather, he continues to play his flute in the rubble and has survived, it is suggested, to tell his tale. More strikingly, Cordelia is seen tending to Lear (later, he will tend to her) in an extended sequence that, in an affirmation of 'socialist leadings' and 'generalized humanitarianism', uses water as a metaphor of resurrection and reveals the protagonist in alignment with the people.[4] As Kozintsev himself remarks in an assessment of his vision, the play 'gives rise to faith; the evil times will pass'.[5] Arresting in this regard is the mixed nature of responses to the question of whether or not *King Lear* is an ultimately redemptive work, with theatre and film directors engaging with the issue by taking contrary approaches.

Emerging from that mixture of responses is a corresponding variety of representational methods. In keeping with their distinctive readings of *King Lear*, theatrical and filmic productions are technically individuated. *Korol Lir*, essentially realist in method, still departs, where necessary, from filmic verisimilitude: as an example, one might cite the storm scene in which Lear is shot from above, suggesting the possibility of an overarching divine perspective, and the engineered amplification of his voice, which points to the universality of his condition. As befits its construction of *King Lear*, Brook's film is informed by camera work

communicative of alienation, fragmentation and despair. Static compos-
itions later give way to a dizzying plethora of shooting styles, from in-
and-out of focus shots and alternating between white and black to
accelerated zooms and oddly-angled viewpoints, all indicative of madness and breakdown. The director's experimental cinematography has
been condemned as gratuitous in some quarters; scrutiny of the film,
however, reveals a filmic procedure that is precise and directed in orientation. The image of the drowned rats, for example, nicely dovetails
with Lear's acknowledgement of the 'Poor naked wretches' (3.4.29),
while the surrealist dropping of the protagonist in death from the frame
of representation both denies reparation and is analogous to a failure to
progress. At the opposite end of the spectrum in terms of experimenta-
tion is the much more conventional 1983 *King Lear* with Laurence
Olivier: the repeated use of close-ups suggests that this is a subjective
narrative (characters think, ponder and grow). No less ameliorative is
the outward-moving shot towards the end which shows the characters
en masse. Inclusion, finality and a sense of community is implied in the
camera's pondering on a society that is coming to terms with itself.

Underpinning all of the productions is the centrality of the Lear role.
Interestingly, for many, playing Lear is construed either as the achievement of a kind of professional ascendancy (one thinks here of Ian
McKellen in the part) or as the swansong to a Shakespearean career (as
in the case of Olivier's rendition of the role). Certainly, Olivier as Lear,
as the 1983 television production demonstrates, is the structuring prin-
ciple, with his age (he was seventy-five at the time) a governing deter-
minant of explanation. 'Which [. . .] doth love us most?' (1.1.49), Lear/
Olivier demands playfully, the idea being that the character and the
actor have rehearsed these lines on many previous occasions. During
the storm scenes, an emphasis on Lear's physical frailty (he is lifted onto
a bed by his depleted retinue) directs a similar attention to the blurred
lines separating the performing body and the Shakespearean construction. Vulnerability is on display, as when we see the naked Lear skinning
a recently caught rabbit: the theme of monarchy brought low gains in
intensity from the spectacle of a renowned actor stripped of accoutre-
ments and placed before the camera's exposing eye. Moving back in
time, earlier renderings of the drama are preoccupied not so much with
the player's intertextual resonances as the king's relation with his world.
In its first half, for example, *Korol Lir* discovers Lear as sadly removed
from his subjects: at his first appearance, the protagonist is seen hiding
behind a mask (a metaphor for his separation and blindness), and in a
later scene he is glimpsed ascending a tower to announce the banish-
ments (a sense of distance is stressed). Paul Scofield as Lear, in the 1971
Brook film version, is less ethereally placed as he is pejoratively

cast – monotone, gruff and antipathetic. 'Know that we have divided [. . .] our kingdom' (1.1.35–36), his and the film's first words, bear out in their punning ('know'/'no') both the production's mood and a more pervasive conjuration of negativity. More recently, Ian Holm in the stage-inspired 1998 television version plays Lear as angry and peremptory: 'Give me the map there!' (1.1.35), he exclaims, the accompanying drumbeat of his fingers on the table suggesting that this is a ruler who does not brook hesitation. All of these productions bear witness to an impulse to make readable and accessible the Shakespearean preoccupation with pride and regality. How best to communicate Lear's inflated sense of himself? Directors and performers enlist means that are contextually dependent, with verbal emphasis and visual detail functioning to clarify Lear's essential traits. Silent representational business is particularly forceful in these respects: hence, in the most recent television *King Lear* (2008), as in the stage version from which it emerged, Ian McKellen enters attired in gold as a cardinal blessing the crowd, the implication being that this is a personality vainly self-absorbed and concerned above all with an aggrandized public image.[6]

Of course, key to any representation of Lear in performance is the character's relation with his daughters. Gender questions are amply foregrounded in *King Lear*: the play in its theatrical and screen realizations is responsive in kind and offers a test-case for changing attitudes towards constructions of female will and patriarchal control across the twentieth and twenty-first centuries. The televisual *King Lear* of 2008 and its theatrical predecessor are abundantly pertinent to this discussion: in particular, the representation of an incensed Cordelia (Romola Garai), who rises during the protagonist's opening peroration, brings into the arena of debate both the 'untender' (1.1.106) accusation with which she is charged and the issue of the constraints placed on a woman's behaviour. As the production makes clear, moreover, this is no stereotypical reading, for, as a later scene establishes, women's roles are realized at several levels: welcomed by Gloucester (William Gaunt), for example, Goneril (Frances Barber) and Regan (Monica Dolan) are discovered as cradling their wine glasses in self-satisfied fashion even as their facial expressions convey emotional shading and self-doubt. Productions often equate the situations and motivations of the Goneril and Regan characters. The 1998 television *King Lear* reveals the sisterly pair hugging and dressed identically in grey; the 1983 Laurence Olivier realization has Goneril (Dorothy Tutin) and Regan (Diana Rigg) entering as one and, throughout, filmed together as species of twin. Via such strategies, Goneril and Regan are streamlined into a composite of comparability (as opposed to the generally more-variegated Cordelia), even if, in the play, the two elder daughters are carefully distinguished.

Crucially, a common denominator of productions of *King Lear* is a drive towards establishing an entry-point for an engagement with the condition of daughter, although that orientation is tempered by the moral polarities that representation inevitably brings to the fore. Thus, the 1971 film version (again taking energy from Brook's theatrical predecessor) allows for a moment of empathy with Goneril (Irene Worth): Lear's knights, genuinely riotous and unruly, break up their hostess's castle, and she is noticeably excluded from and perturbed by the masculine complexion of noise and disorder. (The idea was taken up in the production of *King Lear* directed by Rupert Goold in 2008 at the Everyman Theatre, Liverpool, in which Lear's followers were portrayed as dangerously violent football supporters.) As might be expected, the Kozintsev *King Lear* of the same year addresses the gender question more subjectively and sentimentally. It is of a piece with this production's ideological investments that Cordelia's self-questioning should be realized as a voiceover (this stresses her silence and interiority) and that she should be represented as marrying the King of France in an interpolated scene characterized by a sense of sanctification. Women, it is implied, are ensnared in multiple ways in institutional operations and in the permutations of fatherly pronouncement.

The situation of daughter is often associated in productions of *King Lear* with the predicament of related kinds of oppressed figure. 'One cannot portray the life of a king without portraying the life of his subjects', declared Kozintsev (p. 34), a sentiment amply borne out in his 1971 *Korol Lir*: here, processions of beggars (we do not know if they are victims of dispossession or followers of a pilgrimage) show that the king has to be read according to surrounding material factors and, more specifically, illuminate the director's Soviet schooling – as John Collick states, his espousal of 'populist themes' and his insistence on the 'corrupting processes of absolute power'.[7] Material forces, and the protagonist's potential for tyrannous dereliction, are hinted at again in the images of the properties and goods he takes on progress, such as hunting dogs and birds of prey. Of course, this is a subtly gradated politics: other productions can be more assertive and locally referential. The set for the *King Lear* staged by Imre Csiszár in Hungary in 1981 was a 'decaying factory' suggestive of the shortcomings of communist rule, while, in the RSC production of the play directed by Adrian Noble in 1982, searchlights, combat boots and visual reminders of a bombed-out East European city betokened a context of revolutionary aftermath.[8] More commonly, Lear's relation with the political is mediated via his intimacy with the Fool character. In the 1983 television production, the Fool (John Hurt) speaks to Lear from behind his throne (he is the nagging voice of conscience or the flea in the ear); the 1998 television realization has the Fool (Michael Bryant) as an older man speaking in a rural accent (his is the history of the land); and the 2008 television reading discovers the Fool (Sylvester McCoy) putting egg shells on his eyes, an index of his master's inability properly to see. Theatrical productions take a similar tack: when, in the 1982 RSC production, Lear (Michael Gambon) accidentally kills the Fool (Antony Sher), who has taken refuge in a dustbin, it is implied that the dependent classes have ever been treated as just so much rubbish and that political inadequacy manifests itself not so much as continued ignorance as unwitting destruction. These are productions that make a virtue of the manifold ways in which Lear fails family and people alike; they are also productions that finds in the Shakespearean narrative meanings and applications that are resolutely contemporary.

Shakespearean Spin-Offs

King Lear, as a core component of the Shakespearean corpus, has attracted textual reinventions as well as classic approaches, noticeable appropriations in addition to faithful renderings. As Yvonne Griggs notes, the play operates as a 'source of inspiration', with interpreters in various media 'selectively employing elements of its narrative and its language'.[9] By way of introduction to a cluster of recent *King Lear* postmodern adaptations, I focus briefly on the film, *King Lear*, directed by Jean-Luc Godard in 1987; this work, apparently, had its genesis in an agreement (signed on a napkin) between the filmmaker and Cannon Films, but when the subsequent – conventional – production fell into difficulties, an alternative version of the play which flouted cinematic rules was created. Accordingly, throughout *King Lear*, the pressure of external influences, whether through voiceovers or taped conversations, is alluded to, amounting, at times, to what Peter Donaldson has described as a scattering and recomposing of the 'paternal body of the text ... [a] deconstructive artistic practice'.[10] How to adapt *King Lear* for the cinema? This is the overriding concern animating a series of onscreen announcements, such as 'Fear and Loathing' or 'An Approach', titles which testify to the play's historical associations, the contingent nature of its messages and an auteur-led desire to make Shakespeare speak. There are numerous ways, both discontinuous and contradictory, the film implies, whereby the play can be reinvented.

If there are types of *Lear*, there are also varieties of Lear. Norman Mailer and his daughter Anne stand first for Lear and Cordelia; later their roles are taken by Burgess Meredith (who appears as Don Learo) and Molly Ringwald; and, given his canonical filmic credentials, even the director himself, playing Professor Pluggy, might be said to signify the Shakespearean patriarch. The idea is that there is no one point of reference for the interpretative encounter. But Lear, the film suggests, can only come into proper existence/s when *Lear*, which has been destroyed following a nuclear disaster, is memorially reassembled. Hence, the film playfully canvasses the attempts of the aptly named William Shakespeare Junior the Fifth (Peter Sellars) to recover the sacred literary artefact; this, as the frequent images of Promethean fire suggests, is essentially a search for origins. In the process of seeking out the lost 'original', the key identifying features of any literary utterance are aired and debated. Authorship rears its head in invocations of the 'father' and shots of hands being photocopied; by the same token, the role of language is highlighted in the notebook jotting, 'HEAR NO LEAR THING', an injunction that testifies to the power of the word. Inheritance, posterity and representation – all come together in an imaginatively linked series of images, actions and imperatives.

As Shakespeare's *King Lear* is a seminal text, so, too, has Godard's *King Lear* been importantly generative. For example, Cordelia, who labours under a veil of silence, is described in the film in terms of com-modity fetishism ('a little bit of flesh') and lives in expectancy of being 'delivered' (which translates as emancipated from male domination). In this respect, the film forms an alliance with related films and theatrical ventures that have as their *modus operandi* the simultaneous freeing up and prioritizing of the woman's perspective. In *Lear's Daughters* (1987), for instance, a play devised by the Women's Theatre Group, Regan is imagined as pregnant by Lear (he has also, it is implied, raped the other daughters) even as a space is created for female condemnation of an abusive history.[11] Throughout, in fact, as when *King Lear* interleaves stills of male filmmakers and images of Joan of Arc, Godard colours his preoccupations with a gendered awareness; in particular, the focus on a number of daughters is part-and-parcel of the film's absorption in its most pressing preoccupation – the capacity of cinema to reproduce culture.

Emerging from the narrative attention to the place of the voiceless woman in Godard's *King Lear* is a corresponding interest in later Shakespearean appropriations in forms of exploitation. Four films, *A Thousand Acres* (dir. Jocelyn Moorhouse, 1997), *The King Is Alive* (dir. Kristian Levring, 2000), *King of Texas* (dir. Uli Edel, 2001) and *My Kingdom* (dir. Don Boyd, 2002), turn to Shakespeare's *King Lear* as a basis for exploring linked examples of authority and injustice in modernity and, in so doing, pass judgement on the influence of the father, histories of imperialism and the persistence of past practices in present arrangements. *A Thousand Acres* (1997) is a case in point: based on Jane Smiley's 1991 Pulitzer Prize-winning novel of the same name, the film, which sets Shakespeare's narrative in the American Midwest, implicitly posits the traditional-style farming methods of Larry Cook/ Lear (Jason Robards) over and against the newer 'organic' agriculture of Jess Clark/Edmund (Colin Firth), who is envisioned as an ambiguously heroic figure. From this scenario, the film elaborates a storyline centring upon the coercion of women and the ways in which female bodies, and their reproductive potential, are dictated to by the combined forces of patriarchy and industry. The cancers that have plagued the lives of Rose/Regan (Michelle Pfeiffer) and her mother are thus associated with Larry Cook/Lear's interference with the order of things, as when Jess/ Edmund objects to the continued use of a toxic 'fertilizer' and asks Ginny/Goneril (Jessica Lange), who has had five miscarriages, 'Didn't your doctor tell you not to drink the water here?' The implication is that 'nature', which is broadly conceived and metaphorically treated in *A Thousand Acres*, has been ravaged by the incursions of men and that the transmission of the family line has been blighted as a result. *The King Is Alive* (2000), which details the attempts of a party of tourists stranded in the Namibian desert to stave off disaster by enacting *King Lear*, also concerns itself with a brutalizing reification of the land's resources, although here the theme assumes a colonialist complexion. The abandoned mining town of Kolmanskop, which serves as set for *The King Is Alive*, is testimony to a now-eclipsed diamond industry and, more generally, as Thomas Cartelli and Katherine Rowe note, to 'the barren legacy of the European scramble for Africa'.[12] Reinforcing these associations is the way in which, at the close, the tourists are finally rescued by a lorry of local soldiers and workers. It is a charged moment in its summoning of an idea of deliverance, but it is also one that gains energy from a reversal of a familiar power dynamic, for it is the indigenous inhabitant, rather than the non-indigenous visitor, that asserts control. Such a conjuration of European and African relations recalls the early nineteenth-century wars in Namibia between German forces and the Herero and Nama peoples in which three-quarters of the population died, suggesting that, for *The King Is Alive*, *King Lear* functions most powerfully as a document that endorses the importance of social and ethical accountability. The protagonist's epiphany, we recall, arguably occurs when he acknowledges 'Poor naked wretches [. . .] That bide the pelting of [the] pitiless storm' (3.4.29–30).

The persecuted poor are the immediate point of reference for *King of Texas* (2001), a Turner Network television production which takes the *King Lear* story to the Old West – in particular, to the post-Alamo/pre-Civil War period when Texas operated as a republic. The opening shot of two bodies hanging from a gnarled tree suggests both criminality and the meting out of authoritarian principles: this is confirmed when we later learn that John Lear/Lear (Patrick Stewart) has had executed starving Mexicans who were caught trespassing on his territory. At once, therefore, *King of Texas* politicizes and ethnicizes the Shakespearean construction of the connection between the king and his subjects, with the film engaging this concern in terms of character (Lear is the archenemy of the Mexican landlord, Menchaca [Steven Bauer], who also stands for the King of France) and geography (the Rio Grande in is the boundary that, ideally, keeps the rival constituencies separate). Exploitation takes on racial meanings in the scene where the black Rip/Fool (David Alan Grier) is abused by Warnell/Oswald (Richard Lineback), who declares, 'I wouldn't want no slave to foul this water by drinking from it'. Tied to a tree and whipped, Rip is saved by Lear, who intervenes to protect his 'property'. Because it recalls the earlier hanging of the Mexicans, the scene (a version of the play's trade in insults between Oswald and Kent) implies both that practices of stigmatization filter downwards across the historical white majority and that a variety of subjugated groupings are imagined as synonymous in the film's recreation of ideology. Via these sequences, *King of Texas*, it might be suggested, exposes to critique the imperialist policies of George W. Bush, who also boasted a Texan affiliation. For, even though Lear is constantly praised for his expansionist and materialist ambitions, he signally fails to acquire greater possessions: the scenes in the desert, where the protagonist loses his bearings, offer a potent realization of a leader who cannot find his way. And, when we recollect that the ranch of Westover/Gloucester (Roy Scheider) is adorned by a giant 'W' initial, it is tempting to detect in the film's patriotic governors a presidential parallel.

Where *King of Texas* analogizes Texas, *My Kingdom* (2002), a British film that reworks *King Lear* as a modern gangland tragedy, invokes and applies the associations of Liverpool. Filmed in and around the city, *My Kingdom* delights in lingering over shots of the famous 'Three Graces' (the Royal Liver Building, the Cunard Building and the Port of Liverpool Building) on the waterfront, embodiments of the city's commercial ascendancy, success as a port and rich maritime history. That Liverpool's wealth was built on the slave trade is important: intertextually, at least, the location of filming brings to mind once again *King Lear*'s own preoccupation with issues of marginality and occlusion. The Lear figure, Sandeman (Richard Harris), is first discovered watching a western on television, suggesting that he, too, is caught up in the repercussions of imperialism, that he, in a place of transit and embarkation that enables business, is a modern-day entrepreneur. Such a reading finds support when Sandeman, reflecting on the drug-empire over which he presides, states: 'Smell that, steam ships, iron shavings [. . .] thinking about the past, this great city, mine'. It is unclear if the drug lord is represented as ruminating upon his own past or the city's; either way, the two are enfolded, and the implication is that the Liverpool of the present, taking energy from its previous incarnations, is somehow or other Sandeman's creation.

But that connection with place in *My Kingdom* is ultimately pejorative. Indeed, in *A Thousand Acres*, *The King Is Alive*, *King of Texas* and *My Kingdom*, the Lear character is consistently portrayed as flawed in relation to the broader environment, with his personal shortcomings visiting themselves upon kin, community and society, alike. In *My Kingdom*, for example, Liverpool is simultaneously rendered at the level of decline. Images of dilapidated buildings and abandoned warehouses abound and, as one character declares, the city is characterized by 'no work [. . .] no future'. Because Sandeman claims Liverpool as 'mine', he, it is implied, must bear a generous measure of responsibility: the protagonist's wife is murdered by a hoodlum, a product of the ghettoized system that drug use has engendered. Similarly, the juxtaposition in the film of sumptuous gentlemen's residences or luxury flats (the proceeds of criminality) and dingy hotels brings into visual play the idea that Sandeman's brand of mercantilism has been critically divisive. *King of Texas*, too, makes the point that the Lear character's derelictions have wider effects. Hence, the resentment of Mrs Susannah Lear Tumlinson/Goneril (Marcia Gay Harden) and Mrs Rebecca Lear Highsmith/Regan (Lauren Holly) is precipitated in part by their father's favouring, above them, his son (who, in the background fiction to the film, has died before the action commences). The extinction of the male line becomes a repressed subtext, an unconscious prompt to consigning the daughters to a type of parental neglect.

Perhaps the most forceful realization of a Lear-like abnegation of proper care is found in *A Thousand Acres*. The ghosts of Godard's *King Lear* and related theatrical interpretations – such as the Royal National Theatre production of 1986 which, as John Russell Brown notes,[13] was made infamous by its suggestions of Lear's 'incest' – inform the representation, in this film, of a series of appalled and appalling revelations. Charges of being 'dumb', accusatory stares, references to secrets and a sense of gathering tension culminate in Rose/Regan's admission to Ginny/Goneril, 'he [Lear] went into your room at night [. . .] He was having sex with you [. . .] we had sex', and in Ginny/Goneril's later statement, 'It happened like you said'. An imaginative development of the construction of the failing father, the discovery in *A Thousand Acres* of domestic abuse takes to its furthest extreme the concern with a transgression of the familial compact. Indeed, such is the orientation of this film that conventional expectations are undermined, with the moment of epiphany being reserved not so much for Lear as for his offspring who are finally able to confess to and own the implications of their early upbringings. *The King Is Alive* is also pertinent here: the film preoccupies itself with the ways in which, through the performance of *King Lear*, characters are enabled either to ascend to improved versions of themselves or to confront long-established psychic imperfections. Hence, Amanda (Lia Williams), who initially appears mousy and apologetic, pinpoints in the Fool's extemporized satire a means of speaking out against her bullying husband: 'I knew you were a pig', she observes, 'for once I'm absolutely clear-headed'. Yet there are also in the diverse assembly of beleaguered Americans and Europeans Lear-like figures who repeat the same old Shakespearean mistakes. Ashley (Brion James), a California socialite, is openly identified by Henry (David Bradley), a British theatre producer, as Lear, and it is a sad indictment that the former appears as muddled and suffering from alcohol-related withdrawal symptoms, ultimately dying of his condition. The bluff and self-satisfied English father, Charles (David Calder), also features as a postmodern variant on Lear, not least when, having sexually exploited Gina/Cordelia (Jennifer Jason Leigh) and been rejected by her, he urinates on her corpse: it is an ultimate act of disaffection, defilement and madness. *The King Is Alive* stresses the perennial and more contemporary meanings aroused by Lear's excesses by reproducing his prevailing traits, and imaginative transformations of them, across a range of character equivalents.

But where is Shakespeare in the postmodern return to *King Lear*? By what means is the Shakespearean utterance detected in filmic language? What purpose is served by the mobilization of *King Lear* in a contemporary setting? And does that mobilization endorse or undo the canonical wisdoms the play is said to enshrine? In *A Thousand Acres*, the contours of *King Lear* are in evidence throughout; at the same time, however, the film repositions many of the play's key set-pieces, not least at the close where a trial functions as a test-case for the coming to terms with culpability. *King Lear*, too, of course, contains a trial scene (a fantasy encounter that takes place, essentially, in the protagonist's own mind), and it is this that *A Thousand Acres* imaginatively elaborates. The film makes of the trial a high point; it shows the ways in which private conflicts enter the public sphere; and it fashions from a Shakespearean episode a dénouement that accords with some of the generic requirements of mainstream Hollywood cinema. *My Kingdom*, by contrast, conjures the Bard more directly. The well-known pronouncement from *King Lear*, 'As flies to wanton boys are we to the gods; / They kill us for their sport' (4.1.37–38), appears at the start as an inter-title, a strategy that helps to promote the action's absorption in the gratuitous violence of gangsterdom, to advertise a legitimizing Shakespearean affiliation and to suggest an interpretative approach that recognizes the arbitrary operations of constituted authority. Later, in the film proper, the customs and excise officer, Quick/Gloucester (Tom Bell), commenting on the dispossessed situation of Sandeman, declares, 'Humanity must perforce prey upon itself, / Like monsters of the deep' (4.2.50–51). The transposition of the line from Albany in the play, which arraigns Lear's daughters for their barbarity, is instrumental in the film in ratifying Sandeman's sense of outrage and draws a heightened attention to the internal dissolution of the protagonist's empire. At this point, as elsewhere in the film, the presence of a Shakespearean quotation is integral to the reinforcement of certain kinds of moral polarity, and it is not accidental that Quick/ Gloucester's moment of perception makes all the more horrific the episode of his blinding that ensues soon afterwards. Thus, when Jug/ Cornwall (Jimi Mistry), confronting the vengeful father of a drug-addict he has tortured and murdered for pleasure, attempts to wriggle off the hook by citing Portia's sentiment from *The Merchant of Venice*, 'The quality of mercy is not strained', an audience is alerted to the possibility of another kind of justice being enacted, albeit one sullied by criminality: Liverpool does harbour manifestations of reconstruction and reform, *My Kingdom* suggests, even if they are caught up in some of the very processes they would ostensibly eradicate. The Bard as a route to recovery is given its most far-reaching statement in *The King Is Alive*. As Mark Thornton Burnett states, 'the play beyond the film is figured as a source of origin and connection, with Shakespeare at some level filling the place of the "missing transcendental" in the global marketplace'.[14] Shakespeare serves social uses, the film suggests, and we repeatedly see this in action: characters model the lessons of the play to their own situations, adopting the lines of *King Lear* in multiple therapeutic applications. The title of the film, in this connection, comes into its own: Lear is alive, one might argue, Shakespeare has life, the works remain transferable, and *King Lear* still possesses the power to communicate.

Addressing the imputed power of the Shakespearean text brings us back full circle to the question of the redemptive *King Lear*. Interestingly, all of the films under discussion here would seem to approve, although with differing emphases, the notion of an underlying and informing Shakespearean narrative that holds out the prospect of amelioration amid devastation, revival in the face of apocalypse. *The King Is Alive* constitutes a salient instance. The film takes as its governing metaphor the idea of a bus journey that has gone off course and of lives that have similarly strayed: as Carolyn Jess-Cooke states, the action is populated by characters at the 'end of their morals, marriages and selves'.[15] It goes on to show, by the end, survivors who articulate *King Lear* meaningfully as a community for the first time: the language, and what it signifies, has been internalized. The deepest engagement with the play occurs in a moment when its content comes fully to shadow a lived experience. Even Kanana (Peter Kubheka), the local tribesman who has overlooked the proceedings, speaks openly (rather than in a voiceover) at the close, suggesting that he, too, has been incorporated within *King Lear*'s expressive orbit. Operating in this manner, *King Lear* is realized as a work that facilitates vision: certainly, this is the case in *King of Texas*, which commences with evocations of myopia (Lear is unable to 'see' according to his daughter, Claudia/Cordelia [Julie Cox]), and concludes with assertions of untrammelled sight. As the Gloucester character, Westover, states: 'I was blind before. I couldn't see'. Properly to see, it is suggested, is akin to a moral reformation and, in this respect, *King of Texas* accords fully with the notion that *King Lear* might ultimately be considered as affirmative. Tempering the deaths of Lear and his youngest daughter, for example, is the brief cross-ethnic romance of Menchaca/France and Claudia/Cordelia (which is so elaborated as to hint at the virtues of a more pluralized demography) and the survival of Westover/Gloucester and his son, Thomas/Edgar (Liam Waite), with the note of positivism struck by the latter in his remark, 'I'll be keeping watch'. Embracing purposefully the film's absorption in vision, this closing observation points up the key role of the action's inheritor and hints at the preservation if not guardianship of a society newly aware of abiding values.

In a discussion of what she terms the 'postnostalgic Renaissance', Courtney Lehmann notes of *My Kingdom* that the film erodes 'identity' in its conjuration of 'the centrifugal energies of globalization, the paranoia of post-9/11 culture, an imploding cycle of neglect and [. . .] the fear that the apocalypse has already arrived'.[16] Provocative as her argument is, Lehmann's reading ignores, I think, the dynamics of the concluding scene, which is notable for simultaneously isolating and enfolding the Lear character. Sandeman is pictured walking to the end of a lonely jetty; in the same moment, Jo/Cordelia (Emma Catherwood) turns to move in the opposite direction. Seemingly centred upon disunity, the sequence in fact approves a species of reconciliation, for Jo, we recall, has successfully renounced her drug habit, while the wordlessness between father and daughter conveys a deeper affinity. As the camera pans outwards to show us, once again, the 'Three Graces', the sequence takes on the flavour of an urban benediction. To survive trauma and disaster is to declare the importance of personal worth, *My Kingdom* suggests, and *A Thousand Acres* follows suit. Crucial here is the fact that Ginny/Goneril dominates the proceedings via her retrospective interpretation of events: it is her perspective that is privileged, and the whole amounts to an elaboration of her autobiography. Informed engagement with what was prior ('I remember' and 'I was remembering' are loaded refrains) permits the emergence of a new-found female self-confidence, while the narrative more generally unfolds in such a way as to grant the woman, for the first time, a shaping voice. Of course, in elaborating these points of view, and as befits the genre to which it subscribes, *A Thousand Acres* is sentimental; to adopt a formulation of Yvonne Griggs, because the film is represents a 'melodrama [or] [. . .] "women's weepie"', its political resonances are often blunted (p. 34). *A Thousand Acres* is entirely typical of the other films discussed here – *The King Is Alive*, *King of Texas* and *My Kingdom* – in departing, at the close, from a Godard-like model. All four works bypass a more post-modern approach to *King Lear* in ultimately subscribing to realist, and mutedly assuring, endings; in this sense, they stand as rich and revealing examples of the reinvention of *King Lear* that stimulate and surprise in their decisions and directions.

Intercultural Performances

With the exception of *Korol Lir*, this study has confined itself thus far to productions and appropriations of *King Lear* in the English language. What happens when Shakespeare's play is transported to a culture and representational system to which it bears no immediately obvious affinity? How does the introduction of a non-English linguistic register function to mediate the Shakespearean word? And to what extent does a fusion of styles and forms amount to a reimagining of the 'Shakespearean'? Commenting on intercultural performance, Li Lan Yong notes that the movement of Shakespeare across boundaries and borders 'is not only predicated upon some degree of ignorance, unfamiliarity and incomprehension for every spectator but also calls into question how our discourses of cultural entry or access are inseparable from discourses of mastery'.[17] It is such responses and reactions – and the notion of a promotion of cultural self-consciousness – that I wish to pursue and tease out across the body of three Asian incarnations of *King Lear*, *Ran* (1985), *Lear Is Here* (2000, 2004, 2007) and *Iruthiattam* (2001).

Immediately obvious in *Ran*, and marking the film out as distinctively Japanese, is the use of landscape. At the start, four horsemen are glimpsed stationary on the grassy sward of a mountainside, and, when this is later revealed as Mount Fuji, it becomes clear that the direction is oriented towards an approximation of the play and recognizably non-Western scenes and locales. The technical dimensions of the film are similarly conceived. In the great battle sequence at the Third Castle devoted to the destruction of Hidetora/Lear's (Tatsuya Nakadai) troops, the only sound heard is of the accompanying music; this diegetic form

of representation recalls the aural strategies of some forms of Noh theatre and shows the ways in which, in *Ran*, violence, although graphically
illustrated, is also arrestingly aestheticized. As elsewhere in *Ran*, to
encounter the film is to make significant adjustments in resources of
familiarity and comprehension and to begin a process of re-schooling
or re-tutoring as part of our intellectual engagement. The use of primary colours is no less pertinent: Hidetora/Lear's three sons, Tarô
(Akira Terao), Jirô (Jinpachi Nezu) and Saburô (Daisuke Ryû), who
substitute for Goneril, Regan and Cordelia, are attired in yellow, red and
blue, respectively, meaning that a particular hue is all-important as a
means of identification. The visual is as much a signifier as the linguistic, and the image is as powerful a force of communication as the word.
Later in the film, when the formal opening actions have been overtaken
by the chaotic expressions of Hidetora/Lear's madness, a theatrical field
of reference is additionally apparent. In the rocky wilderness, the protagonist appears heavily made-up and emphatically wild-eyed, almost
as if he is wearing a disguise; the seemingly exaggerated look of Lear
points to his continuing disconnection from things, while his artificially
fashioned countenance once again brings Noh to mind and the deployment of masks as indexes of stereotypical character traits.

Throughout this translation of *King Lear*, felicitous recreations of
Shakespearean situations are in evidence. Interestingly, however, *Ran* is
not strictly 'Shakespearean' in inspiration; as Judith Buchanan observes,
the film also rephrases the narrative of 'the sixteenth-century warlord
Môri Motonari (1497–1571) who furnished Kurosawa with the Japanese
half of his Anglo-Japanese [. . .] tryst'.[18] Hence, in any assessment of
Ran, we need to be sensitive to the overlapping of plots from different
cultural origins, to issues of cross-fertilization and to the presence of
other paradigms and histories in variations on the (to Western eyes, at
least) recognizably central storyline. In terms of the Shakespearean play,
Ran inverts, augments and concentrates. Saburô, for instance, speaks
truths Cordelia never could, as when he pronounces of his father,
'Pathetic, he's aging', while Jirô/Regan makes an impact because both
caught in a filial relation to Hidetora/Lear and defined in terms of fraternal resentment: condemning his elder brother, for example, he
laments, Edmund-like, 'I have had to grovel at his feet all my life'. Typically, in such dialogue, it is the workings of authority that rankle. Having parted with his territories, Hidetora/Lear visits his eldest son, only
to discover that his place has been taken by Kaede (Mieko Harada), his
daughter-in-law: 'Am I to sit below you?' he exclaims, continuing, 'Who
do you think I am?' At once, of course, this episode operates as an emo-
tionally charged retelling of Lear's inability to relinquish power, but it
is also enlivening because of its gendered ingredients: Hidetora is

constructed as enraged in that he is forced to give up a physical position as man and head of the family, a process that involves the questioning of identity itself. Gender as a point of reference for *Ran* presents itself more forcefully in the ways in which Kaede, who is linked to materialism, individualism and unresolved rage, is twinned with Sué (Yoshiko Miyazaki), who is married to Hidetora/Lear's eldest son and, throughout, is associated with calm, Buddhist temples and inner peace. Both women, in the backstory to the film, are the victims of Hidetora/Lear's destruction of their respective families, and both function symbolically as divided female responses to a psychic cataclysm of tragedy and bereavement. In this, as at other points in *Ran*, there is a strong Shakespearean component, for Kaede, in her vengefulness, brings Goneril and Regan to mind, while Sué, in her devotion and forgiveness, appears as infused with Cordelia's spirit. *Ran* is at its most expressive, indeed, in the elaboration of such figurations, which mix and match the premises of one of the precursor narratives and Japan-centred ideologies and typologies.

What this amounts to is a pointed application of the local. The suicide of Hidetora/Lear's concubines encourages an audience to ponder the cultural implications of *hara-kiri*; similarly, a focus on the codes of the samurai warriors means that we are invited to read *Ran* inside a paradigm of the *jidai geki*, the genre to which the film belongs.[19] Once again, the film encourages a learning curve of cultural familiarization in order to gain interpretative awareness. The local is invoked, too, in the flute played by Tsurumaru (Mansai Nomura), Sué's blind brother: the instrument invariably accompanied, as John Collick maintains, the warrior/reaper ghost figure from Noh drama (p. 184). In its welding of the local and more universal scenarios that carry the film into generalized currencies of meaning, *Ran* achieves an extraordinarily rich impact, not least at the close: here, Tsurumaru, having been led to a precipice, is left unattended. Although a scroll revealing an image of the Buddha is nearby, there seems less consolation in the tracking of the camera outwards to show the helpless figure as a form in silhouette that resembles rubble: Kurosawa splits his concluding construction between the idea of a ghost that may yet return and the prospect of a larger condition of human desolation.

Performed as a one-man piece in Paris (2000), Taipei (2004) and New York (2007), *Lear Is Here*, a reinvention of *King Lear* by the Taiwanese theatrical practitioner, Wu Hsing-Kuo, is a riveting addition to intercultural Shakespearean appropriation.[20] In his single-handed recreation of Lear and the majority of the rest of the cast, Wu's essential method, as Li Lan Yong notes, is to draw upon the 'full tilt of Beijing Opera's heightened physical expression, dance and athleticism' (p. 545).

Thus it is that Wu deploys *jingju* operatic conventions such as mincing gait, falsetto voice and flapping costume sleeves to approximate Goneril's flattery of her father, with movement and impersonation working as expressively as voice and aural timbre. *King Lear*, the play, is divided by Wu into three parts: the first concerns Lear, the second concentrates on the interrelations of the assembled characters and the third comprises a personal reflection from the director-actor himself. Such reorganization has the effect of foregrounding the main character and the performer who occupies the interpretation's imaginative centre. We begin with Lear, and we end with Wu: commencement and conclusion feature as powerful framing devices. In addition, because *Lear Is Here* starts with the protagonist, we are forced into a peculiarly immediate confrontation with the reverberations of his conduct. Hence, Wu's shaking body gestures are quickly apparent as a realization of madness; his rapid hand and eye movements stand in for accelerated dialogue; and the formality of his mime points towards an inflated sense of the character's royalty. Visual signifiers are enhanced by a carefully orchestrated and syncopated soundscape, as when Lear exclaims, 'Daughter, I did you wrong!' and a thunderclap explodes in the background. The whole, as devised by Wu with the assistance of his collaborators in Taiwan's Contemporary Legend Theatre (which he founded), is indicative of a world in dissolution, in society in a state of disrepair. Typically, the point is enunciated via physical action – somersaults communicate inversion, the loss of clothes points to destitution, an illusion of running conveys exile and flight.

Obliged to recognize the ways in which a specific dramatic language embodies preoccupation and theme, spectators become conscious of the production's absorption in meta-theatrical considerations. 'I am back!' and 'Who am I?' – some of the questions posed in *Lear Is Here* – remind us of the actor beyond the part, the performer at the heart of the representation. This is because it is not always easy to separate out the constituent aspects of the enterprise: for instance, lines such as 'They want me to believe I am of this place!' and 'Am I Lear's ghost?' could refer to the fictional story but might equally well signify the situation of Wu in his social and cultural locations: the dividing-line between the two is intriguingly muddied. There is, in these compressions, a resonant personal statement. As Alexander C. Y. Huang argues, Wu finds in *King Lear* an opportunity to comment both on his 'uneasy relationship with his *jingju* master' and on the tensions arising from practising an 'artform commonly seen as an embodiment of the Chinese nation' in a Taiwanese setting.[21] It is arguably for these reasons that *Lear Is Here* dwells in some detail on the role of the Fool (Wu/the Fool asserts, in a telling statement of pride, that, although a 'dog', he is still 'dignified'), on cultural expressions of father-son relations (as in the repeated 'Bow to the parents' formulation) and on motifs of occupation and dispossession (as actor, Wu berates, at the close, his 'prison with four walls'). *King Lear* is expanded in such reflections into a study of the after-effects of a theatrical apprenticeship (in which issues of authority and paternalism are troublingly inscribed), of colonially inflected processes of subordination and exclusion, and of the potential for emancipation and liberation. Both the history and the present-day status of Taiwan as a Chinese territory are implicitly debated in *Lear Is Here*; by the same token, precisely how the Taiwanese subject might articulate himself/herself in a context of vexed and overlapping national identities becomes a *raison d'être* of the production's imaginative conception and performed unfolding.

A final example of the Asian appropriation of *King Lear* comes from India. *Iruthiattam* (or *The Final Game*) is an adaptation of Shakespeare's play in Tamil by Indira Parthasarathi and was directed for performance by R. Raju in 2001 for the Arangam theatre company.[22] This is a *King Lear* for and of the people, with the production's dominant style showing a keen indebtedness to *terukutoo*, the street theatre form common in India's southeastern regions. An emphasis on clowning, extravagant movements and ironic imitation marks the genre, epitomized in the market-like atmosphere, indigenous costumes, use of popular song and generally uncrowning approach to the play. Lear's entrances and exits are characterized by fanfares of drums and trumpets and by his pretending to ride on a chariot: such are the signifiers of a whimsical personality and of a comic isolation from real affairs. At every turn, the Fool, who is known as the *komali* or *vidushaka*, mocks this self-absorption: Lear is represented as highly pleased by the flattery of the Goneril character, so much so that his satirical servant is seen scratching his master's back in a gesture that exposes and explodes a susceptibility to honeyed words and rhetorical massage. As for Lear's daughters, they are identified via a problematic relation to customary cultural practice (neither of the elder daughters, as they should, touches their father's feet in deference) and by exciting assertions of self-will. Arguably the production's most creative transformation is reserved for the Cordelia character, who strikes Lear during his opening peroration, who is husbandless and who interrogates her father on the deleterious political reverberations of a division of the kingdom. Her prominence accords with the way in which she is spared her generic death and lives on to rescue Lear from the storm. 'Forgive me', the repentant Lear requests; 'You don't need to suffer: come', is Cordelia's reply. In the place of tragic separation, this production stresses reconciliation and continuity, the vital interlocking and co-dependency of the public and the private, and the extent to which *King Lear* can be moulded and fashioned to suit and discover culture-specific truths. As such, the play is constructed as highly attuned to reinvention possibilities, establishing itself as a malleable source text for a confrontation with the familial disputes, gendered struggles, political discussions, territorial arguments, representational experiments and textual uncertainties symptomatic of a global modernity.

Notes

1 See Alexander Leggatt, *King Lear*, Shakespeare in Performance, 2nd edn (Manchester and New York: Manchester University Press, 2004), p. 92; Roger Manvell, *Shakespeare and the Film* (London: Dent, 1971), p. 84.

2 *King Lear* (Conflated Text), in *The Norton Shakespeare*, ed. by Stephen Greenblatt, Walter Cohen, Jean E. Howard and Katharine Eisaman Maus (New York: Norton, 1997), All subsequent references in this essay are to this edition and appear in the text.

3 Samuel Crowl, *Shakespeare and Film: A Norton Guide* (New York and London: Norton, 2008), p. 159.

4 See Yvonne Griggs, *Screen Adaptations: Shakespeare's 'King Lear': The Relationship Between Text and Film* (London: A. & C. Black, 2009), p. 77; Kenneth S. Rothwell, *A History of Shakespeare on Screen*, 2nd edn (Cambridge: Cambridge University Press, 2004), p. 178.

5 Grigori Kozintsev, *Shakespeare: The Space of Tragedy*, trans. by Mary Mackintosh (London: Heinemann, 1977), p. 254.

6 See John Russell Brown, *'King Lear': A Guide to the Text and the Play in Performance* (Basingstoke: Palgrave, 2009), p. 124.

7 John Collick, *Shakespeare, Cinema and Society* (Manchester and New York: Manchester University Press, 1989), pp. 129, 141.

8 Dennis Kennedy, *Looking at Shakespeare: A Visual History of Twentieth-Century Performance* (Cambridge: Cambridge University Press, 1993), p. 303; Samuel Crowl, *Shakespeare Observed: Studies in Performance on Stage and Screen* (Athens: Ohio University Press, 1992), p. 125; Leggatt, *King Lear*, p. 78.

9 Griggs, *Screen Adaptations: Shakespeare's 'King Lear'*, p. 27.

10 Peter Donaldson, *Shakespearean Films/Shakespearean Directors* (Boston: Unwin Hyman, 1990), p. 190.

11 See Amy Scott-Douglass, 'Theatre', in *Shakespeares after Shakespeare: An Encyclopedia of the Bard in Mass Media and Popular Culture*, ed. by Richard A. Burt, 2 vols (Westport, CT and London: Greenwood, 2007), II, p. 779.

12 Thomas Cartelli and Katherine Rowe, *New Wave Shakespeare: Shakespeare on Screen* (Oxford: Polity, 2007), p. 151.

13 Brown, *'King Lear'*, p. 122.

14 Mark Thornton Burnett, *Filming Shakespeare in the Global Marketplace* (Basingstoke: Palgrave, 2007), p. 111.

15 Carolyn Jess-Cooke, '"The Promised End of Cinema": Portraits of Cinematic Apocalypse in Twenty-First-Century Shakespearean Cinema', *Literature/Film Quarterly*, 34.2 (2006), 161–68 (p. 165).

16 Courtney Lehmann, 'The Postnostalgic Renaissance: The "Place" of Liverpool in Don Boyd's *My Kingdom*', in *Screening Shakespeare in the Twenty-First Century*, ed. by Mark Thornton Burnett and Ramona Wray (Edinburgh: Edinburgh University Press, 2006), p. 73.

17   Li Lan Yong, 'Shakespeare and the Fiction of the Intercultural', in *A Companion to Shakespeare and Performance*, ed. by Barbara Hodgdon and W. B. Worthen (Oxford: Blackwell, 2005), p. 527.

18   Judith Buchanan, *Shakespeare on Film* (Harlow: Pearson, 2005), p. 80.

19   See Kathy Howlett, *Framing Shakespeare on Film* (Athens: Ohio University Press, 2000), p. 115.

20   Portions of the performance may be viewed on the 'Shakespeare Performance in Asia' website at http://mit.edu/shakespeare/asia/collections/videoclips.html.

21   Alexander C. Y. Huang, *Chinese Shakespeares: Two Centuries of Cultural Exchange* (New York: Columbia University Press, 2009), pp. 196, 220.

22   Extracts from a video of the performance can be viewed on *Shakespeare in India: 'King Lear'* (2006), a multimedia CD-ROM produced by Poonam Trivedi of the University of Delhi. The discussion here is much indebted to Trivedi's CD-ROM commentary. There is no accompanying cast list.

CHAPTER THREE

The Current State of Thinking on *King Lear*

Philippa Kelly

Since the year 2000, substantial critical scholarship has been devoted to the subject of *King Lear*, with the MLA international database listing over the past nine years 548 Lear-related articles, as well as 151 critical monographs having substantial reference to the play (somewhat less than the 635 articles and 194 books in the ten-year period before that). Shakespeare's great play has in recent years continued to be mined for what it can yield in connection to power, familial relationships, love, repentance and remorse, as well as for its reflections on the relentlessness of death that stands in the face of all wishing.

Religion at Stake

From the very first scene of the play when an angry old man swears by the gods and 'the operation of the orbs', *King Lear* alludes to the questionable role of gods in the world, and, indeed, in the cosmos. What kind of universe is governed by any god whose earthly representative (the king) could act with such flawed human rashness? And what kind of gods could permit such abuse of old, foolish men by their 'thankless' children? In the last decade, several scholars have contributed to long-standing conversations about the role of the gods in *King Lear*. In 'The Cause of Thunder: Nature and Justice in King Lear', Paul Cantor suggests that the play ultimately validates natural law rather than any divine law: 'The characters who scorn conventional laws as merely arbitrary distinctions turn out to behave criminally, even among themselves.'[1] In Cantor's view, Lear is forced to rethink his assumption that nature supports human justice, and that the characters around him fall into place in terms of a divinely ordered conception of humanity. David Beauregard suggests that to see *King Lear* as an indictment of divine justice is to interpret the play in terms of late seventeenth-century ideals. The play, for him, is less about the gods than about humans: it is not about the deafness of the gods, in other words, but about the malevolence of men and women. This theological position, Beauregard notes, had considerable currency during the Middle Ages and the Renaissance.[2]

Stephen Regan and Graham Martin, in their book chapter '*King Lear*', suggest that the structure of *King Lear* affirms the value of spirituality, as opposed to the reductionism of materiality: 'Once Lear has abandoned his real power', he can no longer make his system of nature serve his needs. Nature, they suggest, will not heed him, however eloquent his appeals.[3] As they see it, the shift in Lear's character from sheer materialism to spirituality occurs after he goes mad: prior to this point, his bartering of love for land is grounded in materiality, while the descent into madness exposes him to a Nature deaf to any cry that 'I gave you all', blind to any suggestion that love can be measured and banked. John Hughes, in 'The Politics of Forgiveness: A Theological Exploration of *King Lear*', draws on the political structure of *King Lear* to reflect upon forgiveness as a social and political practice. Hughes argues that neither conservatism nor radicalism triumphs within the play, but rather that both sides – those who adhere to the bonds of loyalty and those who subvert them – share the same understanding of materialism that prevents them from engaging in forgiveness. If Cordelia did not perceive materialism as incompatible with love, after all (a perception somewhat ironically shared by her sisters), she would be able to see Lear's love-test for what it is: a scene about love, and not about property. Forgiveness, for her, comes only when she relinquishes her assumptions about what materialism means and what it prevents her from giving.[4]

Over the last century, the issue of *King Lear* and godlessness has been fed by perspectives on existentialism and nihilism that have found much resonance in the howling of the elderly protagonist over the loss of hope and redemption in the play's last scene. (This sense of loss is epitomized in the fact that Cordelia's life – which would have safely 'redeemed all sorrows' Lear has felt – is not, in the end, preserved for her father's comfort [5.3.265–67].[5]) In a recent contribution to this ongoing dialogue, George Walton Williams suggests that although the play was set in pagan times, the audience would have expected a Christian vigilance to be maintained by the gods: so that, for instance, despite Edmund's evil ways, the gods hear his invocations and grant him what he wishes for.[6] In this context, even the gods affirm the play's 'godlessness'. Michael Edwards disagrees with critics who interpret *King Lear* as an expression of a godless existence, contending that the play is 'an eminently Christian work', dramatizing human imperfection as well as the possibility of redemption.[7] Sean Lawrence challenges the very juxtaposition that Edwards and others establish between redemption and pessimism, arguing for the value of a nihilistic overview and perceiving the characters in the play as creating gods in their own images.[8] Lyell Asher suggests that Lear's belated knowledge, which comes too late to redeem him from all sorrows he has felt, compounds the play's tragedy and sense of hopelessness.[9]

There has also been vigorous critical discussion about Shakespeare's connection to Catholic/Protestant theological debates. Katharine Goodland, in 'Inverting the *Pietà* in Shakespeare's *King Lear*',[10] links the play to a general premise that Renaissance secular drama restores the unity disrupted by the Protestant curtailment of Catholic mourning rituals. Thus, when the Reformation banished the corpse from the church, plays like Shakespeare's could restore the symbolic value of this image by placing the corpse prominently onstage. Goodland observes that in *King Lear* the spiritual figure of the mother mourning over the body of her son is replaced by the figure of the father mourning over his daughter – with, of course, far more impact from the howling and wailing by virtue of the fact that Shakespeare's protagonist is a man and not a woman. Frank Brownlow, arguing for Shakespeare as a closet Catholic, maintains that Catholic members of the original audiences to *King Lear* would have interpreted the play as covertly representing their own persecution and suffering. (In Brownlow's view, this representation is substantiated by the betrayal of fathers by children, in particular Edmund's betrayal of the father who so deeply trusts him.)[11]

Frankie Rubinstein suggests that religious issues, and their part in the dynastic rivalry between various British reigns and factions – including Essex's rival court set up in the reign of Queen Elizabeth – have an important place in *King Lear*'s capacity for social commentary. In Rubinstein's view, Shakespeare used the play to expose the way in which religious and political bigotry were eating away at the fabric of British society. Rubinstein illustrates her argument by means of Lear's pivotal speech of Act 5, scene 3, which she sees as a metaphorical allusion to Catholic–Protestant controversy.

> We two alone will sing like birds i'th'cage.
> When thou dost ask me blessing, I'll kneel down
> And ask of thee forgiveness. So we'll live,
> And pray, and sing, and tell old tales, and laugh
> At gilded butterflies, and hear poor rogues
> Talk of court news, and we'll talk with them too –
> Who loses and who wins, who's in, who's out –
> And take upon's the mystery of things,
> As if we were God's spies. (9–17)

Like two religious refugees, devout in their hidden faith (as many Catholics were in a Protestant reign), Lear and Cordelia seek solace in each other's blessing. Lear takes upon himself 'the mystery of things' in his role as one of 'God's spies', and in the words, 'God's spies' Rubinstein hears also 'God's (s)pies' or magpies, whose black and white plumage constituted a frequent contemporary mockery of bishops in their black and white garb.[12] Mark Thornton Burnett considers Protestantism in the context of master/servant relationships in *King Lear*,[13] while Judy Kronenfeld attempts to stand back from the Catholic/Protestant debates about Shakespeare's religious sympathies, arguing that we cannot, for instance, characterize someone as Protestant simply because they use the metaphor of the 'naked truth' to signify true and plain speaking, or the language of the heart; nor can a character be seen as proto-Catholic because he values gorgeous apparel, ceremony and ornate verbal display.[14]

The Politics of Loss

By himself experiencing poverty and the forces of the wind and rain, Shakespeare's player king must have cut an intensely ambivalent figure in the early seventeenth century, suggesting alternately an iconoclastic image of a king who has, in dividing his kingdom, perverted the sacred trust of his office, and the appealing figure of a monarch who has broken recklessly and painfully out of the cosseting environment of his court to expose himself to 'feel what wretches feel' (3.4.34). This is one of the many observations that help to dismantle the centrality of the 'universal man' to whom early-to-mid twentieth-century humanists were addicted, drawing *King Lear* instead into historical understandings of kingship, politics, law and inheritance. For these contemporary historicized points of view, we are hugely indebted to the forces of the new historicism and cultural materialism that flourished in the 1980s and 1990s, schools of thought that made fascinating incursions into understandings about the operations of society, power and politics.

The effects of these critical movements can be felt in the subtle, anthropologically informed arguments put forward by critics like Linda Woodbridge. Discussing the well-known rogue books that conveyed the equivocal nature of Protestant attitudes towards beggary and vagrancy and alluded to major epidemics of the plague, Woodbridge ties *King Lear*'s 'aimless' dramatic structure to the wandering geographical movement of the vagrant.[15] Margot Heinemann considers Regan and Goneril as representatives of parliamentary attacks on royal prerogatives and expenditures. She points out that while a patriarchal view of power – which in her terms endorses kingly authority with the prerogatives of the father – is strongly present in the play, it is by no means unchallenged: Lear, the 'wise' father, pig-headedly refuses to listen to wise counsel, and thus, exposes his poor judgement.[16] Lisa Hopkins, in 'Lear's Castle', considers the figure of Robert Dudley, Earl of Leicester, whose shadowy presence can be discerned in *King Lear*. Himself beloved by two sisters, the Earl of Leicester finds a doppelgänger in the figure of *King Lear*'s Edmund; while other correspondences, including that of names and of parallel poison plots, are also to be found.[17] Kaara L. Peterson devotes twenty-three pages to Lear's lines concerning *hysterica passio* (2.4.56–57), which have long been seen as a sign of Lear's emasculation in the course of his suffering. She considers a range of interpretative manoeuvres to conclude that these lines reflect a 'misdiagnosis' on the part of the old king that is 'Shakespeare's method of sending an intelligible message to his audience about the king's errant mind, not his errant womb'.[18] Simon C. Estok contributes to geopolitical conceptions of fatherhood in the play by examining the relationship between *physical* space (Lear's control of his kingdom) and the emotional unboundedness of a world that is slipping out of his control – and, indeed, out of control altogether.[19]

Several recent historically informed essays on *King Lear* hinge on the issue of property. Heather Dubrow interprets the play's lawless world as invoking a widespread social anxiety over housing and dislodgement that occurred along with property invasions and land disputes, as exemplified when Gloucester is driven from his house.[20] William O. Scott imagines a seventeenth-century legal context for Lear's abdication and division of his kingdom, bringing out some of the problems and ironies that result from his choice.[21] Harold Leon Craig considers the political implications of the distribution of Cordelia's suitors in the play's first scene. He grants some plausibility to Lear's initial intention to divide his kingdom, with the most opulent third going to Burgundy as a buffer between Albany in the north and Cornwall in the south.[22] Stephanie Chamberlain's study of inheritance laws elucidates in the first scene of the play Lear's gross miscarriage not only of judgement, but of justice.[23]

Psychoanalysis has, over the past decade, continued to contribute to conversations about *King Lear*. Catherine Belsey has recently deliberated on 'the paradoxical relationship between pain and joy in the experience of art', speculating on the linguistic misunderstandings that lie at the heart of the play. Belsey suggests that these misunderstandings display the gap between language and emotion: the unreliability of language is what silences Cordelia and leads her father to the 'unspeakable' pain of his final 'unheroic' speech (that is, a speech that fails to position itself heroically).[24] Paul Kahn argues that psychoanalysis 'fits' the play only in

failure of language

counterpoint to politics. *King Lear* is in his view most aptly appreciated when politics and psychology are entwined. His study of *King Lear's* 'political psychology' develops the notion that 'the play explores the issue of what a commitment to political order does to, and requires of, the soul'. This marriage of politics and psychology, Kahn argues, enables us to link the play no less relevantly to modern democratic contexts than to Shakespeare's contemporary political contexts.[25] In the course of Kahn's painstaking scene-by-scene analysis, some idiosyncratic and valuable insights emerge: he notes, for example, that while in the play's first scene love is a form of ritual that serves the two older sisters' intense interest in the theatre of the state, later in the play this dynamic is reversed so that law, for them, serves the theatre of love (150). Zdravko Planinc also appeals to a more psychologically oriented view of what is politically at stake in the play. He suggests that *King Lear's* deepest insight is found in the fact that the king's desire to master his own death – to 'crawl towards death' in his own way – almost costs the destruction of love, and of his self, altogether.[26] And Alan Rosen has studied the psychological and thematic implications of the play's unique dramatic ending. Rosen examines the psychological effect of the occurrence of the climax early in the play instead of at the end, where it traditionally occurs.[27]

Family Matters

How does *King Lear* reach today's audiences? In order for the impossible brutality of the play's action and the misogynistic, self-centred rantings of the aged protagonist to have emotional resonance, Lear has to be someone whom we do not just theorize about, but *care* about. And ultimately, we are asked to care about Lear as a character not because he represents a certain political system or theology, nor even because he depicts the image of a king who has lost everything: we care about him because he is *a father* who has lost everything: a father who, as Ewan Fernie has suggested, runs from shame in the first scene and comes finally to some acceptance of it as he embraces his folly and the daughter he dismissed as wayward.[28]

In the end, then, *King Lear* is a play that can live at the heart of any family. Laurence Olivier once said:

> [Lear's] just a selfish, irascible old bastard – so am I [. . .] My family would agree with that: no wonder he's all right, they would say, he's just himself, he's got just that sort of ridiculous temper, those sulks. Absolutely mad as a hatter sometimes. [. . .] When you're younger, Lear doesn't feel real. When you get to my age, you *are* Lear in every nerve of your body.[29]

Lear is king and not-king, superman and everyman, an internal conflict built into the social psychology of fathers across the centuries and all over the world.

The subject of family remains the focus of many important publications on the play, and some of the most powerful recent arguments link the emotional impact of family dynamics with historicist understandings of statehood. Meredith Skura observes, indeed, that whereas the *Leir* precedent for Shakespeare's play concentrates on how to judge and repair discord, Shakespeare's play concentrates on what discord *feels* like. Examining the two plays (*King Lear* and its *Leir* precedent), Skura finds in Shakespeare's play a more complex father/child relationship than in the *Leir* play because Shakespeare's father *and* child are both sinned against and sinning. Skura argues that in order to complicate the relationship between Lear and Cordelia, and, indeed, between Lear and his three daughters, Shakespeare has moved outside the *Leir* precedent to Michel de Montaigne's writings about fathers and children who compete for scarce resources. Skura also traces the influence on Shakespeare of Harsnett's ideas on demonic possession, which would have helped the dramatist to understand what it feels like to be possessed.[30] Bruce Young argues that critics should be sceptical about homologies that associate early modern fatherhood with patriarchal alienation rather than tenderness and gentleness (so that in Young's terms Lear violates conventional understandings of father/daughter relationships rather than endorsing them).[31] From an altogether different perspective, Neville F. Newman considers the role of Cornwall as a surrogate father in *King Lear*, contrasting his willingness and certain kind of competence with the ineptitude displayed by the two 'natural' fathers, Lear and Gloucester.[32]

Philippa Kelly contributes to the series of minigraphs *Shakespeare Now!* (series editors Simon Palfrey and Ewan Fernie) with a volume entitled *The King and I*. Kelly uses the book's personal account of her life within an Australian family to examine, via the lens of *King Lear*, Australian issues of loss, ageing, indigenous rights, prisons, cultural humour and, as an overarching theme, the concept of banishment, that state of enforced alienation that is so difficult for humans anywhere to bear. Although it emerges from Australia, the book illuminates these themes for audiences and general readers as they relate to families everywhere.

Very important to recent studies of the family was the publication of Jane Smiley's *King Lear*-based novel, *A Thousand Acres*, in 1991, a powerful story detailing the relationships between two abused elder daughters who finally take a stand against their tyrannical patriarch. In Smiley's reading of Shakespeare, Lear relentlessly hogs the stage, allowing insufficient space and sympathy for the characters of his daughters ever to be developed. A *Thousand Acres* pushes Lear to the margins of the story altogether, requiring that, as a man who has committed incest, the father, and not his much-maligned older daughters, take on the narrow space of unequivocality. I mention Smiley's novel here because it has continued to provoke critical speculation over the past decade, with Caroline Cakebread, James Schiff and Nicholas Kostis and Claudine Herrmann all contributing to ongoing interest in the incestuous implications of Lear's relationship to his daughters.[33] Yvonne Griggs focuses on the movie version of *A Thousand Acres*, contending that the close of the film reflects the more upbeat cinematic conventions of melodrama rather than the tenuous resolutions offered by either Smiley's novel or Shakespeare's play.[34] (Interestingly, Richard Proudfoot, in his article, 'Some Lears', which concerns the links between nineteenth-century revisions and rewritings and the ways in which *King Lear* spoke to the late twentieth century, asks some questions that are vey useful to conceptual understandings of the appropriation employed by Smiley.[35])

King Lear, the Globe and Stagecraft

Over the last century, there has been a great revival of a play once thought too large and grotesque for the stage, and the last ten years have added substantially to this interest. In summer 2001, Shakespeare's Globe staged *King Lear*, starring Julian Glover, with the storm scene memorably portraying Lear and the Fool struggling across the stage yoked together by a rope. In 2007, Ian McKellen, who had begun his career on the Shakespeare stage and moved into lucrative film roles in *X-Men*, *Lord of the Rings* and *Richard III*, returned to the stage in Trevor Nunn's internationally touring production of *King Lear*.

King Lear's recent appeal for the stage has given extra volume to the ever-flowing stream of material on stagecraft. Discussions of stagecraft remain fertile because they elucidate and expand our understandings of the play's thematic resonances. In 2005, Simon Palfrey's *Doing Shakespeare* began with the question: 'We want to know why he [Shakespeare] has such a towering reputation, and to judge for ourselves whether the work deserves such acclaim rather than meekly taking it on trust.'[36] Palfrey's book gives a welcome opening to the subject of what 'words' and 'characters' (the titles of the two main sections of the book) 'do', and of how Shakespeare himself cues us to understand his plays and appreciate their complexity. In *Shakespeare in Parts*, with Tiffany Stern,[37] Palfrey considers Shakespeare as the author of performance texts. Given that he conceived of his plays 'in parts' for individual actors from his own company – each of whom learned his role from a 'part-script', plus cue words or phrases signalling his re-entry into a speech-act – the actor's acquaint-ance with his character developed privately. Shakespeare, therefore, wrote with this process in mind. 'In the disjunctions and discrepancies between play-text and part-text', Palfrey and Stern argue, 'in the false starts and mistaken attributions that ensue, Shakespeare is often script-ing a battle for understanding, definition and recognition that carefully reconstitutes the most elemental challenges of achieving sustainable self-hood' (p. 118). In relation to *King Lear*, the authors consider textual examples – like Gloucester's 'tis strange, strange' in 1.2 (of the Q text – the Folio may have excised one 'strange' for reasons of space) – that serve as structural and thematic cues. Gloucester's repetition of the words serves as a cue for Edmund's entry, while also displaying both the old man's droning befuddlement *and* his son's sense of purpose as he enters to 'take charge' of the plot (241–42).

Lisa Hopkins[38] examines the function of letter-writing in *King Lear*, noting that there are thirty-three references to letters in the play, and that the use of letters (sometimes seemingly redundant, as when Edgar is assumed to have written his brother a letter when they are living in the same castle) helps to advance and often to complicate the plot. But even more importantly, letters – exchanges of opinion by means of report – add to the plenitude and ambiguity of meaning in the play. Andrew Gurr, in the rather loftily entitled 'Headgear as a Paralinguistic Signifier in *King Lear*', seeks to uncover details about the original per-formances of the play via the use of headgear (crowns, coronets and the like, as well as Lear's shedding of traditional headgear in favour of a crown made of weeds). Gurr notes that although we have regrettably little evidence about what the original players in *King Lear* might have worn, the indications about headgear in the text strongly suggest that the playwright expected crowns and coronets to be used not just as monarchical 'hats', but as emblems of individual significance.[39] Bruce Smith, David Warner and Charles Hallet have also offered valuable essays on theatrical production.[40]

Performances of *King Lear* inspire speculation about location as well as about the playtext. Ruru Li, for example, writes about a recent Taiwanese adaptation of *King Lear* that displays virtuosic breadth in an actor trained, in the traditional Taiwanese way, to specialize in single roles. In deciding to base his performance on *King Lear*, the actor con-sciously chose to work against his 'natural' acting tradition, offering a solo performance built on presenting nine different characters from Shakespeare's play.[41] Diane Daugherty discusses a Kathakali perform-ance of *King Lear* that took place in India in 1999, questioning the 'hourglass' model of perceiving theatrical practice as 'imported' into a 'target' culture. The hourglass model sees foreign performance practice as being poured through the neck of an hourglass into the target culture. The target culture is imputed to have a dozen or more filters that regulate the passage of 'grains' of the performance text through which audiences observe the slow rearrangement of the text within the conventions of this target culture. Daugherty suggests an alternative concept: the pendulum model, whereby a complex back-and-forth perceptual motion suggests the malleability, or porosity, of both Indian performance conventions and Western story.[42] Poonam Trivedi, in a CD ROM entitled *Shakespeare in India: 'King Lear'*, considers the attraction of *King Lear* for Indian performances. She suggests the importance in Indian history of folklore to do with Lear-like themes of banishment, suffering and exile. Trivedi addresses five trends in the performance of Shakespeare in India: English-language Shakespeare, localized Shakespeare, universalized Shakespeare, indigenized Shakespeare and postcolonial Shakespeare. She sees *King Lear* as a foundational text for Indian audiences: each interpretative mode has been used for performances of the play in India, and not always in English. After independence in 1947, indigenous theatrical versions came to predominate, accompanied by a greater range of linguistic approaches. The multiplicity of these types of *King Lear*, Trivedi suggests, highlights the depth, breadth and versatility of 'Shakespeares' in Asian culture and understanding, and deepens our understanding of the culture itself.[43]

King Lear on Screen

'If we think of genre as a "vehicle" in a literal sense', comments R. S. White, 'we might make the loose analogy that the same people can travel in either a car, a train or an aeroplane. And that *King Lear* can travel in a family saga or a western.'[44] In a recent chapter that focuses on *King Lear*'s connection with Hollywood, White gives a wry and thoughtful analysis of the business of adapting *King Lear* for film. And what does it mean to explore Shakespeare as a historicized original? Terms like 'adaptation', 'appropriation' and 'spin-off' all describe a relationship to a premised 'original' text. For Daniel Fischlin and Mark Fortier the verb 'to appropriate' is weighted with a sense of coercion, while 'spin-off', 'transformation' and 'off-shoot' implicitly favour the authenticity of an original text.[45] 'Adaptation' emerges as the most useful term, distinguishing 'a generalized cultural activity that posits reworking in new contexts as more characteristic of cultural development than are originality in creation and fidelity in interpretation' (5). 'Adaptation', in other words, gets away from the pejorative to convey a sense of elasticity.

While not all adaptations of Shakespeare are films, all films of Shakespeare are in some sense adaptations. The screen provides a medium for which the playwright never had the capacity or intention, allowing the director, via a camera, to manipulate visual perspective beyond what is possible for the stage. Grigori Kozintsev put it well when he said of the cinematic medium: 'The advantage of the cinema over the theatre is not that you can even have horses, but that you can stare closer into a man's eyes'.[46] In Trevor Nunn's recent movie version of the production starring Ian McKellen, camera close-ups played McKellen's demonic self-centredness for all it was worth.

In an article on *King Lear* and genre films, Yvonne Griggs notes that because of the play's preoccupation with redemption, it is 'tailor-made' for adaptation as a genre film that highlights the issue of 'indeterminate space'. By this, she refers to the use of space less as connoting 'place' than as connoting a value system, a zone of dramatic conflict, in which the protagonist struggles to realign his views with the perspectives held by the community at large.[47] While Griggs's analysis is highly intellectualized, more interesting to me is Simon J. Ryle's discussion of film adaptations of *King Lear*'s Dover Cliff scene, in which he calls the scene a 'non-space'.[48] It has often been recognized that Gloucester's imaginary fall invokes the early modern practice of textualizing stage space: it plays with the notion of the willing suspension of disbelief, through which the imagination is called on to embody spaces and objects that are unavailable to the players on Shakespeare's stage. In the non-presence of the cliff, Gloucester can *dramatically* (in a play within a play) enact a cathartic fall. In this sense Edgar's improvisation both tests and protects his father. Paying particular attention to Peter Brook's 1971 adaptation, Ryle investigates the possibilities within film adaptations for recreating and recasting Edgar's protective improvisation.

Over the last ten years, some of the famous late twentieth-century film adaptations of *King Lear* have continued to inspire critical attention. As well as the Ryle study of Brook's film, there is also Antonio Teixeira's exploration of it in the context of national identity.[49] Kenneth S. Rothwell, in *A History of Shakespeare on Screen: A Century of Film and Television*, uses Brook's film to illustrate the many features that might otherwise unconsciously shape the viewing experience: Rothwell discusses the 'discontinuities, zoom-fades, accelerated motion, freeze frames, shock editing, complex reverse-angle and over-the-shoulder shots, montage, jump cuts, overhead shots, silent-screen titles, eyes-only close-ups and hand-held as well as immobile cameras'.[50] A number of articles have been published on Kurosawa's *Ran*, a stunning Japanese adaptation of *King Lear* that remains in the very top few foreign adaptations of Shakespeare.[51] Attention has also been given to Jean-Luc Godard's 1987 *King Lear*,[52] which featured the film's back story in the 'text' of the film itself. Godard experienced legendary difficulties with

his star and co-star (Norman Mailer and his daughter), and Godard's
film itself becomes an exploration of the impossibility of resurrecting
his film from its disastrous inception (in which the two key actors left
the set after the very first day of shooting). Three articles in the last decade have also addressed Kozintsev's famous adaptation of *King Lear*.[53]

Editions of *King Lear*

Since the year 2000, there have been a number of new editions of *King
Lear*, including a CD ROM edited by Jacky Bratton and Christie Carson,
and produced by Cambridge University Press in 2000. The CD ROM
offered the first electronic opportunity to access a Shakespeare play
together with its apparatus – including comprehensive performance
history contributions by Carson, Jay L. Halio, Dennis Kennedy and
Philippa Kelly. The CD ROM was quickly over-run by advances in technology, however – not the least of which was the internet, whose fluidity both 'updates' and quickly 'dates' electronic material – and Cambridge
did not follow up with its planned series of single-play CD ROMs.
Complete Works editions like the Norton Shakespeare have proven
very popular, with side-by-side Q1/F1 texts of *King Lear* that treat them
as separate plays, while also making it very easy to see at what points,
and in what ways, the two versions of the play diverge. (In the Norton
edition, Stephen Greenblatt also provides a beautiful introductory essay
to the play).[54]

Editions by Alexander Leggatt[55] and Jay L. Halio were republished in
the last decade (2004 and 2005, respectively) with updated introductions.[56] In 2002, Philippa Kelly published the first general-audience
playtext to be prepared by a woman,[57] which had a narrow distribution
for the Australian market. (It also offered a complete history of *King
Lear*'s performances in Australia). In 2005, Claire McEachern published
with Longman an accessible edition with an astute and creative Introduction,[58] and in 2007 Raffel Burton published an edition prefaced with
an essay by the ubiquitous Harold Bloom.[59]

Richard Knowles added to our knowledge of the Quarto/Folio versions of *King Lear* in 'The Evolution of the Texts of *King Lear*',[60] while
R. A. Foakes, in 'The Reshaping of *King Lear*', considers the debate
about which text (Quarto or Folio) is more authoritative, and what was
the involvement of Shakespeare's hand with each. (Foakes concludes
that revisions were made to the Quarto, possibly by scribes, in order to
compose the Folio.[61]) *King Lear*'s structure is also interestingly illuminated by a glance at Christopher Marlowe's *Tamburlaine*. In 'The End of
II Tamburlaine and the Beginning of *King Lear*', Mark Hutchings details
the similarities between the two plays in regard to the request for a map,

the division of property and the disinheriting of one child, suggesting that Shakespeare found in the dying Tamburlaine an analogue for his play.[62]

Debts to the Aged

Since the year 2000, world events – 9/11 and the global crisis, to mention two of the major forces – have made for a decline in the world economy and for a shaking of the supremacy of Western nations. This weakening of the capitalist world has progressed in counterpoint to the advances in medicine that have meant that elderly people have begun to live longer than they ever have before. It is now not unusual for an elderly person to live to 85, 90, even 95 years old, and deaths of people in their 70s are generally accepted as premature.

King Lear carries a message increasingly pertinent to this context. What do we 'owe' to the aged? Lear's plight brings up so many of the weaknesses of age: loss of judgement, loss of control and loss of dignity – the loss of authority over others, and a diminished capacity to 'author', or control, oneself. How do we value age when its material usefulness has been superseded and is often perceived to be in deficit? With the social impact that is attached to the sheer number of the aged, there has emerged a critical interest in *King Lear's* capacity to speak to the precarious relationship between humanity and material resources. '[W]hat shocks us every time is to learn that Cruelty, as Blake tells us, has a human heart', writes Lore Segal of the play. 'In Vienna, when I was ten years old, we watched our next-door neighbors turning into monsters.'[63] Sean Lawrence, in 'The Difficulty of Dying in *King Lear*', observes that Lear 'express[es] his heroism not by choosing his death but by choosing not to die'. He chooses to endure, and in this sense he attempts to make his existence meaningful through his own powers of resistance and acceptance.[64]

There has also been a renewed interest in *King Lear's* relevance to the subject of vagrancy and poverty in Shakespeare's England, as can be seen in essays by David Teimist, Charles Hallet, James Tink, Paul Efalu and Adrian Poole,[65] as well as the *King Lear* chapter of Linda Woodbridge's book on vagrancy (mentioned above).[66] Michael Shurgot considers the subject of vagrancy in terms of stagecraft, suggesting that Edgar remain naked for the entirety of 3.4 in order to bring across the true meaning of vulnerability in this play: 'unaccommodated man' would be displayed alone, vulnerable, without any protection whatsoever.[67] In the figure of the naked Poor Tom, Lear can confront not only the poor wretches of whom he has 'ta'en so little care', but his own vulnerability.

Feminism and *King Lear*

Feminist sensibilities depend largely on what differences are being marked in an interpretation of *King Lear* – whether it be by asking questions, disrupting stereotypes or, perhaps, by focusing on conventionally marginal characters or features – and on the way(s) in which these differences affect one's overall sense of how a production works. Critics impatient with feminist interpretations of *King Lear* often see these interpretations as narrow-minded political commentaries offered by members of a stubborn interest group. However, if we consider, for example, that Lear's redemption is enacted at the cost of Cordelia's interest as a character, then Lear's youngest daughter can emerge in a fuller interpretative light. Beyond her moving reunion with Lear and her 'no cause, no cause' in the play's fourth act, we never (at least in the Folio text) get to hear of what Cordelia thinks. In the final act of the play she is given no lines at all, just a report of her untimely death and an account of how good and gentle and quiet she was: 'Her voice was ever soft, / Gentle and low, an excellent thing in woman' (5.3.246–47). When we listen to this summation of Cordelia by her father, are we not tempted to agree with Valerie Traub that the cost of redemption in Shakespeare is 'a complete capitulation to masculine terms as well as the resurrection of the faulty structure of sexual dualism'?[68] How can such capitulation make the play at all relevant to audiences in the new millennium, struggling with the meanings ascribed to gender and equal opportunity, and trying to stay attuned to the inherent biases of a gendered system that still needs to declare women 'equal' to a standard transparently established by men?

In drawing attention to approaches that favour or naturalize masculinity, feminist perspectives can add interest and controversy to standard readings and productions of the play, wresting it out of the hands of the two elderly patriarchs and their devotees, and giving it over to innovative female actors and critics. Carol Rutter suggests, for instance, that while certain dramatic moments (like the death scenes in *King Lear*) conventionally play out gendered expectations of female subordination, these expectations can be acknowledged and complicated by 'smart actors' who learn how to 'collaborate with [Shakespeare] to author themselves'.[6] Does contemporary feminism assume masculinity as a natural Shakespearean default-position for 'important' themes and speeches, so that attention to female roles requires challenge and subversion?

[margin handwriting: Good question]

Several critics have presented (necessarily abstracted) early modern contexts for understanding gendered performance. In the early 1990s Lisa Jardine had argued that women in Shakespeare's plays are purely the effect of masculinity, with boy actors playing the woman's part for 'a male audience's appreciation'.[70] A decade later Dympna Callaghan observed, 'A representational schema that understands sexual difference completely within the parameters of masculinity does not require women: it occurs entirely within a material economy of males', leaving 'woman' as a body that is defined in masculinist terms.[71] She suggests that this is not always a negative thing: 'this cleavage between femininity and women in the process of male mimesis need not involve the denigration of women as such. For while the premise of all-male performance is misogynist – in that it is based on the exclusion of women, who are placed entirely outside its circuits of representation – in its execution the performance of femininity might even champion women'.[72]

In response to arguments about how far women are included or excluded, Jill Dolan opens a quite different perspective by contending that feminists would do well to cease 'considering the stage as a mirror of reality'. Once we let go of mimetic expectations, 'we can use it [the stage] as a laboratory in which to reconstruct new, non-genderized identities'.[73] But what does the term 'non-genderized identities' mean, exactly? Ideally, it would seem to suggest that staged identities need not be constrained by gendered associations; that we can look at Shakespeare's stage with something *other* than the bleak summation that we are dealing with a play so implicitly 'masculinized' that women were not even intended to play their own (narrow) gender identities; and that we can conceive of the stage as a 'laboratory' that seeks to achieve *more* than the goal of putting women in the space that men used to occupy. In tune with this opinion, Sarah Werner aptly suggests that 'feminism' refers to 'those actors, directors and performances which strive to question received assumptions of Shakespeare's depiction of and appropriateness for women'.[74] In Werner's terms, feminist thought facilitates a re-thinking, or a reopening, of established opinions and perceptions about female roles and audiences. This kind of flexibility might serve to question what is ascribed to gender in the play, highlighting, for example, Lear's description of tears as 'women's weapons, water drops' (2.2.443), his allusion to emotion as the 'menstrual "mother" that swells up towards his heart' (2.2.225), and his famous revulsion at the 'sulphurous pit . . . burning, scalding, stench, consumption' (4.5.122).[75] It might also enable us to challenge assumptions that the sisters embody essential qualities,[76] that the play's 'universal' questions about age, control and suffering are implicitly masculine,[77] or, alternatively, that misogyny in *King Lear* is less the property of the play than that of the gender-inflected ideas and terminologies imposed by critics.[78] Some excellent feminist studies can cause us to question how we see women in Shakespeare, and how we see women in general. Elizabeth Schafer,[79] Juliet Dusinberre[80] and Phyllis Rackin[81] all seek to open dramatic doors for women rather than mourning their closure, suggesting, in the process, a diversity of positions from which we might re-evaluate the ways in which Lear and his daughters speak to men and women of today.

More than any other of Shakespeare's plays, perhaps, *King Lear* continues to live on in critical debate. Perhaps this is due partly to how often the play is 'done' at school; or to the fact that argument generates counter-argument. But it is also because the play is so stark in its outlines, so rich in possibility; and because its extremes of behaviour are discomforting to the extent that they compel some kind of understanding. *King Lear* offers no excuses for its grotesqueries, and no assurance of redemption. The explosion at the play's beginning gives way to a cold, bare world where youthful characters unveil their ambitions and the elderly, and their followers, are forced to endure; where those who are loyal (and those who are not) meet their deaths and we, in the audience, are left to stand with Albany and Edgar as witnesses to 'this great decay'.[82]

In memory of my brother John Kelly, lawyer and humanitarian, 24–3–1960 to 30–12–2010. 'Let distribution undo excess, and each man have enough.'

Notes

1   Paul Cantor, 'The Cause of Thunder: Nature and Justice in King Lear', in *King Lear: New Critical Essays*, ed. and intro. by Jeffrey Kahan (New York: Routledge, 2008), pp. 231–52 (p. 233).

2   David N. Beauregard, 'Human Malevolence and Providence in *King Lear*', *Renascence: Essays on Values in Literature*, 60.3 (Spring 2008), 199–224.

3   Stephen Regan and Graham Martin, 'King Lear', in *Shakespeare: Texts and Contexts*, ed. by Kiernan Ryan (London: Macmillan, 2000), pp. 241–76 (pp. 264–65).

4   John Hughes, 'The Politics of Forgiveness: A Theological Exploration of *King Lear*', *Modern Theology*, 17.3 (July 2001), 261–87.

5   All references to the text of *King Lear* are from *The Norton Shakespeare: Based on the Oxford Edition*, ed. by Stephen Greenblatt, Walter Cohen, Jean E. Howard and Katharine Eisaman Maus (New York and London: Norton, 1997).

6   George Walton Williams, 'Invocations to the Gods in *King Lear*: A Second Opinion', *Shakespeare Newsletter*, 51.4 (250, 2001–2002), pp. 89 and 106 (Reply to 2001–1–2010).

7   Michael Edwards, '*King Lear* and Christendom', *Christianity & Literature*, 50.1 (Autumn 2000), 15–29.

8   Seán Lawrence, 'Gods That We Adore': The Divine in *King Lear*', *Renascence: Essays on Values in Literature*, 56.3 (Spring 2004), 143–59.

9   Lyell Asher, 'Lateness in *King Lear*', *Yale Journal of Criticism*, 13.2 (2000), 209–28.

10 Katharine Goodland, 'Inverting the Pietà in Shakespeare's *King Lear*', in *Marian Moments in Early Modern British Drama*, ed. by Regina Buccola and Lisa Hopkins (Aldershot: Ashgate, 2007), pp. 47–74.

11 Frank Brownlow, 'Richard Topcliffe: Elizabeth's Enforcer and the Representation of Power in *King Lear*', in *Theatre and Religion: Lancastrian Shakespeare*, ed. by Richard

Dutton, Alison Findlay and Richard Wilson (Manchester and New York: Manchester University Press, 2003), pp. 161–78.

12   Frankie Rubinstein, 'Speculating on Mysteries: Religion and Politics in *King Lear*', *Journal of the Society for Renaissance Studies*, 16.2 (June 2002), 234–62.

13   Mark Thornton Burnett, 'King Lear, Service and the Deconstruction of Protestant Idealism', in *The Shakespearean International Yearbook, Volume 5: Special Section, Shakespeare and the Bonds of Service*, ed. by Michael Neill (Aldershot: Ashgate Press, 2005), pp. 66–85.

14   Judy Kronenfeld, *King Lear and the Naked Truth: Rethinking the Language of Religion and Resistance* (Durham and London: Duke University Press, 1998).

15   Linda Woodbridge, *Vagrancy, Homelessnes, and English Renaissance Literature* (Urbana and Chicago: University of Illinois Press, 2001).

16   Margot Heinemann, 'Demystifying the Mystery of State: *King Lear* and the World Upside Down', in *Shakespeare and Politics*, ed. by Catherine Alexander and Intro. by John Joughin (Cambridge: Cambridge University Press, 2004), pp. 155–68.

17   Lisa Hopkins, 'Lear's Castle', *Cahiers Elisabéthains: Late Medieval and Renaissance Studies*, 62 (October 2002, xi), 25–32.

18   Kaara L. Peterson, '*Historica Passio*: Early Modern Medicine, *King Lear*, and Editorial Practice', *Shakespeare Quarterly*, 57.1 (Spring 2006), 1–23.

19   Simon C. Estok, 'Shakespeare and Ecocriticism: An Analysis of "Home" and "Power" in *King Lear*', *AUMLA: Journal of the Australasian Universities Modern Language Association*, 103 (May 2005), 15–32.

20   Heather Dubrow, ' "They Took from Me the Use of Mine Own House": Land Law in Shakespeare's *Lear* and Shakespeare's Culture', in *Solon and Thespis: Law and Theater in the English Renaissance*, ed. by Dennis Kezar (Notre Dame, IN: Notre Dame University Press, 2007), pp. 81–98.

21   William O. Scott, 'Contracts of Love and Affection: Lear, Old Age, and Kingship', *Shakespeare Survey*, 55 (2002), 36–42.

22   Harold Leon Craig, *Of Philosophers and Kings: Political Philosophy in Shakespeare's Macbeth and King Lear* (Toronto: University of Toronto Press, 2001).

23   Stephanie Chamberlain, 'She Is Herself a Dowry': *King Lear* and the Problem of Female Entitlement in Early Modern England', in *Domestic Arrangements in Early Modern England*, ed. and intro. by Kari McBride (Pittsburgh: Duquesne University Press, 2002), pp. 169–87. See also Dan Brayton, who examines the ritualistic exchange of filial love for property and the thirst for power, 'Angling in the Lake of Darkness: Possession, Dispossession and the Politics of Discovery in *King Lear*', *English Literary History*, 70.2 (Summer 2003), 399–426.

24   Catherine Belsey, 'Psychoanalytic Speculations on the Pain and Joy of Tragedy: The Case of King Lear', in *Reconstructing Pain and Joy: Linguistic, Literary and Cultural Perspectives*, ed. and intro. by Chryssoula Lascaratou, Anna Despotopoulou and Elly Ifantidou (Newcastle upon Tyne: Cambridge Scholars, 2008), pp. 339–55.

25   Paul W. Kahn, *Law and Love: The Trials of King Lear* (New Haven: Yale University Press, 2000), p. xi.

26   Zdravko Planinc, ' . . . This Scattered Kingdom: A Study of *King Lear*', *Interpretation: A Journal of Political Philosophy*, 29.2 (2001/2), 171–85.

27   Alan Rosen, '*King Lear* Without End: Shakespeare, Dramatic Theory, and the Role of Catastrophe', in *Dislocating the End: Climax, Closure and the Invention of Genre* (New York: Peter Lang, 2001), pp. 6–26.

28   Ewan Fernie, *Shame in Shakespeare* (London and New York: Routledge, 2002).

29   Sir Laurence Olivier as quoted in Alexander Leggatt, *King Lear*, pp. 127–28.

30   Meredith Skura, 'Dragon Fathers and Unnatural Children: Warring Generations in *King Lear* and Its Sources', *Comparative Drama*, 42.2 (Summer 2008), 121–48.

31 Bruce W. Young, 'King Lear and the Calamity of Fatherhood', in *In the Company of Shakespeare: Essays on English Renaissance Literature in Honor of G. Blakemore Evans*, ed. and intro. by Thomas Moisan and Douglas Bruster, appendix by William H. Bond (Madison: Fairleigh Dickinson University Press, 2002), pp. 43–64.

32 Neville F. Newman, 'Shakespeare's *King Lear*', *The Explicator*, 60.4 (Summer 2002), 191–93.

33 Caroline Cakebread, 'Remembering *King Lear* in Jane Smiley's *A Thousand Acres*', in *Shakespeare and Appropriation*, ed. by Christy Desmet and Robert Sawyer (London and New York: Routledge, 1999); and James Schiff, 'Contemporary Retellings: *A Thousand Acres* as the Latest *Lear*', *Studies in Contemporary Fiction*, 39.4 (1998), 367–81; and Nicholas Kostis and Claudine Herrmann: 'The Dramatic Motive of Incest in *King Lear*', *Shakespeare Studies* (Tokyo, Japan), 39 (2001), 22–58.

34 Yvonne Griggs, ' "All Our Lives We'd Looked Out for Each Other the Way That Motherless Children Tend to Do": *King Lear* as Melodrama', *Literature/Film Quarterly*, 35.2 (2007:2), 101–7.

35 Richard Proudfoot, 'Some Lears', *Shakespeare Survey: An Annual Survey of Shakespeare Studies and Production*, 55 (2002), 139–52.

36 Simon Palfrey, *Doing Shakespeare* (London: Arden Shakespeare, 2005), p. xi.

37 Simon Palfrey, Tiffany Stern, *Shakespeare in Parts* (Oxford: Oxford University Press, 2007).

38 Lisa Hopkins, 'Reading between the Sheets: Letters in Shakespearean Tragedy', *Critical Survey*, 14.3 (2002), 5–13.

39 Andrew Gurr, 'Headgear as a Paralinguistic Signifier in *King Lear*', *Shakespeare Survey*, 55 (2002), 43–52.

40 Bruce Smith, 'Speaking What We Feel about *King Lear*', in *Shakespeare, Memory and Performance*, ed. by Peter Holland (Cambridge; New York: Cambridge University Press, 2006), pp. 23–42. David Warner, '*King Lear*', in *Performing Shakespeare's Tragedies Today: The Actor's Perspective*, ed. and intro. by Michael Dobson (Cambridge: Cambridge University Press, 2006), pp. 131–42.

41 Ruru Li, ' "Who Is It That Can Tell Me Who I Am? / Lear's Shadow": A Taiwanese Actor's Personal Response to *King Lear*', *Shakespeare Quarterly*, 57.2 (Summer 2006), 195–215.

42 Diane Daugherty, 'The Pendulum of Intercultural Performance: Kathakali *King Lear* at Shakespeare's Globe', *Asian Theater Journal (Assoc. for Asian Performance, Honolulu, Hawaii)*, 22.1 (Spring 2005), 52–72.

43 Poonam Trivedi, *Shakespeare in India: 'King Lear'*: A Multimedia CD-ROM (2006). Available from poonamtrivedi2004@yahoo.com].

44 Robert White, '*King Lear* and Film Genres', in *Renaissance Poetry and Drama in Context: Essays for Christopher Wortham*, ed. by Andrew Lynch and Anne M. Scott (Newcastle: Cambridge Scholars Publishing, 2008), pp. 317–32 (p. 324).

45 Daniel Fischlin and Mark Fortier, eds, *Adaptations of Shakespeare: A Critical Anthology of Plays from the Seventeenth Century to the Present* (New York: Routledge, 2000).

46 Grigori Kozintsev, *'King Lear:' The Space of Tragedy: The Diary of a Film Director*, trans. from the Russian by Mary Mackintosh, intro. by Peter Brook (London and Berkeley: Heinemann Educational, California University Press, 1977), p. 55.

47 Yvonne Griggs, '*King Lear* as Western Elegy', *Literature/Film Quarterly*, 35.2 (2007), 92–100.

48 Simon J. Ryle, 'Filming Non-Space: The Vanishing Point and the Face in Brook's *King Lear*', *Literature/Film Quarterly*, 35.2 (2007), 140–47.

49 Antonio João Teixeira, 'The Construction of National Identity in Shakespeare's *King Lear* and Its Filmic Adaptation by Peter Brook', *Ilha do Desterro: A Journal of Language and Literature*, 51 (July-December 2006), 283–99.

50   Kenneth S. Rothwell, *A History of Shakespeare on Screen,* : *A Century of Film and Television* (Cambridge: Cambridge University Press, 1999), p. 151.

51   Yoko Takakuwa, '(En)Gendering Desire in Performance: *King Lear*, Akira Kurosawa's *Ran*, Tadashi Suzuki's *The Tale of Lear*', in *Shakespeare and His Contemporaries in Performance*, ed. and preface by Edward J. Esche, intro. by Dennis Kennedy (Aldershot: Ashgate, 2000), pp. 35–49; and Joan Pong Linton, 'Kurosawa's *Ran* (1985) and *King Lear*: Towards a Conversation on Historical Responsibility', *Quarterly Review of Film and Video*, 23.4 (August 2006), 341–51.

52   Alan Walworth, 'Cinema *hysterica passio*: Voice and Gaze in Jean-Luc Godard's *King Lear*', in *The Reel Shakespeare: Alternative Cinema and Theory*, ed. by Lisa S. Starks and Courtney Lehmann (Madison, NJ: Fairleigh Dickinson University Press; London: Assoc. University Presses, 2002), pp. 59–94; Thaïs Flores Nogueira Diniz, 'Godard: A Contemporary *King Lear*', in *Foreign Accents: Brazilian Readings of Shakespeare*, ed. by Aimara de Cunha Resende (Newark, NJ: Delaware University Press, 2002), pp. 198–206; also Jessica M. Maerz, 'Godard's *King Lear*: Referents Provided Upon Request', *Literature/Film Quarterly*, 32.2 (2004), 108–14. (Maerz argues that while deconstruction, structuralism and modernist auteurism are out of fashion in the contemporary academy, they are of central relevance to Godard's own artistic and critical practice and to the film's historical moment.)

53   David Margolies, '*King Lear*: Kozintsev's Social Translation', in *Shifting the Scene: Shakespeare in European Culture*, ed. and intro. by Ladina Bezzola Lambert and Blaz Engler (Newark, NJ: University of Delaware Press, 2004), pp. 230–38; Anthony Lyons, 'Visible Spirits: Kozintsev's Cinematic Art in *Koral Lier/King Lear*', *Use of English*, 55.1 (Autumn 2003), 27–36; and Mark Sokolyansky, 'Grigori Kozintsev's *Hamlet* and *King Lear*', in *Shakespeare on Film*, ed. and intro. by Russell Jackson (Cambridge: Cambridge University Press, 2000), pp. 199–211.

54   William Shakespeare, *Works*, ed. by Stephen Greenblatt et al. (New York: Norton, 1997).

55   Leggatt, *King Lear*.

56   *The Tragedy of King Lear*, ed. by Jay L. Halio, New Cambridge Shakespeare rev. edn (Cambridge; New York: Cambridge University Press, 2005). See also Halio's essay, 'The Study of Shakespearean Playbooks', in *Acts of Criticism: Performance matters in Shakespeare and his contemporaries: essays in honor of James P. Lusardi*, ed. by Paul Nelsen and June Schlueter (Madison, NJ: Fairleigh Dickinson University Press, 2006), p. 275.

57   Philippa Kelly, *The Bell Shakespeare 'King Lear'* (Sydney: Halstead Press, 2002). I should note here that Jacky Bratton published an excellent actors' edition of *King Lear* in 1982. I have never yet seen an actors' edition so thoughtful or comprehensive. *King Lear*, ed. by Jacky Bratton, Theatre History Edition (Bristol: Bristol Classical Press, 1982).

58   William Shakespeare, *The Tragedy of King Lear*, ed. by Claire McEachern (London; New York: Pearson Longman, 2005).

59   William Shakespeare, *King Lear*, ed. by Raffel Burton, with an essay by Harold Bloom (New Haven, CT: Yale University Press, 2007), pp. xxxiv, 215.

60   Richard Knowles, 'The Evolution of the Texts of *King Lear*', in *King Lear: New Critical Essays*, ed. and intro. by Jeffrey Kahan (London: Routledge, 2008), pp. 124–54, 374.

61   R. A. Foakes, 'The Reshaping of *King Lear*', in *King Lear: New Critical Essays*, pp. 104–23.

62   Mark Hutchings, 'The End of II *Tamburlaine* and the Beginning of *King Lear*, *Notes and Queries: for readers and writers, collectors and librarians*, 47.1 (March 2000), 82–86.

63 Lore Segal, '*King Lear*, Several Little Boys, and An Old Crazy Woman in My Mother's Nursing Home', *Parnassus*, 26.2 (2002), 29–30.

64 Sean Lawrence, 'The Difficulty of Dying in *King Lear*', *English Studies in Canada*, 31.4 (December 2005), 35–52 (p. 49).

65 David Teimist, '"Fortune, That Arrant Whore, Ne'er Turns the Key to th' Poor": Vagrancy, Old Age and the Theatre in Shakespeare's *King Lear*', *Cahiers Elisabéthains: A Biannual Journal of English Renaissance Studies*, 71 (Spring 2007), 37–47. Charles Hallet, '*King Lear*, Act 3: Storming the Stage', in *Acts of Criticism*, ed. by Nelsen and Schlueter, pp. 126–43; James Tink, '"Expose Thyself to What [*sic*] Wretches Feel": The Figure of Bare Life in *King Lear* and *Timon of Athens*', *Shakespeare Studies* (Shakespeare Society of Japan), 43 (2005), 37–61; Paul A. Efalu, 'Rethinking the Discourse of Colonialism in Economic Terms: Shakespeare's *The Tempest*, Captain John Smith's Virginia Narratives, and the English Response to Vagrancy', *Shakespeare Studies*, 28 (2000), 85–119; Adrian Poole, 'The Shadow of Lear's "Houseless" in Dickens', *Shakespeare Survey*, 53 (2000), 103–13.

66 Woodbridge, *Vagrancy, Homelessness, and English Renaissance Literature*.

67 Michael W. Shurgot, '"The Thing Itself": Staging Male Sexual Vulnerability in *King Lear*', *Shakespeare and Renaissance Association of West Virginia Selected Papers*, 22 (1999) (www.marshall.edu/engsr/SR1999.html#A20)

68 Valerie Traub suggests a counterbalance to this despondency, arguing that precisely *because* women were the negative presence of a masculine positive, this left them free to play out sexual orientations with unusual fluidity, identifying with male, female and transvestite roles in Shakespeare's plays. Valerie Traub, 'Jewels, Statues and Corpses: Containment of Female Erotic Power in Shakespeare's Plays', in *Shakespeare and Gender: A History*, ed. by Deborah Parker and Ivo Kamps (London: Verso, 1995), pp. 120–41.

69 Carol Rutter, *Enter the Body: Women and Representation on Shakespeare's Stage* (London and New York: Routledge, 2001), pp. 26, 140.

70 Lisa Jardine, 'Boy Actors, Female Roles, and Elizabethan Eroticism', in *Staging the Renaissance: Reinterpretation of Elizabethan and Jacobean Drama*, ed. by David Scott Kastan and Peter Stallybrass (London and New York: Routledge, 1991), pp. 57–67.

71 Dympna Callaghan, *Shakespeare Without Women: Performing Race and Gender on the Renaissance Stage* (London and New York: Routledge, 2000), p. 51.

72 Callaghan, *Shakespeare Without Women*, pp. 51–52.

73 Qtd Elspeth Goodman, 'Women's Alternative Shakespeares and Women's Alternatives to Shakespeare in Contemporary British Theatre', in *Shakespeare, Feminism and Gender*, ed. by Kate Chedgzoy, New Casebooks (London: Palgrave, 2001), pp. 70–92 (p. 88).

74 Sarah Werner, *Shakespeare and Feminist Performance*, Accents on Shakespeare series (London and New York: Routledge, 2001), p. 107n.

75 Elizabeth Schafer, for instance, points out *King Lear's* 'vividly expressed and poetically effective misogyny, much of it voiced by Lear himself'. Noting that Lear's tirade against women is positioned late in the play when sympathy for the elderly king is riding high, she says, 'Negotiating this moment without endorsing . . . Lear's deep-seated loathing of women's sexuality presents a serious challenge.' *MsDirecting Shakespeare* (London: Women's Press, 1998), p. 128. In Coppélia Kahn's terms, Lear's misogyny gives way in the course of the play to a revelation of his 'hidden dependence on mothering'. 'Magic of Bounty: *Timon of Athens*, Jacobean Patronage, and Maternal Power', in *Shakespearean Tragedy and Gender*, ed. by Shirley Nelson Garner and Madelon Sprengnether (Bloomington: Indiana University Press, 1996), p. 138.

76 Graham Bradshaw (who has, by the way, written extensively and with great insight about many Shakespeare matters) offers a possible case in point: 'nothing that happens in *King Lear* makes us doubt that there is an essential difference between Cordelia's nature and that of her sisters.' *Misrepresentations: Shakespeare and the Materialists* (Ithaca: Cornell University Press, 1993), p. 216.

77 The valorization of Lear as universal man was most famously expressed early in the last century by A. C. Bradley, who referred to a feeling which haunts us in *King Lear*, as though we were witnessing something universal, a conflict not so much of particular persons as of the powers of good and evil in the world: A. C. Bradley, *Shakespearean Tragedy* (London: Macmillan, 1904), p. 262. Harley Granville-Barker wrote likewise of a 'larger synthesis' that suggests a universal relevance to Lear's moral progress: Harley Granville-Barker, 'King Lear', in *Shakespeare Criticism 1919–1935*, ed. by Anne Ridler (London: Oxford University Press, 1936), p. 293. John Middleton Murry, in the 1950s, saw the 'positive theme' of the play as 'no less than the Self and the birth of Divine Love. That comes to pass in Lear, through absolute isolation, through his becoming "the thing itself", through "madness", John Middleton Murry, *Shakespeare* (Jonathan Cape: London, 1956), p. 338.

78 Ann Jennalie Cook argues for Shakespeare's 'quicksilver elusiveness' and aversion to the 'orthodoxies of his time': *Making a Match: Courtship in Shakespeare and His Society* (New Jersey: Princeton University Press, 1991), pp. 261–63, while Juliet Dusinberre argues, in contrast, that the period in which Shakespeare lived was itself more proto-feminist than is conventionally perceived by feminists. She sees feminist thought in the period as a Puritan reaction to King James's misogyny: *Shakespeare and the Nature of Women*, 2nd edn (New York: St Martin's Press, 1996), esp. pp. 2–19.

79 Schafer, *MsDirecting Shakespeare*.

80 Juliet Dusinberre suggests that we might see Shakespeare's women as able to assist contemporary women in defining their own relationship to male-authored ideas about coherent selfhood. Juliet Dusinberre, Third Preface to her book, *Shakespeare and the Nature of Women* (New York: Palgrave Macmillan, 2003), pp. xx–xxi, xxii.

81 Rackin suggests that feminist scholarship might now speak so thoroughly to academic qualifications and credibilities that, 'adopted as a conceptual tool by women and men without a serious political commitment to feminist political agendas, criticism designated as "feminist" . . . can just as easily be used to naturalize women's oppression as to oppose it', 'Misogyny Is Everywhere', *A Feminist Companion to Shakespeare*, ed. by Dympna Callaghan (Oxford: Blackwell, 2000), p. 47.

82 *King Lear*, in Shakespeare's *Works*, ed. by Greenblatt et al., V.iii.297.

CHAPTER FOUR

New Directions: Promised End?
King Lear and the Suicide-Trick

Lori Anne Ferrell

Critics always introduce their thoughts on *King Lear* by confessing themselves dismayed, confused, appalled, outmatched – and wanting more. This is no recent literary turn. 'I was, many years ago, so shocked by Cordelia's death, that I knew not whether I ever endured to read again the last scenes of the play', wrote Samuel Johnson – in a postscript to his enduring 1765 edition of the play. 'The fierce dispute / Betwixt Damnation and impassioned clay / Must I burn through' lamented John Keats in 1816, as he sat down to read – once again. 'To see Lear acted', wrote Charles Lamb in 1810, 'has nothing in it but what is painful and disgusting.' No doubt he had just returned from the theatre. No doubt he planned to return.[1]

What accounts for this censorious fascination, for what A. C. Bradley called *King Lear*'s 'comparative unpopularity'? According to Bradley, it was due

> not merely to the extreme painfulness of the catastrophe, but in part to its dramatic defects, and in part to a failure in many readers to catch the peculiar effects to which I have referred – a failure that is natural.[2]

A Failure That Is Natural

More than a century ago, Bradley derived his theory of tragedy in large part from reading *Lear*, and even now we cannot shake off his haunting suggestion: that this great tragedy is great precisely because it is failed, because it dares present us with failure – of a life, of our understanding, of dramatic action – testing the limits of our capacity to acknowledge, let alone comprehend. We look again, wincing through our fingers. Perhaps this time the *promised* end will come.

No. Perhaps this time the promised end will be *different*.

Studies of *King Lear* have long dealt with the problem, so acutely described by Bradley, by presenting its failures – of the man and of the play – as, somehow, heroic. It has been glossed as a model of Christian sacrifice (against those refreshingly immodest Augustan-age critics who complained that it had few redeeming features), and it has been parsed as a model of humane redemption (against twentieth-century critics who have argued for its uncanny anticipation of Beckett, and the theatre of the absurd). That human failure is the engine that drives tragedy is a literary-generic commonplace; that the ultimate destination of any tragedy is death is another. But the most persistent commonplace is that this trail of failures and deaths has, somehow, transcendent purpose. In *King Lear*, however, the purpose of the journey seems so unclear as to render its concluding pile-up of death not so much meaningless as curiously over-elaborated, even for tragedy. Even for seventeenth-century English tragedy with all its bloody-mindedness. Even for Shakespeare's late tragedies, which were, structurally speaking, overly complex and, dramatically speaking, almost surely unsuccessful in their day.[3]

We need to reassess the meanings of failure, despair, and death in this play, given their near-giddy overrepresentation: characters die in battle, die from poison, die of heartbreak. The annihilation of souls is meted out in ways that acknowledge and then exploit the bounds of tragic irony. Death is made known to us by report, recounted too late, and thwarts not only the characters' expectations but, also and more significantly, the audiences'. His father's heart broke with joy, Edgar says – but well after the fact, and come to think of it, it may have broken from grief. Cordelia is to be executed in the prison cell she shares with her father, Edmund confesses – but, alas, not in time to save her, and, anyway, he was planning to pass the whole thing off as her fault. A dying Lear carries a dead Cordelia out of their shared prison cell – but somehow he missed the hanging. If you follow the First Folio version instead of the 1608 Quarto, he is not even certain that she is dead. Where there is no certainty there can be no closure, and there surely seems no certainty here.

Or is there? This rich set of variations on a cultural theme – possibly *the* largest and most anxiety-producing – the certainty that death comes for all, is best demonstrated in the play's reliance on what, borrowing generic terminology (from early modern comedy or, I suppose, sex farce), I will call the suicide-trick. Like bed-tricks, the suicide-tricks in *Lear* require remarkably convoluted strategies of elaboration and substitution, and they are responsible for moving the play's plot into position – at times when ordinary, believable behaviour simply will not do. And, as in the bed-trick, the suspension of belief is followed immediately by a reaction as logical as it is essentially misguided. Gloucester's abortive suicide at Dover, for example, is driven by a son's design to lie to his father, cruelly *and* to good purpose. The blinded Gloucester leaps – to nowhere; he then has to be convinced that he remains alive.

This is farce at its most painful edge: not simply failing to extinguish one's own life, but also failing to recognize that one has not actually succeeded at this self-sufficient task. In fact, the play's only successful self-murder, Goneril's, merits our attention only because it interrupts the rescue of Lear and Cordelia in prison, in so doing thwarting Edmund's attempt to repeal the suicide-trick he had earlier devised: he is then prevented from preventing its fulfilment. And in having failed to stop her killing, he has also failed to reinscribe that murder as Cordelia's own desperate deed.[4]

What may be clouding – or, better said, crowding – *King Lear*'s tragic vision is, then, the play's elaborate stagings of the act of self-murder: of all the ways of dying both the least certain (to those left behind) and the most (to the successful practitioner thereof). Explaining the juridical meaning of the act, Edmund Wingate noted in 1661 that the Suicide 'destroy[ed] himself out of premeditated hatred against his own life': *felo de se* (felon of himself) thus carried a complexly internalized, but ultimately inescapable logic. Between Intending Suicide and Intended Target, after all, nothing can occur contrary to expectation: within its necessarily limited parameters, suicide cannot make itself a mockery. And so, just as none but those who die by their own hand can commit that specific offence, the offence – so solipsistic, so particular – can admit of no meaning other than its own. One either succeeds or one fails at a self-determined act. There is, it would seem, nothing in between.

Or is there? Shakespeare put these cultural commonplaces and confusions, born of the contemporary social, legal, and religious necessity to determine the meaning of self-murder, under intense scrutiny in his 'Jacobethan' tragedies – staging their sombre consequences in *Romeo and Juliet* and *Othello* and refusing, frustratingly and satirically, to stage them in *Hamlet*. But his most singular treatment of suicide was still to come, deceptively but undeniably staged in the opening act of his next tragic work.

This essay will trace Shakespeare's intently forensic study of self-murder in *King Lear*, beginning with the medieval folktales, early modern literary treatments, and social and religious attitudes that provided him with his dark materials.[5] In it, I will first note the editing out of the folk Cordelia's suicide in the anonymous and anodyne *True Chronicle*

History of King Leir first staged in the 1590s, and then turn to a twist on the theme of self-murder devised in the story of the Pamphlagonian King in the new *Arcadia*, another work of the 1590s. Against this literary back story, I will consider the two printed versions of the Lear play, the Quarto edition of 1608 and the Folio edition of 1623, paying particular attention to the Gunpowder Plot. After completing this sombre circuit, I will reassess the world created by the king in *Lear*'s opening scene – and, in so doing, offer a decidedly eccentric but, as I will argue, entirely justifiable reading of this problematic, terrifying, irresistible tragedy.

Before *King Lear*

Shakespeare first encountered the tale of King Leir when the story was particularly ripe for the retelling, undergoing its first major reconstruction since its medieval move from – or better said, shifts between – oral and written versions.[6] By the end of the sixteenth century, the story of this ancient British king had emerged from shadowy recollections of the pre-Christian past to take on new forms: first compiled by Geoffrey of Monmouth in the twelfth century, it had returned in historical entries in popular chronicles by William Camden and William Harrison; it could be found in the name, *Cordelia*, barely glimpsed in Edmund Spenser's exercise in literary archaism, *The Faerie Queene*; and it could be sung as lines set down in a broadside ballad which began 'King Leir once ruled in this land / With princely power and peace/And had all things with hearts content / That might his joys increase'. This last iteration perhaps best demonstrates the story's transition into a contrived historical consciousness by the early modern period, its expression of what Joyce Carol Oates has called 'folk-wish' now conveyed in the dispersible but also disposable medium created by moveable type.[7]

The time-out-of-mind *Leir* thus gifted enterprising early modern narrators with a bred-in-the-backbone storyline that, in the reign of Elizabeth Tudor, would have possessed an uncanny relevance: *Once upon a time, a king had to divide his kingdom between three children . . .* The chronicle histories recount a familiar tale of paternal miscalculation, filial ingratitude and late-rewarded loyalty. Having regained his kingdom with the help of his youngest daughter, Cordeilla, the Queen Consort of Gaul, Leir rules several years more before dying quietly in his bed. Cordeilla then inherits the throne, thereby setting a political lesson into motion. Deposed by her sisters' sons after her husband dies, *this* daughter of Leir kills herself:

> This Cordeilla after hir fathers deceasse ruled the land right worthilie during the space of five yeeres, in which meantime hir

husband died, and [. . .] hir two nephews Margan and Cunedag
[. . .] disdaining to be under the government of a woman, levied
warre against hir, and destroyed a great part of the land, and final-
lie tooke hir prisoner, and laid her fast in ward, wherewith she
took such griefe, being a woman of a manlie courage, and despairing to recover libertie, there she slue hirselfe.[8]

This late sixteenth-century narrative, told in Chapter Six of the second
book of Holinshed's *Chronicles*, is called *The gunarchie [gynarchy] of
queene Cordeilla, how she was vanquished, of hir imprisonment and selfe-
murther*. In the title alone we find preserved the literary motif that will
survive to inform all subsequent versions of the Lear story: female rule
and its consequences.[9] The historical chronicle of King Leir is a cautionary tale of the consequences of division and dispossession. It is not primarily a story about the love of a daughter for her father, nor, in the end,
is it a story about a king who regains his throne. It is a story about a
woman who is forced to hand over her singular rule of a kingdom to
men, and then dies by her own hand.[10]

The first early modern stage adaptation of this Leir chronicle, *The
True Chronicle History of King Leir*, may have been written by Thomas
Kyd, may have been written by Robert Greene, may have been produced
as early as 1588 by the Queen's Men at the Theatre in Shoreditch. While
he was so influenced by it as to undertake to rewrite it, William
Shakespeare probably did not have a hand in this creation. The play
makes an appearance in Henslowe's diary in the mid 1590s, when,
apparently, it was acted conjointly by the Queen's and the Earl of Sussex's Men at the Rose Theatre. It was twice officially recorded – the same
play but under slightly different titles – in the Stationers' Registers of
1595 and 1605. Its contemporary dramatic history is sketchy, then, and
highly suggestive. This was a hastily produced play probably designed
to take advantage of the Leir tale's resonance with current events – a
parable of why it was unwise to hand over a kingdom before its time,
perhaps, or a story of a royal daughter and her two bad sisters.[11]

What *King Leir* would not or, more likely, could not tell was a story
about the failure of a queen. The Leir play of the 1590s thus opened with
a king who lacked male heirs, but it concluded with his restoration to
the throne – creative choice that risked alerting an audience to the sudden silence in an old story they may have learned by the fire or from
Holinshed.[12] But surely the riskier strategy would have been to produce
any play about a childless ruler deposed by near relatives: folly to stage
in England at politically sensitive times throughout Elizabeth's reign,
but more so now in the extraordinarily unstable 1590s, when kingdom
and Privy Council anxiously contemplated her death without issue or

clear successor. It would have been indecorous at the very least to allude to the ambitions of James VI of Scotland, who, in a blatant epistolary campaign to be named Elizabeth's successor, waged from Edinburgh, had been known to style himself the Queen's 'nephew'.[13] And so, in this anodyne version of the tale, the king's daughter survives. There was no particular honour, after all, to be wrung from Elizabeth's peculiar form of monarchical self-murder: her determination effectively to extinguish not only her portion in it, but also the Tudor body of government altogether.

By *True Chronicle's* final recorded appearance in 1605, however, Elizabeth's choices had taken on a different cast. Literally *and* figuratively: with King James now on the throne of England and old King Leir still dressing the London stage, Shakespeare began filling the empty spaces left gaping in the late Elizabethan play with provocative new lessons. He returned to the sense – if not quite the events – of the chronicle histories, conjuring back the spectre of Cordeilla's prison suicide by having *his* Cordelia defeated in war and killed in captivity. More significant, Shakespeare had Cordelia's bitterest political enemy plot to disguise *his* terrible deed as *her* desperate self-murder. This is Shakespeare's first and simplest suicide-trick in *Lear*, an arresting change rung on the theme sounded in the Cordeilla folk-tale.

Edmund intends Cordelia to be murdered by hanging – the mode most likely in the early modern era to return a verdict of *felo de se*. (Apparently it was impossible for an English court to imagine a victim's being hanged by another's hand – unless, of course, it was the state's.[14]) But nothing so cleverly devised and intended in *King Lear* ever proceeds according to plan. Showing himself surprisingly noble in the throes of his own leave-taking, Edmund reveals his earlier order 'to lay the blame upon her own despair / That she fordid herself' (5.3.253–55).[15] This tantalizing intervention vies for onstage attention with the announcements of the offstage deaths of Goneril and Regan – and fails. Much has been made of Shakespeare's cruel determination to end Cordelia's life against all odds (not to mention the fervent wishes of Dr Johnson and nearly every other member of the play's many audiences), but few pause to consider the significance of the cover-up. For in so plotting, Edmund was adding unwonted disgrace to the death he intended for his victim.

In early modern England, death by what was generally called 'self-murder' was relatively rare. The idea of suicide, however, raised such powerful questions that the concept punched well above the weight of its actual presence in this Protestant and absolutist country. Once honoured (at least by certain Stoic philosophers and some tellers of the old Leir folk-tale) as an act of courageous self-will in the face of implacable fate, 'fordoing' oneself was now considered a crime of perverted self-will, undertaken 'against God, against the king, and against Nature'. This trifecta of offence against majesty had the power to obliterate the traces of the self-extinguished human life in ways nearly inconceivable (except, perhaps, in the feverish recesses of the Gothic novel). As Michael McDonald and Terence Murphy have observed, in early modern England:

> Self-murderers were denied Christian burials; their bodies were interred profanely, with a macabre ceremony prescribed by popular custom. The night following the inquest, officials of the parish, the churchwardens and their helpers, carried the corpse to a crossroads and threw it naked into a pit. A wooden stake was hammered through the body, pinioning it in the grave and the hole was filled in. No prayers for the dead were repeated; the minister did not attend.[16]

These grotesque inversions of Christian practice demonstrate how effectively suicide – with its potential to sever the usual ties that bound the generations of the living and the dead – created and sustained a sense of cultural horror and dislocation, raising the profoundly unsettling questions: not merely why suicide was wrong, or if it could be justified, but also what kind of death was dealt when that death was self-inflicted.[17]

Christian doctrine was clear on the issue, but the Christian Bible was not. Samson pulled down the temple and himself with it in Judges 16; Saul fell on his sword – twice, in fact, as the story is recounted in both First and Second Chronicles; Ahithopel hanged himself in 2 Samuel 17; and Judas did the same in Matthew 27: four men determined to escape shame and retribution; all four also triumphing over circumstances in ways that managed to appear both remorseful and resourceful. Scripture thus taught the perverse lesson that suicide was the one means by which humankind might deny Death its grim and punitive prerogative: to strike without warning, like a thief in the night. Christian theologians, looking elsewhere in the scriptures to construct an authoritative argument against this peculiarly social crime, insisted that suicide challenged God's sole prerogative to judge the quick and the dead. As St Paul (and, following his example, thereafter, Augustine, John Calvin and William Perkins) had argued, men and women were 'predestinated according to the purpose of him who worketh all things after the counsel of his own will'. The progress of human life, and human death, were, in the end, unconditional and non-negotiable.

This offence against the religious duty to accept God's pre-emptively final judgement also demanded judgement of a more secular and posthumous sort: on the legal and financial status of the Suicide. Self-murder was a social crime and thus an evaluative quagmire. Juries had to consider whether or not the self-murdered was in right mind at the time he or she acted; if so, the act was adjudged to be liable to retribution (it was not until the eighteenth century that the act of suicide was considered definitive proof in itself of the ameliorating mental state of insanity). The property of a proven self-murderer reverted to the Crown, placed in ward as fast as Cordeilla's nephews had once sequestered her body. Only a legal finding of mental incapacity or demonic possession could protect the Suicide's heirs from penury and the stripping of their legal status unto succeeding generations. A family so bereaved, then, would need to prove to a church court that *their* self-murderer had been, in fact, murdered: killed by the actions of some-*body* or some*thing* else; or, that the victim had been, in essence, some*one* else – someone quite mad – at the time he or she acted.

In any case, the deceased was now lost to them in ways they could neither comprehend, articulate, nor adequately describe and defend. It is this theme – of suicide as ground for religious deliberation and legal dispute, and, perhaps most unnerving, of suicide's capacity to divide a personality into three parts, labelled The One Who Intended, The One Who Succeeded and The One Who Died – that was called into extraordinary being with Shakespeare's decision to add a second storyline to his Lear narrative.[18] The Gloucester plot functions as an independent tale – it has a beginning, middle and an end, and generates sufficient interest in its own right – but in its precise parallelism and capacity to provide a running commentary on the seemingly incomprehensible, nihilistic arc of Lear's experiences, it becomes one necessary interpreter of the play – in addition, of course, to the audience. As we will see, it allows Shakespeare to make a doubly audacious case for the prosecution: finally exonerating the duke of a charge of self-murder, but in so doing ultimately finding against the king.

Shakespeare neatly lifted the tale that was to become the Gloucester plot from another work of the 1590s, Philip Sidney's *Arcadia* – where, in Galicia, the young heroes Pyrocles and Musidorus meet up with the Pamphlagonian King and his solicitous son Leonatus. Shakespeare found remarkably little to alter in this story. Here he discovered the blinded, sadder-but-wiser father dissuaded from self-murder by his son: a young man born 'of a mother fitte to bear royal children', whose loyalty cannot be extinguished by his sire's misled cruelty. Here he read of a second son, Plexirtus (bastard begotten of a 'base [. . .] concubine'), who once plotted successfully to alienate his father's affection from the trueborn son, then blinded the sire, and usurped his throne. And here he took note of how the *Arcadian* narrative ended: the reconciliation of father and true son, followed immediately by the father's death from joyful heartbreak, followed immediately by a battle between sons, followed immediately by the assumption of a rightful throne, followed immediately by summary judgement – a cascade of decisions and concluding events that somehow manage to remain frustratingly indecisive and inconclusive.[19]

In taking up this precipitate tale, Shakespeare also had to take on its moral –*Arcadia*'s 'un-used [unusual] examples [. . .] of true natural goodness as of wretched ungratefulness'. This moral Sidney ultimately articulated in the playing of a suicide-trick. Defeated, besieged, and threatened with imminent starvation, the bastard Plexirtus, having 'thought better by humbleness to creepe, where by pride he could not march', noose knotted about his neck (in early modern usage, a *plex* was an intricate plait or braid), begs pardon of his brother. The narrator, however, seems convinced that the noose is a mere prop and that Plexirtus's penitent state is a similarly false show of the most tortuously contrived sort: that Plexirtus is not merely faking suicide, not simply faking remorse; but pretending to have reconsidered, and then to have interrupted, an act that, in the first place, was merely standing in for a sincere admission of guilt:

> For certainly so had nature formed him [Plexirtus], and the exercise of craft so conformed him to all turnings of sleights, that though *no man* had lesse goodnes in his soule then he, *no man* could better find the places whence arguments might grow of goodnesse to another: though *no man* felt lesse pitie, *no man* could tel better how to stir pitie: *no man* more impudent to deny, where proofes were not manifest; *no man* more ready to confesse with a repenting manner of aggravating his own evil, where denial would make the fault fouler[20]

We are presented here, then, with a set of simulacra that beg for a grammatical inquest into Plexirtus's motives, wherein the *no man* [. . .] *no man* anaphoric phrasing creates what would seem to be an inextricably self-reflexive and – with all those 'noes' – ultimately meaningless argument. But this, after all, is the argument the act makes in any case, whether honourable or no: self-murder's solipsistic logic compels us to admit our ignorance of another's motive even when we have the facts. And so we find ourselves forced to deliberate: is Plexirtus truly remorseful? Or is this the fiendishly complex ruse of a person so fully in possession of his wits he deserves the severest punishment? Or is such wit, especially when applied to such ends, evidence instead of the over-intricate mental business of insanity, and thus to be exonerated? Is

Plexirtus, in short, to be found responsible for such actions as to have to answer for them? And if so: in this life or the next?

Whatever *our* views on the matter, the preliminary findings do not convince the most important character in the drama: Plexirtus's brother and judge, the new king of Pamphlagonia. Astonishing the narrator (as well as Musidorus and Pyrocles, who immediately depart in search of a less confusing plot to chase after), Leonatus forgives Plexirtus, placing this reprieve in starkest relief by summarily executing Plexirtus's associates, instead. The narrator, concluding with a shrug, offers this tetchy summation:

> Where what submission he used, how cunningly in making greater the fault he made the faultiness the less, how artificially he could set out the torments of his own conscience, with the burdensome cumber he had found of his ambitious desires, *how finely seeming to desire nothing but death, as ashamed to live, he begged life, in the refusing it,* I am not cunning enough to be able to express: but so fell out of it, that [. . .] ere long he had not only gotten pity, but pardon, and if not an excuse of the faulty past, yet an opinion of future amendment.[21]

Well, who *could* be cunning enough to parse those sentences, much less the subtleties of Plexirtus's character? This narrative capitulation wrenches our attention from the storyteller, who is obviously no longer in control, and redirects our attention to the author and his motives. Sidney's choice to outwit his narrator makes an argument in itself: that *we* may never understand the reason for Leonatus's decision – and if we think we can decode the external signs of Plexirtus's repentance, applying all our powers of human reason, we will end up no more the wiser. In other words, we can now parse this tale as an artificially archaic discussion of the inscrutability of divine judgement, with Plexirtus occupying a state somewhere between 'faulty past' and 'future amendment': the suicide trick as Calvinist experience. Perhaps Leonatus believed a lying show; perhaps Plexirtus's offence was unforgivable; but, then again, how can we be sure, forced as we are to take as our only material evidence this intricately plaited signifier of unfinished business?

Plexirtus's 'fine seeming' is a well-tailored trope, turning the suicide-trick into a simile for the complexities of Calvinist doctrines of the human will. Considered in this theological register, Sidney is writing of both the necessity, and the concurrent impossibility, of 'making one's election sure'. By the 1590s, the requirement for such indeterminate questing – the weighing (to return to Sidney's words) of 'faulty past' against 'opinion of future amendment' – had become English

Protestantism's most characteristic, if controversial, teaching. For this practice of piety was governed by a tricksy spirit: in the experiential world of the committed Calvinist, external signs, either of religious regeneration or sinful backsliding, could be as misleading and open to debate as God's judgements were certain, sure, and already complete. Those elected to damnation, William Perkins taught, might confidently feel the evanescent stirrings of a 'temporary faith'; those elected to salvation were often buffeted by doubt unto despair. Only death, which finally disclosed the eternal secrets of election, offered certainty after this lifelong, unsettling process of making election sure.[22]

It is this unnerving sense of the difficulty, the downright impossibility, of second guessing human or divine judgement that Shakespeare takes away from Sidney's Arcadian tale. This cloud of unknowing distorts perceptions of events on Lear's stage. Like all early modern plays, Shakespeare's were written in large part as bravura demonstrations of the arts of persuasion; his characters, marshalling a dazzling variety of tropes and word stylings, make arguments intended to be irresistible – to the characters onstage, and to members of the audience, who adjudicate as external examiners. This is true even, perhaps most of all, when his characters resort to subterfuge and trickery. The problem with *Lear*, then, is not that its onstage people lie to each other or assume disguises; it is that too often they speak past or around each other, producing nonsense; their arguments are thus rendered incomprehensible, resisting and even thwarting not only onstage inquiries, but those of the audience.

King Lear

William Shakespeare's version of the Lear story was entered into the Stationers' Register of 26 November 1607 as 'played before the King's majesty at Whitehall upon S. Stephen's night at Christmas last'. Sometime after that, Shakespeare, his theatrical associates, or Shakespeare in tandem with those associates remade the *King Lear* first printed in 1608, turning it into the version we find in the First Folio of 1623.[23] Between 1608 and 1623, many critics argue, Shakespeare's story of Lear was altered so drastically as to create a new play with new political import: the First Folio version may sharpen the Fool's already shrewd assessments of Lear; cuts one important, if baffling, aspect of the case against women's rule – Lear's 'mock trial' of Goneril; and might revise the meaning of the play's presentation of political intrigue, transforming its military plot from one telling of foreign invasion to one that might just hint at civil war. But placing such significance on these pragmatic edits (the First Folio's editors were not philosophers but stage managers and actors) depends on a very subtle and determined reading. I mention these alterations to point out that they neatly span the same years as those of the effective rule of James VI and I, the monarch dominating the Shakespeare play's opening night and first publication title.

By far the most critical attention has been paid to the First Folio's conclusion where, according to the play's editors in every age, new stage directions and some very subtle edits, in R. A. Foakes's words, '[allow] us to *suppose* Lear *may* die in the joyful delusion of thinking Cordelia is still alive'.[24] Foakes's carefully qualified contention reminds us, poignantly, of the shift in interpretation that has privileged the play's domestic story of failed fathers and dysfunctional families – a plotline, moreover, that also privileges the expression of the father-daughter relationships in the House of Lear over the father-son relationships in the House of Gloucester – since the eighteenth century.

But the Jacobean *King Lear* is not primarily about such affective ties; it would take nearly a century, and the secularization of the concept of monarchy, to shift its familial plot from Metaphor to The Thing Modified. In the early seventeenth century, the play's representation of systemic failure – of loyalty; of counsel; of health; of vision; of any plan, for good or ill, hatched in the traffic of the stage – illuminated a central, all-consuming political theme: the story first told in the folk tale, but now elaborated into intriguing new life. Shakespeare's *King Lear* is about the consequences of what – given his need to proclaim his right to England's throne, advance his theories of kingship, and proclaim a distinctive rhetoric of the analogous indivisibility of the monarch's physical body and his insular kingdom – James VI, and now I, would surely have condemned as an uniquely monarchical act of self-murder.

Any early modern audience – any audience familiar with Richard II's premature parcelling-out of his kingdom to Bushy, Bagot and Green; or the troublesome and lamentable Edward's desire to 'make several kingdoms of this monarchy/And share it equally with you all/So I may have some nook or corner left/to frolic with my dearest Gaveston' (Marlowe, *Edward II*, 1.4) – would have known that the division of a kingdom, by a king still living, and on such careless grounds, was possible to stage but impossible to defend. The need for an audience to negotiate between stage and social possibilities made visceral the ideas generated in *Lear*. Filial disobedience, heinous disloyalty, tumultuous storms, gory blinding and agonizing deaths on or off stage were mere glancing metaphors for an otherwise unspeakable political abandonment.

In 1607, however, a strikingly similar argument, in another realm of discourse, was struggling for political life. A very real king was arguing for the inevitability of England's full political union with Scotland by pulling out one of the better tricks in the absolutist's rhetorical playbook: the metaphoric strategy that equated the bounds of a kingdom with the intrinsic integrity of the kingly 'body'. With this trope, King James could suggest that his opponents wished to see him dismembered, an act of treason. 'No more possible is it for one king to gouerne two Countreys *Contiguous*', this thoroughly irritated king had recently declared, to a Parliament stubbornly dismissive of union despite the king's extraordinary efforts on its behalf, 'than for one head to governe two bodies'. James had been haranguing his advisors, council and polemicists about the union of his two kingdoms since his accession, and at this point the issue, the argument and any hopes for union was proving too weak to prevail.[25]

But what happens when such a puissant metaphor is weighed and found wanting? This was a question that surely disturbed the composure of early modern kings, political theorists and playwrights – all of whom relied on the commonplace that well-wrought words were good as deeds. And to answer it in context, I return to *King Lear* by way of Sidney, and the staging of a second suicide-trick.

On the Dover Cliffs

Shakespeare was so indebted to Sidney for his Gloucester plot that his one extensive elaboration on the *Arcadia*, wherein the remorseful king of Pamphlagonia failed to enlist his son in his own plan to kill himself, is worth examining:

> I craved of him [Leonatus] to lead me to the top of this rock, indeed I must confess, with meaning to free him from so serpentine a companion as I am. But he finding what I purposed, only therein since he was born showed himself disobedient to me.[26]

Here the word 'serpentine' conveys a world of meaning: describing the king, and by extension his plan to kill himself, as diabolical and twisted as Plexirtus and his misleading noose. Under these conditions – a father not only desires to kill himself, but, due to his infirmity, requires the compliance of his son in an assisted suicide – disobedience is transformed into its opposite. Leonatus's refusal, an act of filial rebellion, in fact proves him a true son and rightful heir; it allows Leonatus to gain his father's kingdom. This provides the necessary dramatic counterweight to Plexirtus's demonstrably unfilial act of usurpation.[27]

Shakespeare transformed this passage of Sidney's, with its alluring suggestion of what constituted natural and unnatural relations between child and parent, parent and death wish, into a *tour de force* of the suicide-trick. At 4.6, we find Edgar, still disguised but now 'better-spoken', with the blinded Gloucester, who is in a state of despair brought about by a series of increasingly debilitating shocks: from physical injury – (and this is why, I think, we are meant to see these injuries inflicted); from Edmund's betrayal; and, worst, from his own intolerable recognition that he has disbelieved, repudiated and banished a loyal son. But Edgar refuses to salve his father's soul by revealing his identity, despite the graphic and sanguinary evidence of Gloucester's remorse. While moved, Edgar persists in this stratagem of disguise, stating in an aside to the audience that despite its appearance of vengeful cruelty he must 'trifle' with his father's 'despair' in order 'to cure it'.

This 'trifling' has serious purpose. As they stand safely far from danger, Edgar limns for his father the dangerous and disorienting edge of the Dover cliffs – and in so doing exposes the perilous edge of Gloucester's mental abyss. And so Gloucester believes in the certainty of the death that lies before him, and asks the seeming stranger to deliver a parting apology to the son he believes he has lost forever. Thus repentant, and sure of his fate, he leaps.

Falling harmlessly to the ground, Gloucester nonetheless believes he has plunged fathoms. Observing the entirely conscious man who now thinks he's dead, Edgar contemplates his awful power of suggestion and its effects: how 'conceit may rob / the treasury of life, when life itself / yields to the theft' (4.6.43–45). If Gloucester continues to believe in the force of his own despair, Edgar knows, it *will* be past cure; the tiniest tumble will kill him. 'Had he been where he thought', he muses to himself, '[b]y this had thought been past' (4.6.45–46): past thought, his father would also be past saving.

Edgar's task now is to keep his father 'where he thought' – in other words, in full acceptance of the inevitability of his *death* – while at the same time convincing Gloucester that he has entered nonetheless a vastly different state of *mind*. Pretending to be yet another stranger, Edgar claims to have come upon Gloucester at the bottom of the cliffs and, maintaining the subterfuge, informs his father that the man Gloucester knew as 'Poor Tom' has remained behind, atop the Dover cliffs. Gloucester replies:

> That thing you speak of, I took it for a man;
> often it would say 'The fiend, the fiend'.
> He led me to that place. (4.6.79–81)

Gloucester now associates his momentary belief in the finality of his action with a shape-shifting attack – not by his son but by the Great Deceiver. His son's singular and sustained suicide trick has in fact delivered a marvellous truth, rendered out of any stage trick's formulaic blend of wild surreality and strict logic: Gloucester has been saved. Not from the cliffs, for he still believes – and Edgar has allowed him to hold fast to that belief – his body has somehow endured that buffeting; nor from death, for he believes, reasonably, he should have died from the plunge, but from the only thing truly fatal to him – or, better said, to his soul: the brink of despair. He then expresses his resigned determination to 'bear / affliction till it do cry out / enough' (4.6.77–78); his soul awaits its promised end, and it is not one destined to be in Gloucester's choosing.

Conclusion

If the bed-trick is, in the words of Wendy Doniger, 'going to bed with someone whom you mistake for someone else', the protagonist of the suicide trick goes to death with some*one* else – the person who is not yet meant to die. That these star-crossed partners are one and the same person is a truth as self-reflexive as the act itself, as self-reflective as Calvinist doctrine was required to be. This is the painful and essential lesson Gloucester is vouchsafed through the grace extended to him by a mendacious child.

But this play is supposed to be about King Lear: a man lessoned in quite another way. And how might this reflect on the rule of a contemporary king, James VI and I?

To begin with the real monarch: James's 1607 Parliament thought it entirely possible to leave a kingdom divided; James's invocation of an abhorrent and 'monstrous' body moved them not one whit. Resisting what had been one of the most potent applied metaphors in early modern political discourse, James's new parliamentary subjects refused, stubbornly and finally, to endorse full political union with his kingdom of Scotland. And so the king's dearly cherished political programme, the signature project with which he had introduced himself to his new subjects in 1603 and reiterated in the aftermath of the Gunpowder Plot (wherein the threat of personal and political dismemberment was made frighteningly possible), became the first, and the most, symbolically significant failure of his English reign. He reigned, nonetheless, for another eighteen years: James VI *and* I, a monarch on whose head rested two separate crowns.[28]

As for our fictional king, there were many reasons to commit self-murder on the stage, but in *King Lear*, the act itself was never what it seemed. This brings me to the only important – and invariably unrecognized or denied – successful suicide in *The Tragedy of King Lear*: one that has long tricked us into thinking it not what it is.[29] Commentators are always wondering why, of all the unhappy and unwise characters on his stage, Lear himself resists being drawn down the narrative path towards self-murder. Critics treat Lear's abdication, his claim to be tired of ruling, as a disastrous political choice, or as proof of his senility, or a disastrous political choice that proves his senility – but none see it simply for what it is: an immediate and conclusive act of governmental self-murder.

I am not claiming that Lear's decision sets a *plot* in motion that will eventually and finally produce its doleful and promised end. No: with the division of his kingdom that is his body politic, and his subsequent refusal to allow his daughters and counsellors to call it what it is – self-murder pure and simple, Lear has committed suicide outright. His story begins for us, then, at its end. Playing counterpoint to Gloucester, Lear does not know he has succeeded at his solitary task.

This may sound impossible, or simply irresponsible. But the late plays of Shakespeare abound with just such fantastic impossibilities: ghosts stalk parapets, uxorious men kill for the sake of a handkerchief, and statues come back to life and love again. So surely Lear can continue to tread his stage, a vexed ghost traversing a blasted landscape, self-stripped of all that once proclaimed the massy bounds of his kingdom. This is a man who has to ask at 1.4.211 'who is it who can tell me who I am?'; a king, as Kent sadly observes in 5.3.319, 'usurp'd' from the start, the Nothing that comes of nothing.

Which brings us back, finally, to an earlier question: what happens when a ruling metaphor is tested – to the breaking point? When, in an era moving uneasily between medieval and modern habits of thought, expressions lose their formidable powers of association, their capacity to inspire astonished nods of recognition and assent? As he watched the first production of *King Lear*, King James's rhetoric of union was failing fast; by the time *Lear* appeared in the Folio of 1623 that language was long dead, and the king, acquiescing to political reality, took a linguistic turn. (Absolute monarchs, like the Protestant God, ruled by persuasion; as James had been taught and learned well, only a tyrant resorted to force to impose his will.) In the years intervening, James had elected to declare himself by royal proclamation the head of an imaginary empire he called 'Great Britain'. Despite this brave show – or, better said (and ironically), because of it – he demonstrated what happens when an early modern monarch loses control: not of policy, but of the language of policy. In this particular age of eloquence, such was the most devastating loss a ruling monarch could sustain while yet surviving. Shakespeare illustrated this political reality in Lear's suicide, which was no trick but the real thing.

Notes

Earlier versions of this essay have been presented in a variety of public settings: the 33rd Annual Meeting of The Renaissance Studies Conference at New College in Sarasota, Florida (March 2010), the History and Literature seminar at Jesus College Oxford

(April 2010), and the Institute for Medieval and Early Modern Studies at Bangor University, Wales (June 2010). Many thanks to all who commented. A note of special thanks for insightful reading and intervention is due, as is so often the case, to Lou Ruprecht.

1 Grace Ioppolo, *A Routledge Literary Sourcebook on William Shakespeare's King Lear* (London: Routledge, 2003), pp. 45–47; see also *King Lear*, ed. by R. A. Foakes, 3rd edn (London: Arden Shakespeare, 1997); *King Lear: A Parallel Text Edition*, ed. by René Weis (London and New York: Longman, 1993), p. 1; Charles Lamb, 'On the Tragedies of Shakespeare' (1810), in *The Works of Charles Lamb in Two Volumes* (London, 1818), vol. 2, pp. 25–26, also reprinted in Ioppolo, pp. 50–51.
2 Ioppolo, pp. 55–56.
3 Larry Champion, *Shakespeare's Tragic Perspective* (Athens: University of Georgia Press, 1976), pp. 4, 226.
4 Kent's lines at 5.2, 'Your eldest daughters have fordone themselves / And desperately are dead', conjoin those sisters' fates, making 'irrelevant', as Rowland Wymer observes, 'which was the murderer and which the suicide': *Suicide and Despair in the Jacobean Drama* (Brighton: Harvester Press, 1986), p. 47.
5 Cultural and social histories of suicide in the early modern period are rather more plentiful, but almost never cite *King Lear* to illustrate their cases. If they cite Shakespeare at all, they cite *Hamlet*. And there are surprisingly few studies of suicide in Shakespeare's works, Rowland Wymer's *Suicide and Despair* providing the exception that proves a rule. We have an abundance of critical literature on tragic despair in the religious sense but, as we will see, the theological category *despair*, while similar, can be distinguished in some interesting ways.
6 See the editors' preface and Stanley Wells's introduction to Gary Taylor and Michael Warren, eds, *The Division of the Kingdom: Shakespeare's Two Versions of King Lear* (Oxford: Clarendon Press, 1983), pp. v–x, 1–22.
7 *A New Variorum Edition of Shakespeare: King Lear*, ed. by Horace Howard Furness (Philadelphia: Lippincott, 1880).
8 R. Holinshed, *The Second Booke of the Historie of England* (London, 1587), reprinted in Geoffrey Bullough, ed., *Narrative and Dramatic Sources of Shakespeare* (New York: Columbia University Press, 1978), p. 319.
9 That this mode of dying is here presented as honourable may reflect certain classical influences on Holinshed, but by the late sixteenth century the act inspired more fear and bewilderment than admiration. Another contemporary rendition of Cordelia's plight, in John Higgins's *The Mirror for Magistrates* of 1559, concluded with an admonition against 'dispair for any prison pine or paine / If they be giltless let them so remaine / Farre greater follye is it for to kill / Themselves despairing, then is any ill.' Reprinted in Bullough, *Narrative and Dramatic Sources*, p. 332. I am indebted to Scott Lucas for his suggestion of an alternate traditional reading from *Mirror for Magistrates*, and to Phil Withington for his observation about the classical influence on Holinshed.
10 This is, of course, not to claim that this is the only reading possible of Leir's (or, for that matter, Lear's) meaning. Disputes over land division and inheritance were a topic of deep concern in this period, and thus form another, more historically accurate (strictly speaking) contextual source for the anxieties expressed in the early modern story and plays. Many thanks to Professor Clive Holmes for this pragmatic and sensible observation.
11 *King Leir* facsimile of the 1605 edition (London: Oxford University Press for the Malone Society, 1908); Jay Halio, *King Lear: A Guide to the Play* (Westport, CT: Greenwood Press, 2001).

12   But cf. Muir, who once famously claimed the omissions would have merely confused and alienated the audience.

13   Mark Kishlansky, *A Monarchy Transformed: The Penguin History of England, 1603-1688* (London and New York: Penguin, 1997); James I, *The Letters of James VI and I*, ed. by G. P. V. Akrigg (Berkeley and London: University of California Press, 1984).

14   Paul Seaver, 'Suicide and the Vicar General in Early Modern England', in *From Sin to Insanity: Suicide in Early Modern Europe*, ed. by Jeffrey Watt (Ithaca, NY: Cornell University Press, 2004), pp. 25–47, 195–99 (p. 31).

15   All references are taken from *King Lear: A Norton Critical Edition*, ed. by Grace Ioppolo (New York: Norton, 2008).

16   Seaver, 'Suicide and the Vicar General', pp. 25–37, and Jeffrey Watt, 'Suicide, Gender, and Religion: The Case of Geneva', in *From Sin to Insanity*, pp. 138–57 (p. 148); S. E. Sprott, *The English Debate on Suicide from Donne to Hume* (LaSalle, IL: Open Court, 1961), pp. 1–21; Michael MacDonald and Terence R. Murphy, *Sleepless Souls: Suicide in Early Modern England* (Oxford: Clarendon Press, 1990), p. 15.

17   Edmund Wingate, *Justice Revived: Being the Whole Office of a Justice of the Peace* (London, 1661), p 88. Also quoted in MacDonald and Murphy, *Sleepless Souls*, p. 16.

18   Here I follow not only my own reading of the play but the suggestions made by Ann Thompson, who argues that it is possible to see the Gloucester plot as in narrative terms stronger and more satisfying than the Lear plot: 'Who Sees Double in the Double Plot', in *Stratford-Upon-Avon Studies 20: Shakespearian Tragedy*, ed. by David Palmer and Malcolm Bradbury (New York: Holmes and Meier, 1984), pp. 47–75.

19   Philip Sidney, *The Countess of Pembroke's Arcadia* (1590), Book II, reprinted in *Narrative and Dramatic Sources*, pp. 402–8.

20   *Narrative and Dramatic Sources*, pp. 407–8. Italics are mine.

21   *Narrative and Dramatic Sources*, p. 408.

22   On William Perkins and the concept of the 'temporary professour' of the faith, and on Sidney's literary style of Protestantism see Brian Cummings, *The Literary Culture of the Reformation: Grammar and Grace* (Oxford: Oxford University Press, 2002), pp. 260–63, 270–75; and Lori Anne Ferrell, 'William Perkins and Protestant Aesthetics', in *John Foxe and His World*, ed. by Chris Highley and John N. King (London: Ashgate, 1998), pp. 160–79.

23   *Shakespeare: King Lear*, ed. by Russell Fraser (New York: Signet, 1998). The Quarto version of 1608 (hereafter Q), titled *The True Chronicle Historie of the life and death of King Lear and his three Daughters*, contained 285 lines not included in the 1623 version of the play. (This figure is approximate: there are 167 deviations between ten of the twelve copies extant, all of which show evidence of proofing and text-correction during printing; in 1619 a second quarto, falsely attributed to the 1608 output, appeared as a poorly corrected version of Q.) The 1623 version (hereafter F), retitled *The Tragedie of King Lear*, contains 115 lines not originally found in Q.

24   *King Lear*, Arden 3, ed. by R. A. Foakes (Waltham: Thomas Nelson, 1997), pp. 138–39. Italics are mine. That Shakespeare himself wrote both Q and F was argued strenuously and at great length in Taylor and Warren's *The Division of the Kingdom* (1983) and has inspired some editions of *King Lear* that feature two separate versions, each with its own discrete claims. Editions, and the editorial opinions that made them, have long been divided between volumes that present the two plays side by side, choose between Q and F, or combine their lines. Those that argue for separation tend also, according to Foakes, to inflate the importance of what Foakes still concedes are important differences between Q and F. The argument about F's possibly politic omission of certain references to the French invasion, thereby turning the conflict of

Q into a form of civil war rather than a military strike by another country is Gary Taylor's: Foakes, ed., p. 140.

25   *King James VI and I: Political Writings*, ed. by Johann P. Sommerville (Cambridge: Cambridge University Press, 1994), p. 162.

26   *Narrative and Dramatic Sources.*

27   In Sidney's religious register, his principled refusal would also have reflected the Calvinist dictum, articulated in the final chapter of the concluding book of *The Institutes*, that ungodly governors, like ungodly laws, must be – and thus can be – legitimately resisted, as long as the resisting is done by someone with authority – like a magistrate, or a son only temporarily illegitimated.

28   Lori Anne Ferrell, 'The Sacred, the Profane, and the Union', in *Politics, Religion, and Popularity in Early Stuart Britain: Essays in Honour of Conrad Russell*, ed. by T. Cogswell, R. Cust and P. Lake (Cambridge: Cambridge University Press, 2002), pp. 45–64.

29   See Frank Kermode, for example, in his introduction to *The Riverside Shakespeare*, ed. by G. Blakemore Evans et al. (Boston, MA: Houghton Mifflin, 1974), 1251.

CHAPTER FIVE

New Directions: 'The Wisdom of Nature': Ecological Perspectives in *King Lear*

Anthony Parr

In the twentieth century, and especially after the Second World War, *King Lear* came to be seen as the drama of Shakespeare's that most urgently addressed the concerns of contemporary civilization. The process by which it dislodged *Hamlet* as the most prestigious work in the Shakespeare canon (for literary critics and *cognoscenti*, if not always for theatre audiences or general readers) was extensively analysed by R. A. Foakes in a study published in 1993, which concluded with the prediction that for the immediate future *King Lear* will continue to be regarded as the central achievement of Shakespeare, if only because it speaks more largely than the other tragedies to the anxieties and problems of the modern world.[1] *King Lear* acquired an urgent relevance, Foakes argues, in the post–1960 world of nuclear nightmares and totalitarian repression, and attracted interpretations like Jan Kott's influential reading of the play through Samuel Beckett's *Endgame* and Peter Brook's concurring vision of a brutal wasteland in his 1971 film version, both finding a congruence between absurdist literary models and the bitter ironies of the Cold War. These powerful accounts of *King Lear* have lost some of their force since the fall of the Berlin Wall and now look rather slanted, partly because other cultural trends that flourished in the late 1960s and survived the end of the Cold War have made their own claim on the play. Feminism and psychoanalysis, for instance, find in *King Lear* a highly troubled world but not the geopolitical miasma emphasized by Kott and Brook; multicultural interests have displaced the old East–West axis and led to more diverse and colourful productions and different ways of teaching the play. Yet there have been enough causes in recent history to remember why the darker side of *King Lear* spoke so strongly to modernity during the Cold War: the unfathomable atrocities of Yugoslavia and Rwanda, the *juntas* and ageing dictators that continue to oppress the countries they rule, and the new conceits of the 'promised end'[2] that accompany the rise of fundamentalism and global terrorism. The play does not, of course, depend on these linkages for its artistic importance, and we may have doubts about a criticism that is relentlessly pragmatic in seeking them out. As Foakes's conclusion acknowledges, however, *King Lear* has acquired its modern standing in part through its capacity to be a perceptive witness to the major developments of our time; and it is worth asking why, given the profound attention in the play to the multiple meanings of 'nature', very little attempt has been made to enlist it in thinking about the challenge that many feel is the most urgent faced by the modern world: that of environmental degradation and its potential to undermine large parts of our civilization.[3] In this chapter I want first, by briefly reviewing parts of the critical legacy, to suggest some reasons for this omission, and then to sketch some of the directions in which such an enquiry might proceed.

The threat of environmental catastrophe is not only as immediate today as the nuclear annihilation promised by the Cold War, but is also, I would argue, rather more in tune with the intimations of apocalypse in *King Lear* than were the global confrontations of the recent past. The play is full of reference to a living world that has to accommodate the traumas of the plot, and it resembles *Macbeth* in its imaginative evocation of a realm ravaged and exhausted by human actions – without, moreover, the emphatic sense of deliverance that comes at the end of that play. From the fertile 'champains' and forests allocated to Lear's elder daughters in his carving up of the kingdom, to the quagmires and standing ponds where Poor Tom and his kind eke out an existence; from the innumerable forms of animal life that are imagined into being by nearly all the characters, to the faith that Cordelia invests in medicinal herbs, 'you unpublished virtues of the earth' (4.4.16), Shakespeare conjures a densely imagined physical environment that is more resilient than the vulnerable characters who occupy it, but whose relationship to human needs and designs has become problematic or opaque. Throughout the play, the dramatist portrays his characters' interactions with the natural world either as a source of crisis or as the hardly bearable consequence of human misunderstanding and conflict. We have to be careful not to impose anachronistic concepts on Shakespeare's imaginative world – the word 'environment' was not in his lexicon, and 'nature' had not settled down to mean simply the non-human world – but I think it is significant that *King Lear* was written at a moment when, especially in northern Europe, confidence in the idea of a stable and sustainable eco-system was particularly low. Freak weather events and a run of bad har-vests in the 1590s that brought famine to large parts of England could be, and were, explained in providential terms or as part of a more fun-damental pattern of cosmic disturbance, but explanatory frameworks of this kind only intensified a widespread feeling that the earth, and the human cultures that occupied it, were faced with imminent breakdown. Many suggested that there was a link between abnormalities in the nat-ural world and accelerated change in the socio-political sphere; and although the conditions scarcely existed to explain this ecologically, the awareness of complex interdependence within 'nature' in all its forms, of bonds that are 'too intrince t'unloose' (2.2.73) without injury, is to be found throughout Shakespeare's later work, and achieves some of its most complex and ambiguous effects in *King Lear*. The play addresses fundamental questions about humanity's place in the world that have been skirted until very recently by all developed societies, and not least by parts of the literary-critical establishment in those communities that have found the play an eloquent vehicle for their cultural and political concerns.

The politically inflected criticism of *King Lear* during the past fifty years, obeying the injunction that the best way to understand Shakespeare in our own time is to see him in his, represented a major shift in approach from the days when contextualization was studiously avoided (for example, the possible connections between Lear and the mad George III during the Regency period) and the emphasis fell either on Lear's private agony or on his titanic confrontation with the uni-verse. As Foakes says of this earlier tradition, 'no other work has induced in a succession of critics such an addiction to capital letters, used as a means of claiming a metaphysical grandeur and removing the play from ordinary social and political considerations.'[4] Rescuing *King Lear* both from philosophical inflation and from narrowly psychological readings was a challenge that was eagerly embraced by new historicists and cul-tural materialists, and this academic initiative, anticipated in the early 1970s by left-wing adaptations (like Edward Bond's play *Lear* and Grigori Kozintsev's Soviet film), put the spotlight on issues of govern-ance and social justice, patriarchal authority and family politics, prop-erty rights and land, and thereby sharpened our sense of the play's relevance to modern concerns. *King Lear* remains for such critics – as it was for Jan Kott and Peter Brook – a potent tool for investigating the socio–political realities of the world we inhabit: *the* play for our times. The archaic setting of the action has actually assisted this emphasis, for in this pre-Christian story, as in modern secular cultures, there is no

hint of supernatural assistance or revelation: the characters call repeatedly on the gods but receive no answer, and are forced back on their
own resources. At the same time, however, getting rid of those capital
letters has involved loss as well as gain. *King Lear* is a play of big ideas
and not just a vehicle for ideology (or critique thereof); and loss of
interest in its metaphysical dimension has led to readings that are indif-
ferent to the play's affective power and too often seem narrowly instrumental, using it largely as a pretext for the critic's own political interests,
and displaying, as Kiernan Ryan recently complained, 'an abject neglect
of *Lear*'s qualities as a work of art'.[5] The disregard for aesthetic considerations (widespread in the literary academy for some time and only
now starting to wane) seems to be linked to this desire to control literature's frame of reference and make it speak to particular sets of concerns; and it damages our ability to hear in Shakespeare's drama the
complex overtones to what otherwise appears to be a neat and contained diagnosis of human affairs.

In particular, there is a notably regressive element to much of the
revisionist critical effort of the 1980s and 1990s: in rejecting what were
seen as 'establishment' approaches to and uses of Shakespeare, it also
jettisoned the perspectives evident in the titles of earlier studies like
John Danby's *Shakespeare's Doctrine of Nature* and Theodore Spencer's
Shakespeare and the Nature of Man. 'Nature' as an idea or physical reality or ruling context is rarely visible in materialist criticism, perhaps
because its advocates avoid the notion of a traditional order in tune
with natural law, and are strongly in the camp that views all human
activity as self-created, a purely cultural construct. Large questions
about 'Man's place in the universe' or 'in nature' are seen mostly as por-
tentous ways of avoiding awkward political issues. But the result is that
a play like *King Lear* is reduced in scale, and its central perplexities are
simply ignored. Lear's demand about his ungrateful daughters, 'Is there
any cause in nature that / make these hard hearts?' (3.6.74–75) is only
one instance of this play's searching contribution to a debate that was
vitally important to Renaissance thinkers and which continues to
mutate through modern scientific research and sociological theory.
And while it is probably true that the 'big' questions about nature and
the cosmos sat more comfortably with a generation of literary critics
who were little concerned with questioning the political status quo,
nonetheless to regard them as having been superseded by the efforts of
more radical commentary, with its discourse of hegemonies and subversion, is to ignore the fact that deconstruction – at least in literary and
cultural studies – has largely left intact habitual human attitudes to and
treatment of the natural world. (As Stephen Greenblatt remarked in

quite another context, in such writing 'there is subversion, no end of subversion, only not for us'.)[6] The question of humanity's place in nature will not go away, and what is startling about so much cultural theory and criticism is its sheer anthropocentrism: the continuing assumption that the world exists for our needs and purposes. I shall come shortly to the history of that assumption insofar as it bears upon *King Lear*. Meanwhile, it is worth remarking that the mid-twentieth-century critics of Shakespeare who were interested in ontological questions (like 'the nature of nature') were writing at the same time as intellectual historians like Rosalie Colie and Hiram Haydn, scholars whose work investigates the Renaissance roots of our most enduring ideas about physical reality and the nature of being, and is constantly aware of the importance of aesthetics in moulding beliefs and sensibilities. Theirs was not an activist scholarship, but in explicating the ways in which Europeans shaped their mental world in a crucial period of human development, they opened up questions about our place in the natural order that more 'political' criticism appears to regard as settled.

'Nature', then, is an established, if latterly neglected theme in criticism of *King Lear*; but this line of approach needs to be reformulated if it is to be useful to an environmental reading of the play. Shakespeare's action encompasses virtually every aspect of this notoriously slippery concept, from the 'state of nature' that orthodox thinkers saw as being 'the forerunner to the Law' and untouched by divine grace,[8] to the 'natural' goodness that Gloucester mistakenly sees in Edmund and Lear rediscovers in Cordelia. Nature is the howling wilderness into which Lear is cast in Act 3, and it is the 'bestial' behaviour that tears out Gloucester's eyes, but it is also a pristine state from which the failings and inequities of civilization can be observed, and a physical reality that can be investigated to discover the secrets of existence. The sheer complexity of early modern conceptions of nature testifies to a human culture that was thinking very hard about its role in creation, at a moment when European societies were making the difficult transition from one relatively stable world-view, that of mediaeval Christianity, to another, the model offered by seventeenth-century science. Of course, the instability that accompanied this intellectual ferment in Tudor and Early Stuart England prompted many to reaffirm old certainties, in particular an orthodox conception of natural law, and in later centuries the same conservative impulse among literary critics often attributed this traditional view to Shakespeare. It is faithfully reproduced, for instance, in Edwin Muir's declaration that Lear and his allies represent 'an order of society so obviously springing from the nature and needs of man that it can also be called natural' – a certainty whose implications are a major obstacle to ecological thought and which was certainly questioned by sceptical thinkers in the early seventeenth century. A similar idea is expressed in more complex fashion by A. P. Rossiter, comparing Shakespeare to Wordsworth in the racy style of his published lectures:

> The play is not an allegory, but we can allegorize it without distortion. The magical King, who is Order and Right Reason, tears out the keystone of Authority; and the arch of State, of piety (in the widest sense) and Kind-liness (affection *and* nature, the 'law of Kynde') collapses. But Nature is double; and from this collapse an *under-nature* surges over the world, making good, as it were, Edmund's claim: 'Thou, Nature, art my goddess', and also his kind of priority, for he is a 'natural son'.

Rossiter's idea of an 'under-nature' captures something important in *King Lear*, something akin to the 'multiplying villainies of nature' that are invoked early in *Macbeth* and then proceed to engulf the kingdom. He is responding to an energy and sense of 'terror' in Shakespeare's play that he finds only intermittently in Wordsworth's vision, which is for the most part (he claims) 'Nature as something comfortably in our English pockets'. Rather: 'Think of what the Black Death was, and poliomyelitis [. . .] And then of human rage, obsession, mass-hysteria; of heartless craft and treachery [. . .] This terror in Nature is only an element in the whole, but one which caught some of the great sixteenth-century artists by the throat and bore them away.'[10] This is finely expressed; but Rossiter, like Muir, assumes too readily that order and reason can be identified with a benign natural power that is invested in state and crown. In the process, all the elements that oppose Lear are effectively demonized: they become an 'under-nature', a swarming, subterranean force that rushes in when authority is undermined. This turns *King Lear* into too orthodox a document of Christian humanism and displaces an insight into the play's exposure of the frighteningly volatile nature of everything, including Lear's own titanic rage and disproportionate suffering. Virtually every development in the plot of *King Lear* is a challenge to belief in a stable, divinely ordained system, and while we can counter Rossiter by finding in the play a subversive attitude to Jacobean social and political orthodoxies, what seems to me more interesting, and timely, is Shakespeare's deeper questioning of the premises of civilized human life and its sustainability on the terms by which it defines itself.

Pessimism and Progress

The traditional Christian view of creation was of a world made by God for humankind, but a world that fell along with Adam and Eve, thus introducing an element of tension into human relations with the natural world. Mankind might be sovereign, but over an intractable environment, for the earth had degenerated since the human rebellion against God: nature was hostile in many of its forms, and even domestic animals, previously willing servants, had often to be coerced.[11] Human authority was renewed after the Flood, at which point its relationship to nature was redefined: people became carnivorous and aggressive in their designs on the environment, because now they had to be. Renaissance negotiations of this traditional outlook were many and varied, but (to oversimplify) two can be isolated for our purposes: a cautionary approach to the idea of a sustainable universe, and the more confident outlook of early modern science. First, the belief in a fallen nature of which mankind is a part was in many ways intensified in post–Reformation concerns about the imperfection of the sublunary world, and this led in sceptical sixteenth-century thought to a widespread belief in entropy, a sense of the earth running down. It is a spirit that finds its way into the play, in Gloucester's pessimistic belief that 'We have seen the best of our time' (1.2.112), and perhaps also at the end where apocalyptic fears shadow Edgar's final declaration that 'The oldest hath borne most; we that are young / Shall never see so much, nor live so long' (5.3.299–300). In late Tudor England these anxieties intensified with the approach of the century's end and the anticipated death of Elizabeth I, and appeared to be confirmed by abnormalities in the heavens (an unusual number of comets and eclipses) and natural disasters on earth. As John Norden put it in 1600, describing 'Nature's fearful alterations':

> The *Sunne* and *Moone* eclipsed ne'er so much,
> *Comets* and strange *impressions* in the *ayre*:
> The *tydes* and swelling *flouds* were never such:
> The *earth* doth tremble, *Nature* doth impayre [. . .][12]

These sentiments are very common in late Elizabethan writing, and often read like intimations of imminent ecological collapse, born of a fear that nature's laws, supposedly invariable, are breaking down as a result of universal corruption. Gloucester's view is representative of this widespread eco-pessimism: faced with Edgar's apparent treachery, he declares that

> These late eclipses in the sun and moon portend
> no good to us. Though the wisdom of Nature can
> reason it thus and thus, yet nature finds itself

[handwritten margin notes: "Christian history of Mankind" with arrow; "apocalyptic undertow"]

scourged by the sequent effects. Love cools,
friendship falls off, brothers divide [. . .] (1.2.103–7)

What Gloucester means by 'the wisdom of Nature' is something like
'those with pretensions to scientific knowledge', referring to the latest
work in astronomy that thinks it can explain eclipses objectively as
physical events, without astrological implications for life on earth. The
emergent scientific community at which Gloucester thus glances dis-
paragingly was arguing more broadly that superstition must give way to
proper investigation of natural phenomena, and for the replacement of
a value-laden geography with one in which nature is morally neutral
and without purpose. This more assertive and modernizing response to
a fallen world also finds a voice in the play, when Edmund declares his
allegiance to Nature (ironically deified as his 'goddess') and ridicules
his father's credulous reliance on astrology: "This is the excellent fop-
pery of the world, that [. . .] we make guilty of our disasters the sun,
the moon and the stars, as if we were villains on necessity, fools by
heavenly compulsion [. . .] [. . .] An admirable evasion of whoremas-
ter man, to lay his goatish disposition on the charge of a star! [. . .]
(1.2.118–29)'.

As historians and critics who have discussed this clash of 'Ancients
and Moderns'[13] make clear, what was ultimately at issue was the via-
bility of popular belief in the 'organic' theory of the world's senescence: the assumption that the earth was subject to decay and
extinction in the same way as an individual living creature. Breaking
such an idea had significant implications for the development of ecological thought.

The 'wisdom of Nature' carries little weight with Gloucester because
he needs to make sense of troubling developments in the world and science does not offer him any prospect of ameliorating the 'sequent
effects', which he stubbornly goes on insisting are caused by eclipses. Yet
he is not unaware of the progressive objection to his position. We can
see here the outlines of a dilemma familiar to us from modern climate
change debates: the desire, even the need, to reject what science tells us
because its implications for our way of life are too disturbing. The fact
that Gloucester's predicament is the reverse of ours, since he is up
against an expert view that *denies* any connection between natural phenomena and human activity, is perhaps a measure of the development
of environmental science over the past four hundred years; but this does
not alter the basic problem he articulates. Gloucester's habitual outlook,
which is basically ecological in the sense that it believes in an organic
connection between human actions and the external world, and is

rooted in the mediaeval belief in an animate universe, is being challenged by a rationalist philosophy that denies what are for him (and
were for many of his contemporaries) holistic explanations of reality;
and he is psychologically unprepared to abandon it. His position is
doubly insecure, however, in that the widespread perception of a
world in decline could only weaken confidence in a comprehensive
system of natural law that regulated the cosmos and held everything
together. Gloucester's clinging to a belief in portents, in other words,
is something of a refuge, and it is ultimately self-defeating because it
makes him rely on phenomena that are themselves evidence that the
old view may now be obsolete. (This is rather like insisting that a
cold winter disproves global warming when science can show that it
is actually caused by it.) Edmund meanwhile is ready to fill the vacuum created by the collapse of traditional beliefs. His flippancy
reveals not just clear-headed scepticism but a contempt for his father's
spiritual values, providing a perfect illustration of Donne's famous
argument that the undermining of a hallowed belief-system produces
a dangerous hiatus in human affairs, creating existential confusion
('New philosophy calls all in doubt') and fostering an anarchic
individualism:

> Prince, Subject, Father, Son, are things forgot,
> For every man alone thinks he hath got
> To be a Phoenix [. . .][14]

At the same time, Edmund's demolition of his father's beliefs is unanswer-
able in scientific terms, and this raises the question of what vision of
progress is implicit in his particular version of the new philosophy. If it
is true – as I believe it is – that the play's 'imaginative vision is straining
towards the future, not slumped inside the past',[15] this must include at
least some of the activity of the 'new age' to which critics have often
linked Edmund, one of 'scientific enquiry and industrial development,
of bureaucratic organization and social regimentation, the age of mining and merchant-venturing'.[16] We need to ask what this implies historically for the attempt to think about *King Lear* in terms of ecological
ideas.

   The postcolonial view of things tends to hold the European Renaissance responsible for originating most of the sins of modernity, and our
present ecological problems are unlikely to be an exception to this,
given that we can plausibly link them to developments that are identified with the early modern period: the advent of money economies and
the rise of capitalism, the process of globalization that began with the
voyages of discovery, the colonial exploitation of resources, usually with

little understanding of its impact on the environment, and a process of secularization that gradually removed constraints on development and revealed to Europeans what Keith Thomas calls 'a disenchanted world, to be shaped, moulded and dominated'.[17] To think of the modern era as realizing the major implications of processes that began or were greatly accelerated in the sixteenth century makes a good deal of historical sense, and such an overview may help us in charting a viable post–industrial future. But it is important not to extract from Renaissance activities only the grim truths of exploitation and non-sustainability. Reductive views of history can mean that we read the literature of the past reductively as well, particularly when it is as sensitive to contemporary developments as is *King Lear*. We might recall that Jan Kott's view of the play as an endgame, or as modernist nightmare, was not just a response to Cold War politics, but involved a theory of how in the post-medieval world 'impersonal and hostile mechanisms have taken the place of God, Nature and History', and, traditional values having been obliterated, '[a]ll that remains at the end of this gigantic pantomime, is the earth – empty and bleeding'.[18] Shorn of its extravagant rhetoric, this is not very different from the standard critique of Western 'progress' outlined above: the contention that, as Richard Grove summarizes it, 'the advent of mechanistic, analytical or reductionist interpretations of nature and society' in the early modern period 'stimulated destructive attitudes towards an increasingly objectified environment'.[19] It is increasingly obvious to environmental historians and activists alike, however, that sweeping diagnoses of this kind are not very helpful in getting to grips with the difficult legacies of the past, and it should be equally clear that if literature has a role to play in debates about our current predicament, it is because it helps us to think more intuitively about the relevant issues than any analytical discourse, even the ecologically-oriented kind, and reminds us of what is usually wrong with mechanistic approaches. *King Lear* is significant in this respect not because it pinpoints a moment when European civilization took a wrong turn or a fatal step, but because it compels us to participate in the turmoil of ideas that were transforming the social and moral landscape of early modern England, and whose consequences were as yet unknown.

The play certainly offers much evidence of what Grove calls 'reductionist interpretations of nature and society', particularly in Edmund's dismissive treatment of his father's beliefs (as we have seen) and in the ruthless pragmatism with which Goneril and Regan address all their obligations. Lear's bitterly sarcastic plea as the conflict escalates,

> Dear daughter, I confess that I am old;
> Age is unnecessary. On my knees I beg
> That you'll vouchsafe me raiment, bed and food. (2.2.343–45)

is (as usual with Lear) an overreaction to being challenged, but it none-theless registers the arrival of a coldly utilitarian ethic. Shakespeare is careful to indicate the circumstances that generate some of the new ruthlessness. Edmund's marginalization by Gloucester ('He hath been out nine years, and away he shall again', 1.1.31–32) is a product of social developments in post–Reformation England that replaced a more loosely structured and inclusive mediaeval model of the family with one in which the natural son, like the aged father in the households of Goneril and Regan, has no guaranteed place.[20] And if Edmund is a casualty of tighter restrictions on illegitimacy, the two sisters, who are hard-headed enough to take advantage of their new-found opportunities, are also shown to be struggling to reconcile their father's quasi-feudal retinue of one hundred knights with the structure and resources of their modern households (even as she reduces the number of his followers to fifty, Regan argues that 'both charge and danger / Speak 'gainst so great a number' – 2.2.428–29). Moreover, her prudent stance is only superficially in contrast with Lear's largesse in the opening scene. The first and most startling act of 'objectification' in the play, after all, is his carving up of the kingdom like so much real estate, treating land as a kind of commodity to be traded for a calculated statement of love from each of his daughters. We never discover how Lear arrives at the deluded belief that he can do this and yet retain the 'name, and all th' addition to a king' (1.1.137), since the organic theory of the state he is relying on to give him continued authority, one which finds the body politic symbolized in the indivisible person of the monarch, obviously forbids its dismemberment. But the map that he employs to demonstrate his intentions cuts him off from any such awareness, showing him to be 'intoxicated by cartography', as John Gillies suggests, while it 'figures the nation as an available object of desire'.[21] In Tudor and Stuart England, the 'plotting' or surveying of domestic territory in a 'painted paper' could be controversial: surveyors were accused of being 'the cause that men lose their lands: and sometimes [. . .] are abridged of such liberties as they have long used'.[22] (Peter Brook's film powerfully conveyed such a scenario with its long opening shot of massed peasants awaiting the king's decision.) And the surveyor's language ('plenteous rivers and wide-skirted meads' – 1.1.65) that Lear uses to draw a response from his daughters seems calculated to appeal to concerns about wealth and status rather than a proper interest in government. He himself has later to admit that he knows little about the lives of those he ruled ('I have ta'en / Too little care of this' – 3.4.32–33), and the use of the map in the opening scene, overruling in every sense the experience of life on the ground, provides a kind of licence for the thoroughly instrumental handling of power by those who benefit from Lear's abdication.

In the following scene, Lear's 'darker purpose' in dividing the realm gives way to one that is more candidly exploitative. Edmund's declaration 'Legitimate Edgar, I must have your land' (1.2.16) has such a coolly focused quality that it is not difficult to believe he has some very specific ideas about how he might benefit by the acquisition. The landed gentry in Stuart England were increasingly interested in schemes to develop their estates, and the play's early audiences probably needed little prompting to suppose that once Edmund got his hands on his brother's inheritance he would be a typical Jacobean engrosser, turning land to profit through logging, mining and enclosure. Does this mean that they would have treated his ambivalent appeal very much as later generations have done, disapproving of his heartless opportunism but inclined to see him as a man of the future, a harbinger of (possibly unwelcome) change and the embodiment of some vision of progress? The extent to which Edmund has been made to carry such interpretations over the past two centuries is rather remarkable, given that Shakespeare provides only the lightest sketch of his ambitions. Coleridge saw him (rather implausibly) as Napoleon, and used the analogy to develop an assessment of Edmund as a 'revolutionary figure, corrupted in the end [. . .] by his lust for power';[23] and in the twentieth century, as already indicated, the focus tended to be on Edmund as the New Man, the entrepreneur and captain of industry, and on his challenge to the status quo regarding questions of property and inheritance, one that has also been seen as driven by a 'revolutionary scepticism'.[24] There is little hard evidence in the play for any of this, and the susceptibility of the character to these allegorical readings must be found in his initial allegiance to the goddess 'Nature' and the dangerous glamour that attaches to him as a result. Edmund claims to tap into a source of vitality unavailable to more socialized characters, and theatrically he makes good on the claim, claiming our attention with his resourceful plotting and witty adaptation to circumstances. This is what enables him to be the vehicle for seductive ideas. In the soliloquy where he introduces himself to the audience, Edmund's self-promotion as a 'natural' – 'Now gods, stand up for bastards' – is a vigorous piece of free-thinking that keeps company with various contemporary debating points, such as the discoveries botanists were making about the greater vigour of hybrids, and the fashionable ethnography that compared the senescent societies of the Old World with the noble savages of the New. Edmund puts his own spin on that comparison with a claim that creatures like himself

in the lusty stealth of nature take
More composition and fierce quality
Than doth within a dull, stale, tired bed

Go to th' creating a whole tribe of fops
Got 'tween a sleep and wake (1.2.11–15)

– while his contempt for 'the plague of custom' (3) echoes a critique of
social convention that recurs throughout Montaigne's *Essays* and leads
to the latter's celebrated dictum that 'We cannot err in following
Nature' – that is, in obeying our natural instincts and inclinations.[25]
These were influential ideas in Shakespeare's day, especially after the
Florio translation of Montaigne appeared in 1603, and they provided
ready fodder for the sort of pop psychology that Edmund is purveying
here. But in showing the destructive potential of his beliefs, Shakespeare
draws attention to the further implications of the cult of primitivism in
the Renaissance, and its thorny relationship both to traditional notions
of pastoral and to the seventeenth-century endeavour to reform the
study of nature. These three strands of thought were the principal means
by which writers and intellectuals in early modern times sought to
redefine humanity's place in the physical world. They are the 'green'
ideas of their time, and all of them find their way into *King Lear*.

Back to Nature

Renaissance Europe was not in the existential situation that the world
finds itself in today, as it seeks to deal with humanity's physical impact
upon the planet and halt the degradation of the global ecosystem, but
problems associated with economic and social development were multiplying in the sixteenth century, and individual societies responded to
them, and to the disintegration of old beliefs, with cultural ideas that
did much to shape later ecological frames of mind. These ideas ranged
(just as they do now) from a faith in new technologies and knowledge
systems to a repudiation of the artificialities and excesses of modern
life. What they all sought, however, was access to the 'wisdom of nature',
as part of the comprehensive Renaissance attempt to return to the pristine sources of knowledge. As we saw earlier, Shakespeare gives the
quoted phrase to Gloucester (at 1.2.104) in a reference to the efforts of
contemporary science, but it can also usefully be applied to other manifestations in *King Lear* of the human interaction with the natural world,
thereby helping us to come to some tentative conclusions about the
play's traffic in ecological ideas.

As several critics have recently reminded us, the search for Eden,
and the desire in various ways to get 'back to nature', were at the centre
of the early modern effort to renew Western civilization. The nostalgia
for a simpler or more innocent time that is found in virtually all societies was particularly intense in a period when Europe was racked by

doctrinal and epistemological conflicts and undergoing rapid material development, but it was rarely just an escapist sentiment: as Robert N. Watson suggests, English culture was 'infatuated with hopes of recovering some original and authentic reality',[26] most obviously in the work of religious reformation, and its major writers mounted a dynamic response to the challenges posed by social change – for instance, offering environmental alternatives in pastoral and utopian writing to the alienating modern realities of urbanization and capital-intensive farming. At the same time, the new empiricism in scientific enquiry made it possible to think about getting back to nature in practical ways, using rigorous observation and experiment to study the material world, 'God's second book', and thereby rectify the faulty beliefs that inhibited human progress. Richard Grove describes the early modern voyages of discovery as a search for the earthly paradise that would make a vital contribution to the growth of environmental science,[27] and a similar claim is implicit in Francis Bacon's declaration that through the 'arts and sciences' man can repair the Fall and renew 'his command over created things'.[28] For although the Baconian programme of research and development was mechanistic, in the sense that it sought to explain how things worked rather than defining their purpose in a providential scheme, it also saw itself – odd as this may seem now – as an ecological response to mankind's dysfunctional relationship with the rest of creation. The empirical study of earthly phenomena would replace scholastic learning and barren *a priori* modes of enquiry, and restore human beings to an effective stewardship of the natural world. What this meant in practice, of course, was the very control and domination of nature, harnessing its resources exclusively for human purposes, that modern environmentalism seeks to interrogate; and this brings us back to the paradox outlined earlier with regard to Gloucester and Edmund: that it was only by challenging a magical or providential (and in that sense holistic) view of reality that 'rational and measured observations of environmental change', and eventually 'an organised conservationist response', would become possible.[29] In the early seventeenth century, what science and technology were offering, in the most exalted formulation of their aims, was a way back into the earthly paradise, where humankind can bring nature under control through accurate observation and analysis of living phenomena.   *Nature under control*

The optimism of this 'secular recovery narrative', as Carolyn Merchant terms it, seems a long way removed from the mood of *King Lear*, which was after all written several decades before the foundation of the Royal Society; but this does not mean that the play is simply mired in a pre-scientific age whose perplexities were destined to be dispelled. On the contrary, it is thoroughly alert to the way empiricism might change the ways in which we see and investigate things, as Edmund's attack on his father's beliefs indicates, and where its methods are bound to fail. 'Then let them anatomize Regan; see what breeds about her heart' (3.6.73–74), declares Lear, baffled by her lack of 'natural' consideration for him, and obsessed with the thought that surrounding her hard heart – a familiar theological concept –must exist a teeming malignity (like Rossiter's 'under-nature') that can be isolated and perhaps destroyed. As Kent says a moment later, 'his wits are gone' (84), but Lear's bizarre idea is a classic category mistake, of a kind that easily occurs when intangible dilemmas and concerns are redefined as material challenges. The problem of human evil, we know, will frustrate the forensic investigator even more than it does the theologian; there is no wisdom to be had here from the clinical probing of nature. It is a passing moment in the play, and should not be taken as a representative critique of science's claims; but it disturbingly complements, and somehow confirms the violence of Regan's own dispassionate procedure earlier in methodically stripping away her father's last follower ('What need one?'). Rational analysis is open to abuse and misapplication, and like Edmund's demolition of astrology, the sisters' logical reading of Lear's situation overlooks complex human priorities ('O reason not the need') and gives free rein to a remorseless will to power. 'The laws are mine, not thine', snarls Goneril, 'Who can arraign me for't?' (5.3.156–57), and her words imply much more than a simple assertion of authority over her husband. It is the arrogance of newfound authority that thinks it can sweep away traditional scruples and constraints, and the generational challenge that Edmund, Goneril and Regan mount to their elders is harrowing and momentous not just because it does so much physical damage but also because it largely destroys Lear's and Gloucester's belief in a meaningful universe and substitutes only their own brittle regime. The world of *King Lear* is the uncertain space between a dying providential order and a new kind of anthropocentric claim on reality. And at the heart of the rationalist-scientific arguments for human dominion over creation, the play suggests, is a dark contradiction, since they rest on ways of seeing that ultimately deny any moral or ontological basis for privileging human needs. I would argue that in *King Lear* Shakespeare penetrates more deeply into the implications of the new philosophy than any of his scientific contemporaries, intuiting, perhaps, that the denial of final causes in the investigation of nature leads directly to later views of the universe as 'a mechanism of forces devoid of an end',[30] and must imply an ecological system in which humankind has no privileged place.

The play's wary response to technocratic designs on reality extends to what appears initially to be a very different conception of the 'wisdom of nature'. Among the unfamiliar data gathered by the voyages of discovery was the evidence of native peoples in the Americas apparently living in prelapsarian conditions, free of the corrupting effects of civilization. The cult of primitivism that grew out of these stories, which anticipated Enlightenment concepts of 'natural man', played a significant role in encouraging relativist, self-critical thinking among Europeans about the shortcomings of their own societies, but Shakespeare's handling of these ideas is complex. His most sustained engagement with primitivist thinking is in *The Tempest*, where he refuses to ascribe a sentimental nobility to Caliban any more than he endorses the idea of him as sub-human. This cautionary treatment of the primitivist doctrine is anticipated, however, in Edmund's claim to a 'natural' advantage over his peers, since his conduct obviously shows that, *pace* Montaigne, we *can* 'erre in following Nature'; and Shakespeare deepens the analysis by juxtaposing Edmund's glorification of instinct with other characters' more constructive attempts to move beyond custom and find an authen- tic response. Edmund's belief that his impulses and desires are self-justifying is a libertine version of the emphasis elsewhere in the play on transcending formulaic attitudes and conventional codes. 'Speak what we feel, not what we ought to say', declares Edgar at the end (5.3.323), while Gloucester identifies the 'superfluous' man as one who 'will not see / Because he does not feel' (4.1.70–72). The idea that tragedy can probe beyond learned responses and release our deepest (most 'natural'?) feelings is central to the importance in which we hold *King Lear*, and in writing it Shakespeare was surely endorsing Montaigne's stress on inwardness and subjectivity, and acknowledging, as it were, that the extended scope of his own theatrical art has much to do with creating a space for original individual experience. Edmund himself, after all, is a vastly more interesting and credibly motivated character than the Vice figures in morality drama from whom he is descended. Yet it is also true that Edmund's individualism is threatening to these notions of the authentic self, because his identification with nature expresses hostility not only to the social customs that oppress him but also to any intuitions of empathy or altruism (of the kind that finally make him try to save Cordelia 'Despite of mine own nature' – 5.3.242). He is, like Richard III in his punning self-description, 'determined to prove a villain'.[31] The idea that living according to nature makes you free, or contributes to the building of a more successful society, is one that Shakespeare clearly regarded with scepticism, as a key moment in *The Tempest* makes clear: there he virtually transcribes a passage from Montaigne's essay *Of Cannibals* in a speech by Gonzalo on the ideal commonwealth (2.1.145–63) and exposes it to the irony of the other courtiers, while the fraught politics of Prospero's island kingdom are a kind of rebuke to the naive enthusiasm with which Europe had greeted travellers' reports of

stone age societies living in harmony with nature. Edmund's appropriation of primitivist ideas, despite the energy and interest that it generates in the early stages of the play, similarly casts doubt on their ecological
value, for his pact with nature is the sort that licenses a soulless exploitation of others, just as the cultivation of his own 'fierce quality' seems to
be serving a Darwinist creed that fabricates – and fetishizes – its 'natural' origins. (As is often remarked, the Nazis were particularly proud of
their green credentials.) Here, as in so many ways, Shakespeare seems
remarkably prescient about where charismatic ideas and performances
may lead.

Primitivism was the most controversial of the 'green' ideas that were
current during the English Renaissance, because it flirted openly with
the proposition that sophisticated cultures are a kind of aberration from
nature, but it bore a plausible relationship to the more orthodox motifs
of pastoral, which from ancient times had offered the rural retreat as a
salve for the burdens of civilization, and which in the Renaissance
became the genre of choice for debating the moral and philosophical
basis of the good life. In several of Shakespeare's comedies the green
world into which characters flee or are banished becomes a source of
enlightenment and recovery, but in *As You Like It*, which has long been
recognized as a comic companion piece to *King Lear*, this theme is cun-
ningly nuanced, as the exiles in the forest reveal – and are forced to
meditate upon – the delicate contradictions in their attempt to live in
tune with nature. 'Sweet are the uses of adversity', muses Duke Senior as
he welcomes the privations of wind and rain that 'feelingly persuade me
what I am' (2.1.11); but it is the much darker version of this theme in
Act 3 of *King Lear* that really forces the issue, by making the situation of
'unaccommodated man' so stark and ultimately insupportable. In the
extraordinarily original scenes that form the play's central section, the
old king and his companions are thrust out into the storm and reduced
to a previously unimaginable state, seeking shelter in hovels and patch-
ing together a new kind of fellowship in order to survive. It is an extreme
test of the claim of pastoral to undo our alienation from nature.

Despite their banishment from court, Duke Senior and his companions elect to see the forest as a kind of voluntary experiment in simple
living, but for Lear's party there is obviously no such choice. The open
countryside to which they are exposed ('for many miles about / There's
scarce a bush' – 2.2.491–92) is an overwhelmingly threatening space in
which they struggle to survive even briefly. Yet people do live there:
Gloucester's tenant farmer who leads his blinded master at the start of
Act 4, and whoever built the hovel that Kent has discovered as he
searches for Lear (3.2.59–60). Once the old king has grasped that such

environments are the regular habitation of the poor and the homeless, he begins to change perspective:

> O, I have ta'en
> Too little care of this. Take physic, pomp,
> Expose thyself to feel what wretches feel,
> That thou mayst shake the superflux to them
> And show the heavens more just. (3.4.32–36)

Gloucester later concurs: 'distribution should undo excess, / And each man have enough' (4.1.65–66). These sentiments are part of a utopian strain in the play that links it prophetically to progressive movements in the English Revolution and beyond. They seem also to chime with elements in the primitivist argument, equating closeness to nature with authenticity, with the discovery of truth, and reaffirming the importance of feeling and first-hand experience. This dimension of *King Lear* needs to be given its due, for it represents an engagement with what we now call human ecology, or the issue of how people relate to and form part of their environments. But this engagement entails further questions: each man should have enough, but how much is enough? And enough for what? What specifically are human needs, and how far can they be asserted before they turn into anthropocentric vanities? Lear's outburst in response to his daughters' reductionist logic grapples magnificently with the issues:

> O reason not the need! Our basest beggars
> Are in the poorest thing superfluous.
> Allow not nature more than nature needs,
> Man's life is cheap as beast's. Thou art a lady:
> If only to go warm were gorgeous,
> Why nature needs not what thou gorgeous wear'st,
> Which scarcely keeps thee warm. But for true need—
> You heavens, give me that patience, patience I need. (2.4.264–71)

Lear cannot find words to define that 'true need', but he knows that it is not something that can be defined in 'natural' terms: human and animal needs are different, and culture deals in symbols that are essential to self-respect and the preservation of decorum. His daughters' skimpy gowns are apparently invoked as an analogy to his hundred knights, yet Lear's passionate qualification 'But for true need', and his breaking off, suggest a further intuition that luxury and refinement are not the same (and not as important) as the dignity that he is rapidly losing, and that the crisis has challenged his understanding of what it means to be human. It is a more self-centred insight than his later resolve to expose himself 'to feel what wretches feel', but it is also a more radical one. For while Lear's and Gloucester's glimpses into the causes of social misery are important for their personal journeys, these and other moments that are congenial to a Marxist interpretation also prompt the thought that Marx theorized the economic order and relationships between classes but signally failed to reconceive the relationship between humanity and the natural world. Despite its origins in Enlightenment thought, Marxism was throughout the twentieth century largely deaf to the second half of the dialectic formulated by Theodor Adorno and Max Horkheimer, at least in the ecological version of it that Jonathan Bate has proposed: 'Enlightenment's instrumentalization of nature frees mankind from the tyranny of nature (disease, famine), but its disenchantment of nature licenses the destruction of nature and hence of mankind.'[32] We might not expect Shakespeare and his contemporaries to be alert to the latter proposition either, given that the early modern world was necessarily in a different position to our own on questions of development and sustainability, and it would have been difficult then to conceive of civilization physically depleting the resources of the planet. They were, however, more likely than later generations to mourn or be disturbed by the disenchantment of nature, a process that was fully implicit in the emerging science of the period, and in *King Lear* there is a profound engagement with the implications of this epistemological shift that has left us struggling ever since to come to terms with the play's vision of existence.

Notes

1   R. A. Foakes, *Hamlet versus Lear: Cultural Politics and Shakespeare's Art* (Cambridge: Cambridge University Press, 1993), p. 224.

2   *King Lear*, 5.3.261. All references to the play are to The Arden Shakespeare, Third series, ed. by R. A. Foakes (Walton-on-Thames: Thomas Nelson, 1997).

3   Jonathan Bate noted in *The Song of the Earth* (London: Picador, 2000) that environmentalism was the only one of the 1960s movements not to have made a serious impact on literary studies (pp. 71–72). Since his book was published the situation has changed somewhat, but ecocritical attention to Shakespeare has yet to yield substantial results.

4   Foakes, *Hamlet versus Lear*, pp. 57–58.

5   Kiernan Ryan, '*King Lear*: A Retrospect, 1980–2000', in *Shakespeare Survey*, 55 (Cambridge: Cambridge University Press, 2002), p. 10.

6   Stephen Greenblatt, 'Invisible Bullets', in *Political Shakespeare: New Essays in Cultural Materialism*, ed. by Jonathan Dollimore and Alan Sinfield (Manchester: Manchester University Press, 1985), p. 45.

7   See Hiram Haydn, *The Counter-Renaissance* (New York: Charles Scribner's Sons, 1950), esp. chap. 8, and Rosalie Colie, *Paradoxia Epidemica: The Renaissance Tradition of Paradox* (Princeton: Princeton University Press, 1966).

8   Godfrey Goodman, *The Fall of Man* (London, 1616), p. 5.

9   Cited by Foakes, *Hamlet versus Lear*, p. 51.

10 A. P. Rossiter, *Angel with Horns* (London: Longman, 1957), pp. 304–5.

11 Keith Thomas, *Man and the Natural World: Changing Attitudes in England, 1500–1800* (London: Allen Lane, 1983), p. 18.

12 John Norden, *Vicissitudo Rerum* (London, 1600), B4v.

13 R. F. Jones, *Ancients and Moderns* (St Louis: Washington University Studies, 1961), Chapters 2 and 3; Victor Harris, *All Coherence Gone* (Chicago: Chicago University Press, 1949), Chapter 4.

14 John Donne, *An Anatomy of the World: The First Anniversary* (London, 1611), lines 215–17.

15 Ryan, '*King Lear*: A Retrospect', p. 7.

16 John F. Danby, *Shakespeare's Doctrine of Nature: A Study of 'King Lear'* (London: Faber and Faber, 1949), p. 46.

17 Thomas, *Man and the Natural World*, p. 22.

18 Jan Kott, *Shakespeare Our Contemporary*, trans. by B. Taborski (New York: Anchor Books, 1966), pp. 133, 147.

19 Richard H. Grove, *Green Imperialism: Colonial Expansion . . . and the origins of environmentalism, 1600–1860* (Cambridge: Cambridge University Press, 1995), p. 50.

20 See Jeffrey R. Watt, 'The Impact of the Reformation and Counter-Reformation', in *Family Life in Early Modern Times, 1500–1789*, ed. by D. I. Kertzer and Marzio Barbagli (New Haven: Yale University Press, 2001), pp. 125–54 (pp. 148–49).

21 John Gillies, 'The scene of cartography in *King Lear*', in *Literature, Mapping, and the Politics of Space in Early Modern Britain*, ed. by Andrew Gordon and Bernhard Klein (Cambridge: Cambridge University Press, 2001), pp. 109–37 (pp. 119–20).

22 See John Norden, *The Surveyors Dialogue* (1607), 15, 3; and Bernhard Klein, *Maps and the Writing of Space* (Basingstoke: Palgrave, 2001), pp. 51–60, 94–96.

23 Foakes, *Hamlet versus Lear*, p. 76.

24 Jonathan Dollimore, *Radical Tragedy* (Brighton: Harvester Press 1984), p. 198.

25 M. de Montaigne, 'Of Phisiognomy', in *The Essays of Montaigne* (London: David Nutt, 1892), III, 322.

26 Robert N. Watson, *Back to Nature: The Green and the Real in the Late Renaissance* (Philadelphia: University of Pennsylvania Press, 2006), p. 77.

27 Grove, *Green Imperialism*, pp. 3–15.

28 Francis Bacon, *Novum Organum*, ed. and trans. by Graham Rees and Maria Wakely, The Oxford Francis Bacon (Oxford: Clarendon Press, 2004), XI, 447.

29 Grove, *Green Imperialism*, p. 51.

30 Thomas, *Man and the Natural World*, p. 170 (quoting Kant).

31 *Richard III*, ed. by Antony Hammond, The Arden Shakespeare (London: Methuen, 1981), 1.1.30.

32 Bate, *Song of the Earth*, p. 78.

CHAPTER SIX

New Directions: *King Lear* and Protestantism

John J. Norton

In Shakespeare's *King Lear* the humiliation of the protagonist dominates the action of the play. In an essay describing Christian pessimism in *King Lear*, Kenneth Myrick argues that the Elizabethan audience, trained in Reformation theology, would not have been surprised by what unfolds in *King Lear*. Myrick writes: 'One by one, the five villainous characters in *Lear* are destroyed in the exact circumstances in which the Elizabethan had been trained to see and dread the judgment of an angry God.'[1] According to Myrick, Elizabethans would have been familiar with the preaching and the printed sermons of Richard Hooker (1554–1600) and Henry Smith (1550–1591). Smith preached about the 'false security' and 'downfall of evildoers'.[2] In one sermon he describes the process in this way:

> First, God takes him in his fault, that he might see his fault [. . .]
> Then he takes him suddenly, because he contemneth his warning
> [. . .] Thirdly God takes him where he is pleasantest and lustiest,
> and safest [. . .] Vengeance doth stay until sin be ripe, and watch
> the time when they are most occupied, then judgment steps forth,
> like the Angell to stop Balaam in his way, because the punishment
> is more grievous and terrible when they look not for it.[3]

It is in this way, modelled after what Myrick calls the 'tragic sense' or the 'tragic note' of Elizabethan Christianity, that five of the villains in *King Lear* meet their ruin. Myrick is here referring to Goneril, Regan, Cornwall, Edmund and Oswald. The first of these to die in the play is Cornwall, stabbed by the servant who seeks to protect Gloucester. Cornwall's death is not looked for, thus allowing it to take on the 'more grievous and terrible' characteristic as described by Henry Smith. The servant's rise against Cornwall is unexpected:

1st servant:	Hold your hand, my lord.
	I have served you ever since I was a child,
	But better service have I never done you
	Than now to bid you hold.
Regan:	How now, you dog?
1st servant:	If you did wear a beard upon your chin,
	I'd shake it on this quarrel. What do you mean?
Cornwall:	My villein? (3.7.70–77)[4]

Both Regan and Cornwall are surprised at the servant's audacity; Cornwall confessing that this injury comes upon him too early: 'Regan, I bleed apace; / Untimely comes this hurt' (3.7.97–98).

Oswald is the next to die in this list of villains. His death is also unexpected as it is confirmed from his earlier conflict with Kent that Oswald would not be one to draw on someone he thought might prove a good fighter. We witness Oswald run in fear of Kent in Act 2, Kent calling him a coward, a 'lily-livered, action-taking knave [and a] glass gazing [. . .] finical rogue' (2.2.16–19). As an 'action-taking knave', Oswald is claimed to be one who takes legal action rather than fighting; as a 'finical rogue' he would be one who is affected or fussy.[5] In his exchange with Edgar it may be that Oswald is fooled by the dialect Edgar feigns, one of a country peasant, thereby leading Oswald to believe that he would not be a well-trained fighter.[6] Like Cornwall, Oswald also claims that his death is untimely, further betraying his surprise.

In Act 5, both Regan and Goneril die. Regan is secretly poisoned by her sister, clearly an unexpected death, and Goneril, though she kills herself, does so as a desperate act of frustration. Goneril kills Regan so that she may have Edmund for herself, yet in the process discovers that Edmund will not have her. The frustration that overtakes Goneril is unexpected, and her suicide is carried out in a passionate rage.

Edmund's ruin is of a different nature than the previous four. Edmund is faced with his own ruin; he is taken, as stated by Henry Smith, 'in his fault, that he might see his fault'.[7] After being brought to his knees by Edgar, Edmund is charged for his crimes by Albany, to which he confesses:

Edmund:	What you have charged me with, that have I done,
	And more, much more; the time will bring it out.
	'Tis past and so am I [. . .] (5.3.160–62)

He also confesses to Edgar, after Edgar confronts him about the treatment Gloucester is forced to endure:

> *Edgar*:   The gods are just and of our pleasant vices
> Make instruments to plague us:
> The dark and vicious place where thee he got
> Cost him his eyes.
> *Edmund*:   Thou'st spoken right, 'tis true;
> The wheel is come full circle, I am here. (5.3.168–73)

Though it appears that Shakespeare was familiar with Henry Smith's ideas regarding the punishment and judgment of evil men and women, Kenneth Myrick does not claim that Shakespeare was a religious man, nor does he claim that Shakespeare even read the works of Reformation preachers. Myrick writes:

> Whether Shakespeare ever [. . .] heard a sermon by Henry Smith is of no particular relevance. What is important is that Smith and [Bartholomew] Parsons [we can reasonably include Hooker here as well] are representative. It would be absurd, of course, to say that every religious writer of the age was gifted with the tragic sense [. . .] But the frequency of the tragic note in Elizabethan Christianity is undeniable.[8]

In Shakespeare's *King Lear*, we see what Myrick calls the 'tragic note in Elizabethan Christianity' in the fall of the play's antagonists, but I will here extend his analysis, and demonstrate that the impact of Reformation theology on Shakespeare's *King Lear* can be witnessed in the plain dealing of Kent, in the humiliation of the king, and in the compassion of Cordelia.

Lear's Humiliation

As I propose to focus henceforth on what may seem minor elements of Reformation theology, it is important to note that the new doctrines of Protestantism would not have been considered minor to an Elizabethan. As acknowledged by Alison Shell: 'there was considerable personal and literary interaction between individuals of opposing religious views. Catholics and Protestants lived side by side, sometimes spoke to each other without quarrelling, and read each other's books.'[9] In the nature of Kent's plain dealing and in the nature of Lear's humiliation is evidence of Shakespeare's ability to glean from his culture, a characteristic praised in the playwright by Harold Bloom.[10] From the religious storms that rage around him, Shakespeare employs what appears to be the essence of Reformation doctrine. In Shakespeare's *King Lear* we see these passionate teachings played out in the lives of Kent and Lear.

In the first act of the play when Kent confronts Lear in regard to the banishment of Cordelia, Kent understands that the king is exercising poor moral vision:

> *Lear*:   Out of my sight!
> *Kent*: See better, Lear, and let me still remain
>   The true blank of thine eye. (1.1.157–59)

The Arden Shakespeare notes that Kent here invites Lear to look to his servant for good advice. 'See *me* better', is perhaps what Kent implies, as he responds to Lear's command. Kent understands, perhaps, that he alone is able to see the danger that Lear has fallen into. In 'let me still remain', Kent is trying to get Lear to recognize that he is the only one who sees Lear's madness clearly. Offering himself as a potential focal point of sorts, Kent understands that Lear, like a blind man, needs a guide. Ben Schneider, Jr. argues in his essay 'King Lear and the Culture of Justice' that Kent is of the classic plain dealer mould, praised throughout classic literature, the Renaissance, and in contemporary times as one who is unafraid to speak the truth.[11] The spirit of the Reformation is one steeped in the tradition of plain dealing. Martin Luther's very act of nailing his *95 Theses* to the church door in Wittenberg, proclaiming the truth as he saw it, was, in these terms, an exemplary act of plain dealing. In his 'Warning to His Dear German People', the German reformer supports those who would stand up against a corrupt government:

> One might tolerate an evil life; but one can and must not tolerate, much less help to defend, a person who condemns doctrine and God's word and who elevates himself over God. They have disseminated so many doctrinal abominations within Christendom that these cannot be numbered. They repent of none of them, nor do they want to change them, but they openly defend them all and rigorously insist on being in the right. All of that would rest on your neck and conscience. You would make yourself a partner of all such abominations and you would be guilty if you helped to defend them.[12]

Calvin concludes his *Institutes of the Christian Religion* with a warning to those who lack the courage to stand up to a corrupt ruler or king:

> So far is the praise of modesty from being due to that pretence by which flattering courtiers cloak themselves, and deceive the simple, when they deny the lawfulness of declining anything imposed

by their kings [. . .] I know the imminent peril to which subjects expose themselves by this firmness, kings being most indignant when they are contemned. As Solomon says, 'The wrath of a king is as messengers of death' (Prov. 16:14). But since Peter, one of heaven's heralds, has published the edict, 'We ought to obey God rather than men' (Acts 5:29), let us console ourselves with the thought, that we are rendering the obedience which the Lord requires, when we endure anything rather than turn aside from piety. And that our courage may not fail, Paul stimulates us by the additional consideration (1 Cor. 7:23), that we were redeemed by Christ at the great price which our redemption cost him, in order that we might not yield a slavish obedience to the depraved wishes of men, far less do homage to their impiety.[13]

Hooker is no less plain in his writings, arguing that men must know the truth and be willing to stand up for it, be it against priest, king or other guide:

if the guides of the people be blind, the common sort of men must not close up their own eyes and be led by the conduct of such; if the priest be partial in the law, the flock must not therefore depart from the ways of sincere truth, and in simplicity yield to be followers of him for his place' sake and office over them.[14]

We can find models for Kent in all three of these prominent, very plain dealing, writers. While plain dealing was praised long before the Reformation, the religious movement, and especially the work of Luther, Calvin and Hooker, put a new emphasis on the power and honour of speaking the truth plainly and boldly. Just as Huston Diehl claims that the reformers reinvigorated the notion of original sin, 'adamantly insisting that everyone is depraved by nature and sharply critiquing the Catholic ideals of celibacy, monasticism, and good works that imply otherwise',[15] so, too, did the reformers reinvigorate the importance of the plain dealer. It is Luther whose statements about the pope make him the clearest model among Reformation theologians of plain dealing. Luther challenged the Roman powers of his day, wrote profusely about the damage he believed the pope was doing to the church, and made controversial claims about the pope, calling him the 'Antichrist', the 'devil incarnate', and one who 'signifies the terrible wrath of God'.[16] With a Luther-like plain dealing, Shakespeare's Kent is not afraid to step 'between the dragon and his wrath' (1.1.122), even to appear rude and unmannerly:

Lear: The bow is bent and drawn; make from the shaft.
Kent: Let it fall rather; though the fork invade

The region of my heart: be Kent unmannerly
When Lear is mad. What wouldst thou do, old man?
Think'st thou that duty shall have dread to speak,
When power to flattery bows? To plainness honour's bound
When majesty falls to folly. (1.1.142–48)

Kent alludes to himself as one who sees honour in 'plainness', contesting that plain speaking must come before mannerly behaviour. The question Kent poses to Lear is an interesting one, 'What wouldst thou do, old man?' (1.1.145). Kent identifies that the kingdom has fallen into a state of emergency; it is he alone who sees the danger of Lear's request for flattery. Kent claims that this is madness, and his addressing of Lear as 'old man', though an outrageous breach of decorum, is part of what Kent claims to be his duty. Lear's calling on Apollo, the archer god known for clear-sightedness, gives Kent an additional opportunity to press Lear about his poor moral vision:

Lear: Now by Apollo–
Kent: Now by Apollo, King,
       Thou swear'st thy gods in vain.
Lear: O vassal! Miscreant! (1.1.157–60)

Kent recognizes that Lear is unable to see, that his eyes are clouded over with madness. Kent also recognizes that Lear's cry to Apollo is more a cry of exasperation, a taking of the god's name in vain, than a serious cry to the most clear-sighted of the gods. Kent understands that Lear's vision is impaired.

In this opening act Kent is cast in the role of a spiritual physician; Kent has the proper prescription for Lear, yet tragically, Lear is unable to hear his servant's wise counsel:

Kent: Do, kill thy physician, and thy fee bestow
       Upon the foul disease. Revoke thy gift,
       Or whilst I can vent clamour from my throat
       I'll tell thee thou dost evil. (1.1.162–66)

Kent does not seek to win an argument or to be vindicated through his passionate conflict with Lear. Kent, as he claims, is trying to save his beloved king. The language Kent employs, referring to himself as Lear's physician, is the very language employed by Luther in his *Lectures on Romans*. Luther writes:

This is like the case of a physician who wishes to heal his patient, but finds that he is a man who denies that he is sick, calling the

physician a fool and an even sicker person than himself for pre-
suming to cure a healthy man. And because of the man's resistance the physician cannot get around to recommending his skill
and his medicine. For he could do so only if the sick man would
admit his illness and permit him to cure him.[17]

Lear is too arrogant to see that he is sick. Just like Lear, the sick man in
Luther's example proclaims that the person who tries to help him is a
miscreant – a word that *The Oxford English Dictionary* defines more
similarly to heretic and misbeliever than to 'wretch' or 'villain'.[18] Though
Kent seeks to protect the well being of his king, like Luther's sick man
Lear proclaims that his physician is not a proper spiritual guide but
rather a damnable heretic. Kent does not seek honour or power by
claiming to be Lear's physician, rather, through the conflict Kent risks
his life by stepping into Lear's rage. Luther's illustration is meant to
point out man's need to humbly confess his illness, to trust the scriptures and to seek God's grace. Luther further elucidates this concept:

Therefore we need humility and faith. What these words seek to
establish and maintain is solely this, that inwardly we become
nothing, that we empty ourselves of everything, humble ourselves
and say with the prophet, 'Against Thee, Thee only, have I sinned,
so that Thou art justified in Thy words. [. . .] In Thy sight I am
foolish and weak, so that Thou mayest be wise and powerful in
Thy words. [. . .] For all creation teaches [. . .] that no one is
exalted except the man who has been humbled, nothing is filled
except that which is empty, that nothing is built except that which
has been torn down.[19]

Kent's plain dealing and the language he employs to confront Lear bears
a close resemblance to the plain dealing Reformation theologians, and
especially to the writing of Luther. The 'tearing down' of prideful Lear,
still claiming to be more sinned against than sinning long after he has
isolated himself from his family, is the second place we find major
strands of Reformation influence.

The humiliation of Lear comes as a result of his poor moral vision.
There is a desperation that dominates this play, a desperation that
made Samuel Johnson and many others of the eighteenth century glad
of Nahum Tate's revised version of the play. It was Dr Johnson's prediction that playgoers would 'rise better pleased from the final triumph
of persecuted virtue'.[20] Civilized society, in the opinion of Geoffrey
Bickersteth,

had grown too much sophisticated, too consciously aware of its own exquisite refinement, to be capable of responding with any real sympathy 'to the primitive scene, the moral and physical humiliations and the desperate challenge of such a play as *King Lear*'.[21]

It may be, as Stephen Greenblatt writes, that in *King Lear* the Catholic Church is 'revealed to be the persecuted elder brother forced to defend himself by means of theatrical illusions against the cold persecution of his skeptical bastard brother Protestantism'.[22] But Greenblatt's premise misses the more consuming issue at hand in *King Lear*: this is the fact that the humiliation of man, central to the play, was of paramount concern to Protestant writers during the Reformation. That men and women would recognize their sinful state, and that men and women would understand that they were unable to save themselves are two of the chief goals of Luther, Calvin and Hooker. Luther writes:

> Nobody doubts that man with all his faculties was created by the eternal Word of God, as were all other things, and that he is God's creature. Nevertheless there is nothing good in him; this means (as Moses says in Genesis 6[:5]), that all his thoughts and senses with all faculties are continually inclined to evil. Thus although the flesh is truly God's creation it is not inclined to chastity but to unchastity; although the heart is truly God's creation, it is not inclined to humility, to love of neighbor, but to pride and to self-love.[23]

In the opening lines of *Institutes of the Christian Religion*, Calvin writes:

> We are accordingly urged by our own evil things to consider the good things of God; and, indeed, we cannot aspire to Him in earnest until we have begun to be displeased with ourselves. For what man is not disposed to rest in himself [. . .] so long as he is contented with his own endowments, and unconscious or unmindful of his misery?[24]

Hooker follows in the same way, writing thus:

> We are not dust and ashes, but worse; our minds from the highest to the lowest are not right; if not right, then undoubtedly not capable of that blessedness which we naturally seek, but subject unto that which we most abhor, anguish, tribulation, death, woe, endless misery.[25]

In her work on the tradition of common prayer in Elizabethan Christianity, Ramie Targoff cites a passage from Hooker, revealing the Elizabethan preacher's mistrust of the nature of man: '[Common prayer is] a mechanism that successfully moulds the naturally flawed impulses of the worshipper, whose faith can only be stimulated through regulated external forms.'[26] The notion of human depravity stood at the forefront of Reformation theology, and it was this issue that we find played out in Shakespeare's humiliation of Lear.

Luther employs the use of marred human vision to describe the futility of human reason and the truth of human weakness. Luther claims that humans are 'blind' to the truths of God, and the result is that religious institutions oppress their members as Lear oppressed his daughters. As Lear orders each daughter into a posture of confession, he requires of them an offering of praise:

> *Lear:*   Which of you shall we say doth love us most,
> That we our largest bounty may extend
> Where nature doth with merit challenge. (1.1.51–53)

Whether the sisters kneel before their father or stand, they are here ordered to perform an act of religious dedication, to publicly proclaim their love for Lear. Lear's demand parallels what Luther described as the demands of the Roman Catholic Church of the sixteenth century. Luther writes this about the priesthood of his day:

> [Any priest that demands such outward signs of devotion] is as blind as a bat and says that we must fast, pray, sing, and do the works of the law. It continues to fool around in this manner with works, until it has gone so far astray and thinks we serve God by building churches, ringing bells, burning incense, reciting by rote, singing, wearing hoods, having tonsures, burning candles, and by other countless foolish acts of which the world is full, indeed more than full.[27]

Lear's blindness, in many ways symbolic of the blindness of all mankind, is foundational to the human struggle found in the text. Geoffrey Bickersteth refers to Lear's blindness as 'a hideous rashness against the moral order of Nature'.[28] Bickersteth fails to consider the emotional and spiritual implications of Lear's blindness. Lear does indeed lash out at the moral order, but more importantly, he lashes out at the emotional and spiritual order around him. Lear knows himself only 'slenderly', and his understanding of his daughters and other loved ones around him is equally shallow. Lear rushes forward in haste; he rushes forward by what Luther would call the natural light of his own depraved logic. This natural light, or human reason, is marred by sin. Luther writes: 'But the natural light cannot reach so far that it could determine which things are good and which are bad.'[29] Although the thrust of my work here is focused on the character of Lear, it is worth mentioning that Gloucester's physical blindness is included in the play to drive home the point that Lear's tragedy 'is no isolated instance of a single life gone wrong'.[30] Frederick Buechner here moves us towards my central thesis. Lear's story is not an isolated incident, but in some ways a playing out of one of the major theological views of Shakespeare's day: that prideful men are brought into a right relationship with themselves, with others, and ultimately with God only after being brought to their knees through a humiliating experience. Gloucester's physical blindness, acquired at the hand or perhaps the spur of Cornwall, and his literal fall, staged for him by his son Edgar at the imaginary cliffs of Dover, act as a frame for Lear's emotional-spiritual blindness and his ultimate fall.[31] In his essay 'Grief, Authority and the Resistance to Consolation in Shakespeare', Frederic B. Tromly writes the following about Gloucester's fall:

> [Edgar's purpose] was to convince [Gloucester] that there is a divine providence in which his life matters [. . .] Edgar stages a kind of miracle play to convince Gloucester that his attempt at suicide has been foiled by divine intervention [. . .] [the plan was constructed] to save his father from the spiritual death of despair.[32]

Tromly's explanation, though partly accurate, falls short by failing to recognize the historical relevancy of Edgar's 'treatment' of his father. Gloucester, suffering from a depression that an early modern audience would possibly have recognized as melancholy, begs Edgar, disguised as Poor Tom, to lead him to the Dover Cliffs (4.1.73–80). Winfried Schleiner writes that Gloucester's despair bears a similarity to the symptoms of one suffering from schizophrenia, 'with its attendant false images of the world [. . .] fear, pain, and despair'.[33] The scene that follows, and more specifically the remedy that Edgar seeks to apply to his psychologically ailing father, bears a similarity to the remedies employed by Renaissance doctors as well as by Martin Luther to the melancholics that were brought to him for pastoral treatment.

In Act 4, scene 6, Edgar leads Gloucester up an imaginary hill. This scene, involving the deception of Gloucester, is not cruel as Richard Wilson claims,[34] but by Reformation standards, full of grace and mercy. Recognizing the merciful nature of Edgar's staging of Gloucester's fall, Robert Miola describes this 'theatrical fiction' as 'a salvific action performed with costume'.[35] Edgar's ploy to heal Gloucester's imagination through the imagination was consistent with Renaissance psychiatric theory.[36] Edgar must work to entangle Gloucester in an imaginary world:

Gloucester:	When shall I come to th' top of that same hill?
Edgar:	You do climb up it now; look how we labour.
Gloucester:	Methinks the ground is even.
Edgar:	Horrible steep. Hark do you hear the sea?
Gloucester:	No, truly.
Edgar:	Why then, your other senses grow imperfect By your eyes' anguish.
Gloucester:	So may it be indeed. Methinks thy voice is alter'd, and thou speak'st In better phrase and matter than thou didst.
Edgar:	Y'are much deceiv'd: in nothing am I chang'd But in my garments.
Gloucester:	Methinks y'are better spoken.
Edgar:	Come on, sir; here's the place. Stand still. How fearful And dizzy 'tis to cast one's eyes so low! The crows and choughs that wing the mid-way air Show scarce so gross as beetles. Half-way down Hangs one that gathers samphire– dreadful trade! Methinks he seems no bigger than his head. The fishermen that walk upon the beach Appear like mice; and yond tall anchoring bark Diminish'd to her cock; her cock, a bouy Almost too small for sight. The murmuring surge That on th' unnumb'red idle pebble chafes Cannot be heard so high. I'll look no more; Lest my brain turn, and the deficient sight Topple down headlong.
Gloucester:	Set me where you stand. (4.6.1–24)

Gloucester's challenge of Edgar, claiming not to notice any incline and claiming to hear not the sea, but rather a slight change in Edgar's feigned accent, forces Edgar to work even harder at the creation of an imaginary world. The detail he employs, from birds to bugs, fishermen and samphire, creates in Gloucester a confidence in a world that does not exist. Edgar must draw his father from a world of despair into his own world of hope and promise. It is in Edgar's world of hope that Gloucester is redeemed. The old man's fall, and more importantly his redemption, serve as key parallels to King Lear's fall and his ultimate redemption.

Edgar:	Thy life's a miracle. Speak yet again.
Gloucester:	But have I fall'n, or no?
Edgar:	From the dreadful summit of this chalky bourn
	[. . .]
	therefore, thou happy father,
	Think that the clearest gods, who make them honours
	Of men's impossibilities, have preserved thee.
Gloucester:	I do remember now. Henceforth I'll bear
	Affliction till it do cry out itself
	'Enough, enough' and die
	[. . .]
Edgar:	Bear free and patient thoughts. (4.6.55–57, 72–79)

Sixteenth-century records of psychiatric cases and their respective treatments describe patients with maladies of a very similar nature to that of Gloucester. Some patients held strange notions that they had an alternative identity; others believed that they had a unique physical make-up or a dangerous internal problem; still others believed that God had called them to perform different acts of purgation. One patient of Luther's, a case recorded in his *Tischreden*, is described as one who is certain that God has called him to abstain from urinating. The case was handled in much the same way that Edgar handles Gloucester's melancholy. Luther's experience is related thus:

> Then someone came to him saying that he was doing right in castigating his body and that he should certainly stay with his resolve (to serve God and to make himself suffer), for one entered into heaven through many crosses and tribulations. The same person also pretended that he too had taken a vow not to urinate, but that since he had prided himself on this pledge and had thought to gain heaven by it, he had sinned more than if he had urinated; indeed, he had almost become a murderer of his own body. 'Thus all the world will say similarly of you, that you do so out of pride. Therefore give up your resolve and let nature have its course.' In this way he persuaded the melancholic to urinate.[37]

This course of therapy, orchestrated by Luther, involved creating an imaginary world. Like Edgar, Luther sought to save the delusional man by bringing him into another world, a world in which God does not demand men and women to castigate themselves but where men and women are forgiven and blessed with grace. This was in fact what Luther sought to do with the church at large through the Reformation.

Luther sought to offer men and women a paradigm shift, a shift in the way they thought about God, verified by a close reading of scripture. Just as Luther freed his patient, so Edgar freed Gloucester. Although Gloucester claims to 'shake patiently my great affliction off' (4.6.36), in truth his attempted suicide betrays his great impatience with affliction. Gloucester's greatest affliction is his knowledge of his own sin and shame. Just as Luther's patient was afflicted by a false theology – that God wanted him to pay for his sins and earn his forgiveness, so, too, is Gloucester afflicted. Certain that he must pay for his bad behaviour and cognizant of his helpless situation, his inability to fix what he has destroyed, Gloucester seeks to end his own life. Edgar's assurance that the gods have saved Gloucester, that the gods have spared him, allowed him to float down from the great cliffs like 'gossamer, feathers, air' (4.6.49), is all the assurance Gloucester needs in order to live on and accept his fate. Edgar's final command, to 'Bear free and patient thoughts' (4.6.79), is of special significance in light of Luther's connection to this episode. Luther's theology was one that put a particular emphasis on the freedom of the Christian. Free from blame, free from sin, free from damnation, Luther emphasized that the Christian did not need to per- form acts of purgation. Luther emphasized that God's grace was free, and that men and women did not need to earn their salvation. Acts of penance and other forms of castigation, even the purchasing of indul- gences, according to Luther, were not necessary. Luther criticized the Roman church for burdening men and women with harmful theology and for failing to teach of God's free grace and forgiveness.

Gloucester's melancholy, much like the melancholy described in Luther's *Tischreden*, is brought on by a theological misunderstanding. Much like Lear, Gloucester and Luther's patient must be humbled before they can enter into a healthy relationship with God and with others. In the psychiatric terms of the early modern period, Gloucester's broken imagination is healed by a work of the imagination. In the religious terms of the Reformation and the Renaissance, Gloucester and Luther's patient are healed by recognizing what Luther called a man's proper place before God.[38] These men, according to the writings of Luther, were bound by a false understanding of God and by a false understand- ing of themselves. Through a humiliating revelation both men are able to recover their emotional and spiritual vision and to move forward, bearing 'free and patient thoughts' (4.6.79).

Lear's fall can be described in terms of a downward spiral, a move- ment that begins at the banishment of Cordelia. Lear's moral blindness secures him a tenuous position between two competitive daughters. Goneril and Regan have no patience with their father and are grateful to see him choose to leave their homes rather than to stay with a smaller following. While it seems strange to argue in support of Goneril and Regan, Shakespeare does not give us much reason to hate the two sisters in the early stages of the play. When called upon to flatter their father, Goneril and Regan's acquiescence does not seem villainous next to Cordelia's seemingly harsh refusal. Later, when Lear's soldiers are wreaking havoc on Goneril's home, the logic Goneril employs for not allowing her father so many knights is reasonable:

> *Goneril*: This man hath had good counsel – a hundred knights!
> 'Tis politic, and safe, to let him keep
> At point a hundred knights! Yes, that on every dream,
> Each buzz, each fancy, each complaint, dislike,
> He may enguard his dotage with their powers
> And hold our lives in mercy. (1.4.315–20)

At the outset of the play, we see Lear engage his fancy and demand an offering of praise from his daughters. The text gives us every reason to trust Goneril's concern in this passage, for how can we be sure that more 'dark purposes' do not still lurk in the aging mind of Lear? If we take Regan at her word, her home is too small to house all one hundred of Lear's attendants.

> *Regan*: This house is little; the old man and's people
> Cannot be well bestowed.
> *Goneril*: 'Tis his own blame; hath put himself from rest
> And must needs taste his folly.
> *Regan*: For his particular, I'll receive him gladly,
> But not one follower. (2.4.287–92)

Regan is not moved by Goneril's statement of frustration, that Lear deserves to learn his lesson, but insists that she would gladly take him into her home. Even Regan's locking of the doors against Lear, shortly after his departure, seems excusable. She justifies her action by explaining once again that she fears Lear's potential for rage:

> *Regan*:   Shut up your doors.
> He is attended with a desperate train,
> And what they may incense him to, being apt
> To have his ear abused, wisdom bids fear. (2.4.303–6)

In this same passage, Regan echoes Goneril's prophetic word, claiming that Lear will grow in wisdom through a series of injuries, 'O sir, to wilful men / The injuries that they themselves procure / Must be their schoolmasters' (2.4.302–5).

Goneril and Regan do not sin against their father at the beginning of the play. Their flattery, though in many ways contemptible, is part of the courtly life they are a part of. Lear's claim to be 'more sinned against than sinning' (3.2.59) is not true, but instead further evidence of the king's moral blindness, his inability to see himself and the people around him clearly. It may be, as S. C. V. Stetner and Oscar B. Goodman claim, that Shakespeare's audience 'could only view an act of abdication as foolish, irresponsible, and damnable, since it invited civil war and disasters sufficient to rock the macrocosm'.[39] Stetner and Goodman refer to Celestine V, the pope who offered to abdicate his throne and to leave three cardinals in charge, as an historical parallel to Lear.[40] Like Lear, the abdicating pope was also viewed as a foolish man, full of self-interest. Lear is not a wounded soul as he departs from Regan's house, but a wounding soul. He is responsible for the deteriorating family, much more sinning than sinned against.

As the storm tears the clothing from Lear's body, it also takes from him his damning pride. The king is reduced to a humble man, and by act four he begins to speak like a thoughtful man, no longer blinded by pride and even able to give proper instruction to Gloucester:

Lear:	Thou must be patient. We came crying hither:
	Thou knowst the first time that we smell the air
	We wawl and cry. I will preach to thee: mark me.
Gloucester:	Alack, alack the day!
Lear:	When we are born we cry that we are come
	To this great stage of fools. (4.6.174–79)

This is the language of humility, Lear finally seeing himself as he truly is, a fool on a stage. The violence of Lear's humiliation is evidence of its Protestant design. Different from the mild employment of humiliation, as proposed by Aquinas,[41] Lear is not 'using humiliations as a medicine'.[42] The violent humiliation that Lear experiences is one that he has no control over; it is a humiliation that Reformation theologians would attribute to divine grace. Luther describes God as a father that disciplines those he loves with 'scourges and blows'.[43] It is this kind of discipline, according to Luther, that leads to clear self-knowledge and spiritual redemption.[44] In this manner, Lear is reduced to a humble state; his clear self-knowledge is evidenced by the fact that he does not fight to keep his dignity but confesses his human frailty.

Lear:	I know not what to say.
	I will not swear these are my hands: let's see –

> I feel this pinprick. Would I were assured
> Of my condition. (4.7.54–57)

Though he swings in and out of sanity in the final acts of the play, it is certain that Lear is conscious of his human frailty. His expression of self-doubt signals a change in Lear from proud to humbled, before man and before the gods.

Lear's confession draws us back to Regan's statement regarding Lear, that he 'hath ever but slenderly known himself' (1.1.294–95). Lear's confession here indicates that he is not in full possession of himself, that there are things he does not understand about himself and about life. Though Lear does not understand himself completely, his recognition of his own frailty and the frailty of his understanding is evidence of his growth of understanding. As Ewan Fernie writes, through the course of the play Lear moves 'through shame towards relationship'.[45] Lear does not refuse to admit weakness and ignorance, and thus his confession is a model of that which John Calvin describes as the perfect posture of a man.[46]

Lear's fall is compatible with Hooker's view of man, which the preacher expresses in this way, 'But for most men the doom of suffering is a necessity if they are to know the profundities of life.'[47] Though the play ends tragically, Lear leaning over the dead body of his beloved daughter, it may be argued that his sufferings have led him to a place where he can at last experience the greatest profundity of life, true and sincere love for another.

Notes

1   Kenneth Myrick, 'Christian Pessimism in King Lear', *in Shakespeare 1564–1964*, ed. by Edward A. Bloom (Providence: Brown University Press, 1964), pp. 56–70 (p. 67).
2   Ibid.
3   Ibid., pp. 66–67.
4   All references to *King Lear* in this essay are to William Shakespeare, *King Lear*, ed. by R. A. Foakes, The Arden Shakespeare, Third series (Walton-on-Thames: Thomas Nelson, 1997).
5   *King Lear*, ed. by Foakes, 2.2.16, note 16–18.
6   *King Lear*, ed. by Foakes, 4.6, note 231–40. Foakes claims that the accent is one of a West Country yokel.
7   Myrick, 'Christian Pessimism in King Lear', pp. 66–67. Gary W. Jenkins, 'Smith, Henry (ca. 1560–1591)', *Oxford Dictionary of National Biography* (Oxford: Oxford University Press, 2004).
8   Myrick, 'Christian Pessimism in King Lear', p. 61
9   Alison Shell, *Catholicism, Controversy and the English Literary Imagination, 1558–1660* (Cambridge: Cambridge University Press, 1999), p. 16.
10 Harold Bloom, *Shakespeare: The Invention of the Human* (New York: Riverhead Books, 1998), p. 455.
11 Ben Ross Schneider, Jr, '*King Lear* in Its Own Time: The Difference that Death Makes', *Early Modern Literary Studies*, 1.1 (1995), 3.1–49, 24.

12   Martin Luther, *Luther's Works*, ed. by Hilton C. Oswald (Saint Louis: Concordia Publishing, 1972), *XLVII*, pp. 5–16, 30–55.

13   John Calvin, *Institutes of the Christian Religion*, ed. by John T. McNeill, trans. by Ford Lewis Battles (Louisville: Westminster John Knox Press, 1960), 4.20.32.

14   Richard Hooker, *The Works of Richard Hooker*, ed. by John Keble, 3 vols (Oxford: Clarendon Press,1888), I, note 3, pp. 144–45.

15   Huston Diehl, 'Religion and Shakespearean Tragedy', in *The Cambridge Companion to Shakespearean Tragedy*, ed. by Claire McEachern (Cambridge: Cambridge University Press, 2002), pp. 86–102 (p. 91).

16   Luther, *Works*, *XLVII*, p. 346.

17   Luther, *Works*, *XXV*, Romans 15:33.

18   *The Oxford English Dictionary*, 2nd edn (Oxford: Clarendon Press, 1989), 'Miscreant', note 1.

19   Luther, *Works*, *XXV*, pp. 202–3.

20   Stephen Booth, 'On the Greatness of King Lear', in *Twentieth Century Interpretations of King Lear*, ed. by Janet Adelman (Englewood Cliffs, NJ: Prentice Hall, 1978), pp. 98–113 (p. 111).

21   Geoffrey L. Bickersteth, *The Golden World of 'King Lear' (Annual Shakespeare Lecture)* (London: Geoffrey Cumberlege, 1946), p. 5.

22   Stephen Greenblatt, 'Shakespeare and the Exorcists', in *Critical Essays on Shakespeare's King Lear*, ed. Jay L. Halio (New York: G. K. Hall, 1996), pp. 88–121 (p. 110).

23   Luther, *Works*, *LII*, pp. 58–59.

24   Calvin, *Institutes*, 36–37.

25   Hooker, *Works*, *III*, 'A Learned Sermon of the Nature of Pride', pp. 387–88.

26   Ramie Targoff, *Common Prayer: The Language of Prayer in Early Modern England* (Chicago: University of Chicago Press, 2001), p. 48.

27   Luther, *Works*, *LII*, pp. 52, 59.

28   Bickersteth, *The Golden World of 'King Lear'*, p. 23.

29   Luther, *Works*, *LII*, p. 59.

30   Frederick Buechner, *Speak What We Feel* (New York: HarperCollins, 2001), p. 132.

31   In note 3.7.67–69, R. A. Foakes includes a reference to Peter Brook's 1962 production of the play in which Cornwall gouges out Gloucester's eye with a spur.

32   Fred B. Tromly, 'Grief, Authority and the Resistance to Consolation in Shakespeare', in *Speaking Grief in English Literary Culture: Shakespeare to Milton*, ed. by Margo Swiss and David A. Kent (Pittsburgh: Duquesne University Press, 2002), pp. 20–41 (p. 35).

33   Winfried Schleiner, 'Justifying the Unjustifiable: The Dover Cliff Scene in King Lear', *Shakespeare Quarterly*, 36.3 (Autumn 1985), 337–43 (p. 338).

34   Richard Wilson, *Secret Shakespeare: Studies in Theatre, Religion, and Resistance* (Manchester: Manchester University Press, 2004), p. 285.

35   Robert Miola, 'Jesuit Drama in Early Modern England', in *Theatre and Religion: Lancastrian Shakespeare*, ed. by Richard Dutton, Alison Findlay, and Richard Wilson (Manchester: Manchester University Press, 2003), pp. 71–86 (p. 79).

36   Ibid.

37   Martin Luther, *Tischreden, III* (Weimar: Bohlau, 1983), pp. 52–3.

38   Luther, *Works*, *LII*, p. 59.

39   S. C. V. Stetner and O. B. Goodman, 'Lear's Darker Purpose', in *Literature and Psychology*, 18.2–3 (1968), 82–90 (p. 82).

40   Ibid.

41   Aquinas writes the following, describing humiliation as a spiritual discipline, employed by a man or woman to gain humility: 'The spontaneous embracing of humiliations is a practice of humility not in any and every case but when it is done for a needful purpose: for humility being a virtue, does nothing indiscreetly. It is then not humility but folly to embrace any and every humiliation: but when virtue calls for a thing to be done it belongs to humility not to shrink from doing it, for instance not to refuse some mean service where charity calls upon you to help your neighbours . . . Sometimes too, even where our own duty does not require us to embrace humiliations, it is an act of virtue to take them up in order to encourage others by our example more easily to bear what is incumbent on them: for a general will sometimes do the office of a common soldier to encourage the rest. Sometimes again we may make a virtuous use of humiliations as a medicine. Thus if anyone's mind is prone to undue self-exaltation, he may with advantage make a moderate use of humiliations, either self-imposed, or imposed by others, so as to check the elation of his spirit by putting himself on a level with the lowest class of the community in the doing of mean offices' (*The Catholic Encyclopedia*, online at www.newadvent. org/cathen/index.html).

42   Ibid.

43   A Reformation understanding of humiliation is represented by the following excerpt from *Luther's Works*. Luther's description is far more violent and severe than that found in the teachings of the Roman Catholic Church, especially as proposed by Aquinas. Luther writes: 'But we do not understand, and the reason is that the flesh stands in the way. It cannot endure the mortification of itself and hinders the spirit so that it cannot perceive the boundless love and goodwill of God towards us until it comes forth from this struggle and repels the hindrances of the flesh. But the same things are copiously handed down everywhere in Holy Scripture. For it is stated in Rev. 3:19: "Those whom I love, I reprove and chasten." In Prov. 3:11–12 we read: "My son, do not despise the Lord's discipline or be weary of His reproof, for the Lord reproves him whom He loves, as a father the son in whom he delights." These and other statements like them are very striking and memorable. But is it taking delight in a son to strike him with scourges and blows? Scripture certainly teaches this, and experience testifies the same. For those who are good and faithful fathers chastise their sons severely' (*Works, VI*, Gen. 33:1).

44   In the following passage Luther uses the story of Joseph (Gen. 42) to describe the process of humiliation as one that leads to redemption: 'Accordingly, Joseph deals rather harshly with his brothers. It is his purpose to urge them on to repentance and the acknowledgment of their sinfulness, to slay their smugness and drive them to despair by threatening death and punishments of every kind. He does not say that they will render satisfaction for sin in this manner, as the papists prattle. No, he wants to arouse grief and contrition and to induce them to seek health and cleansing for themselves . . . Thus God afflicts us with various disasters, not to punish us, although this really is a punishment. But He takes no pleasure in it. What, then, does He mean by sending so many troubles, vexations, sicknesses and so on? He does this in order that you may be led to a knowledge of your sin' (*Works, VII*, Gen. 42:8).

45   Ewan Fernie, *Shame in Shakespeare* (London: Routledge, 2002), p. 173.

46   Calvin, *Institutes*, 4.20.32.

47   Myrick, 'Christian Pessimism in King Lear', p. 62.

CHAPTER SEVEN

Critical Review: 'Great thing of us forgot'?: New British Angles on *King Lear*[1]

Willy Maley

Messenger:	News, madam.
	The British powers are marching hitherward.
Cordelia:	'Tis known before. (4.4.20–22)[2]

In recent years, critics concerned with *King Lear* as a dramatic depiction of the union of the crowns of England and Scotland at the turn of the seventeenth century, and with it the formation of a new British state which drew on myth as well as history to justify its existence, have been preoccupied with the play's politics. Everyone now agrees *Lear* is a British play, but not whether it is pro- or anti-union or pro- or anti-James, which is where the drama lies. If *Lear* 'deals with a new sense of Britishness subsequent to the accession of James I absent from the English dynastic focus of the history plays written under Elizabeth I', is it a development or denial of the supposedly patriotic and patriarchal line of the earlier histories? Does it complicate our sense of history and nation, and send us back to plays like *Henry V* – a British play in its own right – with a renewed sense of its author as sceptical rather than supportive of national paradigms?[3] New directions often rely on re-opening old routes and roots, and this emerging field of criticism revisits earlier contextual readings from an older historicist tradition. Between the shake-up of Britain in Shakespeare's time and the beginnings of a break-up at the end of the twentieth century, from union to devolution, *Lear* stands as a unique engagement with the politics of division and succession, yet it has been read predominantly as personal tragedy rather than political history, so the strand of criticism that insists on topicality has been submerged. Only now is the weight of criticism such that the British contexts are forced to the surface. In what follows I will map out the field, and ask whether *Lear* takes sides on the union debate, or if Shakespeare's drama is in fact constitutive of the problem of political division in its deepest form.

John Pocock famously characterized British studies as 'the plural history of a group of cultures situated along an Anglo-Celtic frontier and marked by an increasing English political and cultural domination'.[4] That process of cultural domination is mapped out in a series of plays that runs from *Gorboduc* (1561–1562) to *Cymbeline* (1610), a family of dramas that can be extended to include works less obviously engaged with the matter of Britain.[5] The Anglo–Celtic frontier and with it the plural history of Britain is nowhere more evident than in Shakespeare's *King Lear*, 'the most conspicuous example of his turn to British and archipelagic subject matter after 1603'.[6] In the play's two endings, Quarto (1608) and Folio (1623), Albany (Scotland) and Edgar (England) assume the mantle, respectively: 'Two models of monarchical union, Scoto–Britannic and Anglo–Scottish, compete within the fraught, exhausted density of the tragedy's ending'.[7] Do they endorse respectively a new Stuart dynasty and a more balanced partnership? Michael Warren's pioneering essay shows the transfer of dialogue from Albany to Edgar in the transition from Quarto to Folio.[8] Does this redistribution suggest a deliberate shift from Scotland to England in the intervening fifteen years? The play also presents, in its sources and adaptations, Welsh, Cornish, Kentish and even Irish alternatives and challenges to these models. These national and regional identities offer sites of resistance to mainstream metropolitan Englishness. John Kerrigan adds a further layer of ethnicity when he remarks: 'In *King Lear*, the British-Galfridian royal house shares the action with the Saxon-named Edgar and Edmund'.[9] Elsewhere, Kerrigan speaks of 'the Anglo-Celtic double-helix which entwines different versions of the Lear story'.[10] Others have taken up this notion of *Lear* embodying a hyphenated history. As Lyell Asher notes,

> a substantial seam of writing on *Lear* has developed around the idea that the play is on the cusp of a paradigm shift, though notions about what these paradigms are, and who or what represents them in the play, fill a broad spectrum.[11]

While Kerrigan elaborates an archipelagic framework for the play, carefully constructing its historical and theatrical contexts, he does so acutely mindful of the pitfalls:

> It would be fatuous to claim that the irregular, overloaded, speculative world of this tragedy can be reduced to topicality. Yet Lear's

'diuision of the Kingdome' (or, as the Quarto puts it, 'kingdomes') is what triggers the action, and the issue, disconcertingly, returns in the closing moments of the drama.[12]

Is it a matter of *King Lear* being 'reduced to topicality', rather than raised to relevance and resonance? John Draper, one of an earlier generation of contextual critics, unapologetically places the play in its original setting, bluntly insisting on *Lear* as a tragedy of state bound up with Britain rather than a domestic drama:

> The Elizabethans considered public life, the fall of kings and nations, the proper subject for tragedy; and one should look for a theme that is national rather than domestic [. . .] If [Cordelia] is the main figure, and the tragedy be mainly hers, this is crassly stupid dramaturgy.[13]

That nineteenth-century critics' view of the play as 'all pathos and no ethos' is a sign of misreading the map, failing to register that *Lear* is 'one of a series of studies in statecraft'.[14] Of course, in saying that the play is not about Cordelia, Draper offers a gendered vision of history and nationhood, at odds with more recent readings that would see patriarchy and patriotism at issue.

Philippa Berry is among those feminist critics who see in *Lear* a gendering of nation, so that 'female figures of sovereignty enjoy an especial importance in the play's analysis of the new identity of Britain'.[15] According to Berry,

> it is primarily through her absence [. . .] and above all in the muddled and mutable landscape of her digested jointure, that the play indicates the importance of Cordelia as a subtle refiguration of sovereignty as the 'bond' or 'knot' of Union.[16]

Berry offers a British reading of *Lear* that enriches our understanding of the play, providing a useful corrective to Draper's gendered interpretation:

> *Lear*'s figuration of Cordelia as the forgotten middle, or bond of British sovereignty, appears to warn of the dangers of neglecting the deeper meaning both of the political Union and of the unacknowledged relationship of sovereignty to the wasted or disinherited elements of society – a bond which also encompasses a relationship of suffering and death.[17]

When the mother country is threatened, daughters of Albion come into their own.

Lear is a play of doubling and division. Topicality adds texture. As much as in *Cymbeline* or *Hamlet*, the time is out of joint. For Lisa Hopkins:

> There is in *King Lear* a real sense of a pagan Britain, as is seen for instance in Cordelia's order 'A century send forth' (IV, iv, 6), anchoring us firmly back in a time when the customs and terminology of Rome had not yet been forgotten.[18]

This is also a pun for a *fin-de-siècle* moment. Disjuncture extends to genre: '*King Lear*, although invariably referred to as one of the four great tragedies, is equally classifiable as a history, as indeed the varying titles of the Quarto and Folio versions made clear.'[19] Between 'chronicle history' and 'tragedy', Quarto and Folio, England and Britain, *Lear* is a hinge work, troubling and transitional. Surveying criticism of the play, Marion Trousdale concluded that 'History and aesthetics are divided kingdoms'.[20]

In an essay entitled 'Shakespeare and Legendary History', Irving Ribner marked out the differences between Holinshed and Shakespeare, the latter presenting the French invasion led by Cordelia as a thwarted enterprise, in which 'Albany and Edgar, whose sympathies are entirely with Lear and Cordelia [. . .] fight on the side of Britain', because Shakespeare

> wished to affirm that even though one's sympathies might be on the side of the enemy, one's country had always to be defended and that one's country must always be victorious [. . .] *Lear* uses history in order to teach important political lessons; it does so as completely as any of the plays on actual English history, and it is thus, in every Elizabethan sense, a history play.[21]

It may be, 'in every Elizabethan sense, a history play', but *Lear* is neither Elizabethan nor English. Jacobean histories conform to different rules. Samuel Johnson rebuked Shakespeare for 'mingling customs ancient and modern, English and foreign',[22] but *Lear* is preoccupied precisely with what is foreign, and what is domestic.

Visions of Albion and Albany

> To thine and Albany's issues
> Be this perpetual (1.1.64–65)

Anglo–Scottish relations and British history were the stuff of drama long before *Lear*. As James Berg observes, 'Like *Lear*, *Gorboduc* is a division-of-the-kingdom tragedy'.[23] It also foreshadows the Quarto in envisaging a Scottish succession: '*Gorboduc*, which foresees Protestant arguments in later succession tracts and casts a Scot, Fergus of Albany, as an invading usurper taking advantage of the lack of a royal successor, was an early blow in the debate' around the Scottish succession.[24] Conversely, *Lear* is a drama focused on British dissolution resolved by fraternal action, as Albany (Scotland) and Edgar (England) salvage union from the jaws of division. Crucially, in the passage from Quarto to Folio, Albany yields to Edgar. The ghost of *Gorboduc*'s resistance to Scottish succession haunts Shakespeare's play. The letter from Goneril to Edmund that Edgar finds upon Oswald says of Albany: 'There is / nothing done, if he return the conqueror' (4.6.258–59). The key to *Lear* lies in the slip of the tongue between Albion and Albany. As Christopher Wortham reminds us: 'Poets of Shakespeare's day frequently identified Albany with Scotland, among them Spenser in the Lear section of *The Faerie Queene*. In any case, the title of Duke of Albany was a Scottish one and a contemporary reality'.[25] Annihilating Albion was the aim of union as far as James (Albany) was concerned. On 24 October 1604 the Union of Crowns was formalized, but by 1607 it was clear Parliament would not accept the deeper union James desired, so between the first performance of *Lear* on 26 December 1606 and publication of the 1608 Quarto something changed.[26] That Edgar supplants Albany in the 1623 Folio should come as no surprise. 'England' is never mentioned in *Lear*, except perhaps obliquely as 'Albion', yet the 'Great thing of us forgot' is Britain (5.3.235). In the Folio the 'British party' becomes the 'English party' (4.6.245).

The Dukedom of Albany in its early modern form dated from 1398. Henry Stuart, Lord Darnley, took the title in 1563 when he married Mary Queen of Scots. Lilian Winstanley identified Goneril and Albany with Mary and Darnley, and Rizzio with Oswald.[27] Modern critics appear less eager to pursue one-to-one correspondences. By the time Shakespeare wrote *Lear*, Mary's son James was Duke of Albany. As John Draper argues,

> a drama that contrasted England and Scotland separate and miserable over against a united Britain happy and prosperous, must have had a timely meaning; and a Duke of Albany, who, after many trials, is apparently left at the end, benign and powerful, in sole possession, to 'Rule in this realm and the gored state sustain' – this Duke of Albany was surely not a figure displeasing to the eyes of the contemporary holder of that name and title.[28]

Christopher Wortham reminds us of the importance of Albany to James, who 'divested himself of the title and had very recently bestowed it upon his own younger son, the infant Prince Charles, when Shakespeare wrote *King Lear*.'[29] *Lear* depicts a pivotal moment in Anglo–Scottish – or Albion-Albany – relations. As Draper reminds us: 'In October, 1604, James was "proclaim'd King of Great Britain, France and Ireland, that the Name of England might be extinct".'[30] A union that imperilled the very name and nation of England quickly becomes, in Pocock's terms, English political and cultural domination along an Anglo-Celtic frontier.

Claim?

Cordelia and Hibernia: The Irish Context

In William Warner's *Albions England* (1586) and George Owen Harry's *Genealogy of the High and Mighty Monarch, James* (1604) Lear descends from Brutus, but behind Lear also lies a Celtic myth with Irish and Welsh analogues, 'Lir' and 'Llyr' respectively.[31] In the anonymous play, *The true chronicle history of King Leir* (1605), Cordelia was to be married off to 'the rich King of Hibernia'.[32] Who this Hibernian King was we do not know for he quickly disappears from the drama and is absent from Shakespeare's version.[33] A trace of Ireland lingers in *Lear* when the king compares Cordelia to a Scythian, invoking a category understood by contemporaries like Spenser as bound up with Irish savagery:[34]

> The barbarous Scythian,
> Or he that makes his generation messes
> To gorge his appetite, shall to my bosom
> Be as well neighbored, pitied, and relieved,
> As thou my sometime daughter. (1.1.114–18)

In 1681 Irish playwright Nahum Tate rewrote *Lear*, bringing it back into line with the anonymous play of 1605, not bringing Hibernia back, but certainly reviving Cordelia. As has been noted, 'Tate was, if anything, actually "restoring" the "Lear" story's original shape and generic character after its "distortion" by Shakespeare'.[35] Critics have focused on Tate's revision as a royalist rewriting of the play as restoration romance rather than succession tragedy. In Tate's version, 'Gloster speaks pointedly of a "second birth of empire" and of "the king's blest restoration"' (5.6.117–18). As Scott Paul Gordon says:

> That Tate revised Shakespeare to defend established monarchy during the Exclusion Crisis suggests that the original play might have provoked different responses: staging a monarch's fall was dangerous practice, since all spectators might not find Lear's fall

unjust. Those who had no liking for monarchs [. . .] might consider death poetic justice for an imperious monarch who has cared little for his subjects.[36]

Irish painter James Barry rebelled against the Tate reading a century later with his republican rendition through the dramatic depiction of Lear cradling Cordelia while Albany and Edgar, in masculine solidarity prefiguring the future, look on. In Tate's time, James II held the title of Albany. If Tate painted a portrait of *Lear* as royal triumph, then Barry proposed a republican denouement. It is hard 'to make the final scene of Shakespeare's *Lear* tell a republican story', but ending in succession by merit more than birthright would seem to have republican credentials.[37] Kynda Boose sees a fruitless conclusion: 'The only figures who survive to emphasize the sterility of the final tableau are Albany, a widower, and Edgar, an unmarried son.'[38] However, for republicans like John Milton, royal succession was itself sterile compared with the rule of those most fit to rule. Fruitlessness can be overcome by foreign succession or usurpation or by non-lineal ascent. As Christy Desmet reminds us, George Bernard Shaw revisited *Lear* in 1919 in a work that sought to restore female rule: 'As a tragicomedy of private life, *Heartbreak House* sets the sexual/social games played by its denizens against a backdrop of lost empire.'[39] In another Irish version of the play, Marina Carr's *The Cordelia Dream* (2008), a daughter dreams of independence from a father who will not relinquish authority. Like her other oblique takes on Shakespeare – *Portia Coughlan* (1996) and *Ariel* (2002) – *The Cordelia Dream* offers no neat solutions to intractable problems, just a family drama that doubles as an allegory of patriarchy and partition.

Parricide Lost

Earlier incarnations of the Lear story existed in Holinshed's *Chronicles* (1577; 1587), Book II of Spenser's *The Faerie Queene* (1590), and the anonymous play – possibly by Michael Drayton – *The True Chronicle History of King Leir* (1605), but as has been noted:

> The most striking feature of these different legendary and historical narratives, from the perspective of a comparison between Shakespeare and Tate, is that all these versions tell the same story as in Tate's adaptation. The 'King Lear' story is a historical romance narrative of restoration, in all examples but those exemplified by the Shakespearean version.[40]

Versions of the Lear story in Holinshed and Spenser have been well covered, but another significant reading has been overlooked. John Milton's

History of Britain (1670), covering the period from earliest times to the Norman Conquest, offered accounts of three kings that gave their names to Shakespeare plays: Cymbeline, Macbeth and Lear. Milton's history is republican, and, despite its title, anglocentric. *The History of Britain*, whose revealing running header, 'The History of England', suggests its title page was an afterthought, sees Milton writing a jeremiad against monarchy. Misogyny and merit are at war, and Cordelia is one of few female rulers to emerge with any credit:

> Wherin her piety so prosper'd, as that she vanquish'd her impious Sisters with those Dukes; and *Leir* again, as saith the story, three years obtain'd the Crown. To whom dying, *Cordeilla* with all Regal Solemnities gave Burial in the Town of *Leicestre*. And then as right Heir succeeding, and her Husband dead, Rul'd the Land five years in Peace. Until *Marganus* and *Cunedagius* her two Sisters Sons, not bearing that a Kingdom should be govern'd by a Woman, in the unseasonablest time to raise that quarrel against a Woman so worthy, make War against her, depose her, and imprison her; of which impatient, and now long unexercis'd to suffer, she there, as is related, kill'd her self.[41]

Milton praised the modest majesty of Adam:

> in himself was all his state,
> More solemn than the tedious pomp that waits
> On princes when their rich retinue long
> Of horses led and grooms besmeared with gold
> Dazzles the crowd and sets them all agape. (*PL* 5.353–57)

Milton could not sympathize with Lear, but saw in Cordelia a critique of courtly flattery and model of merit. Tate's *Lear* followed close on the heels of Milton's, and Milton's agenda was resistant to the restoration narrative of Shakespeare's sources – and resistant to Shakespeare's appropriation by royalists – making Milton's take on *Lear* of particular interest.

This Darker Purpose I Acknowledge Mine

'England' occurs 245 times in nineteen Shakespeare plays, and 'English' 150 times in seventeen plays, yet 'English' only appears in the Folio *Lear*. Lear's threat to 'resume the shape which thou dost think / I have cast off forever!' (1.4.293–94) might be read as an allusion to the state he apparently renounced when he divided the kingdom(s). The casting out of old names like 'England' and the conjuration of new ones (that are also old) like 'Britain' is fraught with difficulties. Dan Brayton, in 'Angling in the Lake of Darkness: Possession, Dispossession, and the Politics of Discovery in *King Lear*', does some angling himself: 'Lear's test conjures up the ghosts of two distinct but related, arenas of political contestation in early modern England: demonic possession and territorial control'.[42] Brayton himself conjures up what is merely a ghost in the play, namely England, appearing unconcerned by the fact that 'England' – unless 'angling' is a sly allusion by Edgar, not beyond the bounds of belief – is absent from the play. The word 'British' occurs eight times in Shakespeare, five in *Cymbeline* and three in *King Lear*. *Cymbeline* is the only play to feature 'Briton' (nine times) and 'Britons' (eleven). But *Lear* is unique in terms of what happens between Albion and Albany, England and Scotland. Lear's dark materials are the matter of Britain: Lear expresses his 'darker purpose' (1.1.34) with the map; Gloucester's blind world is 'All dark and comfortless' (3.7.84); and Edgar declares that 'Nero is an angler in the lake of darkness' and speaks of 'the dark tower' (3.4.170). For the Fool, 'Out went the candle, and we were left darkling' (1.4.198), when the king is reduced to 'Lear's shadow' (1.4.212). Gloucester's allusion to 'these late eclipses' – 'These late eclipses in the sun and moon portend no good to us' (1.2.97–98) – has been taken to refer to the eclipses of the moon and sun on 17 September and 2 October 1605 respectively, but may also figure the eclipse of Tudor England by the glorious sun of Stuart. The true tale of two eclipses is that of England in the Quarto and Scotland in the Folio.

Edgar and England

Critics have identified the historical King Edgar as a positive image of English monarchy. For John Kerrigan,

> The collaging of periods becomes more explicable when one notices that Jacobean pamphlets about union often cite Edgar (who ruled 959–75) as the monarch who drew the seven kingdoms of Saxon England into a single polity while also laying claim, like James, to a more extensive, British imperium.[43]

Donna Hamilton and Marion Trousdale emphasize the resonance of Edgar not just as a well-regarded English King but as a name with Scottish significance for James's genealogy.[44] According to Hamilton, 'to those who see in *Lear* both a tragedy of individual man and a tragedy of state, the historical Edgars offer an additional context within which to contemplate the thematic reaches of what many have called Shakespeare's greatest tragedy'.[45] According to Meredith Skura,

Even more significant for audiences of Shakespeare's play, the historical King Edgar finally unified the divided kingdom, making all the separate princes on the island pay homage to him. Insofar as Edgar inherits this role, he is like Shakespeare's own new monarch, James I, prince of the newly united realm of Britain and first in a new dynastic line.[46]

Ironically, in *Lear*, it is Edgar who voices one of the play's British allusions:

> Childe Rowland to the dark tower came,
> His word was still 'Fie, fo, and fum,
> I smell the blood of a British man'. (3.4.171–72)

This riddling speech draws on the medieval poem *Le Chanson de Roland* and the fairy tale 'Jack the Giant Killer'.[47] Was King James a giant killer, slaying England in the name of a new British state? Or was he a giant-maker, forging Great Britain out of England's ashes? The question of who was of British blood, as opposed to English, was complex. Britain was a convenient fiction consequent on a dynastic accident. As Linda Colley notes, 'The idea of Britain was invented to give credibility to the union'.[48] The post-Nati debate (Calvin's Case) in the English parliament after the Union of Crowns in 1604 aimed to decide which Scots (for example) counted as 'British', those born after the Union or those born before.[49] After being given the last word in the Folio, Edgar emerged as a laudable model of monarchical authority. As C. B. Hardman observes, prior to Tate's version of *Lear*, 'two contemporary plays [. . .] took Edgar as their subject', Edward Ravenscroft's *King Edgar and Alfreda* (1677) and Thomas Rymer's *Edgar or the English Monarch* (1678).[50] These celebrations of Edgar as King culminate in Tate's royalist revision of Shakespeare's republican ending.

Foreign Invasion as Domestic Salvation

An English lord recites an old saying at the opening of Shakespeare's last Elizabethan English history play, *Henry V*:

> 'If that you will France win,
> Then with Scotland first begin' (1.2.167–68)

He goes on to elaborate:

> For once the eagle England being in prey,
> To her unguarded nest the weasel Scot
> Comes sneaking, and so sucks her princely eggs. (1.2.169–71)

In *Lear* a different scenario presents itself. The weasel Scot comes to England's rescue. W. W. Greg says of the French invasion:

> In the old play of *King Leir*, where the aged monarch is restored to his throne and all ends happily, sympathy is of course wholly on the side of the invaders, and the author does not appear to be conscious of raising any political issue. To Shakespeare, whose dramatic reputation had been built on a long series of patriotic 'histories', such political naivety or detachment was impossible.[51]

But is Shakespeare so simple a patriot, even in the histories? Certainly among the 'British' plays the Roman invasion in *Cymbeline* and the English invasion in *Macbeth* paint a more complex picture.[52] Derek Cohen refreshes Greg's line, arguing that

> when the nation is threatened, even if [. . .] governed by the likes of Goneril, Regan, Edmund, and Albany, most people will choose to defend their country. The neat binary of French and English is complicated and obscured, but it completes a trajectory of oppositionality introduced with Lear's map of a Britain cut into three parts.[53]

Just as in *Cymbeline* the patriots are the wicked queen and her evil son, so the Britons ready to defend the nation against invasion – not all of them against the restoration of the king – are a motley crew. Cohen reminds us that post-Armada the threat of invasion united audiences:

> To choose between Goneril and Regan and Cordelia and Lear seems a simple matter. But the simplicity is a delusion [. . .] further complicated by the fact that the two leading magnates in charge of repelling the invading French are Edmund and Albany, men of opposite inclination who unite in defense of the English state. Albany puts the matter plainly: 'France invades our land, / Not bolds the king, with others, whom, I fear, / Most just and heavy causes make oppose' (V.i.25–7). This speech is present only in the Quarto version (1607–1608), *The History of King Lear* (scene 22, lines 27–9), and does not appear in the Folio (1623). It foregrounds the unresolved ethical and military dilemma Britons must face. For them, in the audience and on the stage, it is a problem with no clear solution. That it is a simple matter for the likes of Oswald, who is driven, according to his last words, by a desire to save England from foreign invasion, makes it only the more complex and difficult.[54]

Greg speaks of an 'Elizabethan audience' and Donna Hamilton of 'Shakespeare's England', but Jacobean Britain draws a more complex figure.[55] Oswald may be of the devil's party, but he is on the side of the Britons rather than the Angles, at least in the Quarto, which has 'British party' in the following speech:

> *Oswald:* Slave, thou hast slain me. Villain, take my purse.
> If ever thou wilt thrive, bury my body;
> And give the letters which thou find'st about me
> To Edmund, Earl of Gloucester; seek him out
> Upon the English party: O untimely death! Death!
> (4.6.243–48)

Shakespeare, too, may be of the devil's party,[56] but is he with the British Party (Quarto), the English party (Folio), or the foreign invasion that seeks to restore the old order? Philip Schwyzer notes the problematic nature of the British references in *Lear*, allusions to 'powers', 'party' and 'blood':

> All three references are rather troubling for British nationalism, those involving Edmund and the army because they seem to associate Britishness with illegitimacy, treachery, and parricide, and Edgar's song because it comes across as an awkwardly self-conscious and perhaps self-consciously awkward substitution of the traditional 'English' for the more politically correct 'British'. Here at last is that precious substance, British blood, extolled by Thornborough, Harry, Harbert, and others. Unfortunately, the blood of the hapless Briton in the song provides him with an identity only inasmuch as it exposes him as prey.[57]

Gloucester's repeated reference to 'brutish' (1.2) puns on British, suggesting no love lost between playwright and new polity: 'GLOUCESTER: Abhorred villain, unnatural, detested, brutish villain! Worse than brutish!' (1.2.73–74). In *The Tempest*, Caliban is 'A thing most brutish' (1.2.344), suggesting there was still mileage in the pun when it came to conflating Britishness and barbarism.

Mapping Britain   → *Connects w/ Gilles*

Everyone knows the Shakespeare play where an ancient British ruler calls for a map to divide the kingdom into three. The scene occurs in *1 Henry IV*, when Glendower, Prince of Wales, declares:

> Come, here's the map: shall we divide our right,
> According to our threefold order ta'en? (3.1.67–68)

This 'threefold order' is taken further in *King Lear*, and recent critics have mulled over Lear's map. According to Gavin Hollis, '*King Lear's* first performances (c.1604–1605) coincided with something of a carto-graphic boom, as a fast developing culture of cartography permeated many levels of English society'.[58] For Dan Brayton, 'the map, like Cordelia's illusory breath on the mirror, is something that is nothing, an emblem of absence that reflects upon the king himself. The map and the mirror become emblems of nothing and loss'.[59] However, most com-mentators see the map as not just metaphor or prop, but as a material text underpinning the play's action. John Gillies stresses the theatrical-ity of cartography.[60] For Terence Hawkes, 'it is precisely at the moment when Lear calls for the map that the play begins to engage with issues of large cultural concern and starts to contribute to their discussion'.[61] Valerie Traub comments on the extent to which *Lear* is a play crafted through cartography.[62] Yet for a play that opens with a map, *Lear* has a disoriented geography. Dover, according to W. W. Greg, is 'the only place mentioned in *King Lear* as connected with the action'.[63] As a meet-ing point it is a strange setting, marked by blindness, disguise and despair, 'as the king attempts to traverse the unmapped, indefinite, and, as A. C. Bradley noted long ago, confused topography of the play's imagined Britain'.[64] For Frederick Flahiff, 'That an imaginary view from a non-existent cliff should be the occasion for the play's most striking instance of scenic writing is not altogether surprising in the topsy-turvy world of Lear's unmade map'.[65] While Greg insists 'there is really no more reason why Gloucester should live near Gloucester than that Albany should live in Scotland',[66] Dan Brayton detects a titular topography:

> Geography and aristocratic identity are inextricably linked in the imaginary feudal social order that the play constructs. We need only glance at the names of the male characters in the first scene, Albany, Gloucester, Cornwall, France, Burgundy, and Kent to see that territory and identity are deeply connected in the aristocratic transaction of power.[67]

Flahiff maintains that map morphs into meal in that opening scene:

> when he commands Cornwall and Albany to *digest* this third (1.1.128), not only does Lear repudiate merit and disregard the apparent precision of his original design; more ominously, he invites his sons-in-law to partake of the strangest of this play's strange meals, one which sees the map become a table-cloth and the kingdom assimilated into the persons of the king's heirs.[68]

According to Gavin Hollis, 'The opening scene of *King Lear* collapses the national into the local by having the titular monarch behave like a landlord', a conflation of state and estate in keeping with the play's blurring of personal and political identity.[69]

Characters embody places, as Ralph Berry reminds us: 'Always one must think of titles as denoting possession of land, and not as empty honorifics.'[70] With Cornwall, Gloucester, Kent, Albany, Burgundy and France circling the crown, England appears as a missing middle, a hole in the heart of Lear's Britain filled in the Folio by Edgar's ascent and Albany's eclipse. That there is neither the name of 'England' in *Lear*, nor 'heath', has not deterred critics from putting them there, but nor should their absence in name prevent us from seeing an England of the mind mapped out in the world of Gloucester and his royal retainers, the lists of wildflowers, Poor Tom, fairy tales and Dover. Moreover, Cordelia's is the prime portion of the map.[71] Britain itself is also absent, as Nicholas Visser notes, for among the male characters addressed by their territory is a notable exception: 'Curiously, one character not so addressed is Lear himself, who is never called "Britain", though the King of France carries the name of his realm'.[72] Lear is associated with the founding of Leicester (Leir's Castle), and Lisa Hopkins detects a link with the Earl of Leicester, making Lear's Britain resemble Leicester's commonwealth, a dystopian vision of autocracy and ruination.[73]

Canon Fire and Regional Dissent

Several critics detect a response to the Gunpowder Plot in the play. According to Nina Taunton and Valerie Hart, 'Shakespeare did not fail to capitalize on the newly erupted scandal of the Gunpowder Treason'.[74] An interesting sidelight on that event comes in Sir Edward Coke's claim at the trial of the plotters in January 1606 that they intended 'the destruction and dissolution of the frame and fabric of this ancient, famous and ever-flourishing monarchy; even the deletion of our whole name and nation'.[75] The deletion of the whole name and nation of England by Britain was already underway. Paradoxically, the process proved reversible. English domination survived the Anglo–Celtic encounter to reign over the expanding British state and empire.

Cornwall and Albany, sometimes viewed as two sides of the same Celtic coin, have different connotations. The Earl of Cornwall was a role occupied in its last two incarnations first by the royal favourite, Piers Gaveston, then by Edward II's second son, Prince John, who died in 1336 before he came of age, and the title with him. Marlowe's play has several allusions to Gaveston as Earl of Cornwall. Mark Stoyle has illustrated the extent to which Cornwall played a crucial role in the transition from

Tudor to Stuart rule, remaining a site of resistance to central authority from the 1490s through to the 1640s.[76] The death of Prince Arthur on 2 April 1502 meant Henry became heir to the throne and in October was duly named Duke of Cornwall, and in February 1503 Prince of Wales and Earl of Chester. A century later, on the accession of James VI, his eldest son, Prince Henry, acquired the title of Duke of Cornwall, while his younger son, Prince Charles, was created Duke of Albany at his baptism in 1605. Henry's death made Charles heir to the kingdoms of Britain and Ireland and he became Duke of Cornwall. Hitherto, Cornwall had trumped Albany. By 1612, the two titles were united in one future king, making Edgar's supplanting of Albany in the Folio less problematic.

If Cornwall was one distinctive English region, Kent was another area with a tradition of political particularity and resistance, with strong local interests often carried to London. The loyal servant banished by his deluded master bids farewell with the words: 'He'll shape his old course in a country new' (1.1.185). Yet even had he not been banished, Kent would have found himself in a 'country new', a newly divided kingdom, while his name locates him in an old county of an old country. Kent's allusion to a 'scatter'd kingdom' (3.1.31) invokes the jigsaw make-up of Britain in the period. Ronald Cooley emphasizes the significance of Kent as a distinctive region:

> Why is Shakespeare's Kent called Kent? It is a little surprising that the question has been so seldom asked, given that *King Lear*'s only precisely named location is in Kent: Dover, where both Lear and Gloucester flee to meet Cordelia and her French army. Names, however arbitrary and conventional, almost invariably evoke specific associations, particularly when they are also aristocratic titles (Kent is, after all, the Earl of Kent), laden with associations linked to the towns, counties, and regions from which those titles are derived.[77]

There is a Britain of the regions as well as the nations, and if a Celtic fringe encircles Lear's empty crown – one that includes Cornwall – then even in a place as English as Dover claims to exceptionality persist. Kent, like Cornwall, was a seedbed of radicalism, with the Wyatt Rebellion of 1554 having its origins there.[78]

Lear's attempt through marriage alliances to make England's Celtic neighbours subject nations runs the risk that the Celtic nations will infringe upon England. Goneril weds Albany, and Regan Cornwall, while Cordelia goes off with France. In *The True Chronicle Historie of King Leir* (1605), the third Celtic neighbour – besides Cambria (Wales) and Cornwall – is initially Ireland, not France. Lear wishes Cordelia betrothed to 'the rich King of Hibernia' (A1), but 'Hitherto she ne'er could fancy him' and so goes off with Gallia. In the *True Chronicle* a noble explains the purpose of the proposed marriages of Leir's daughters:

> To match them with some of your neighbour Kings,
> Bordring within the bounds of Albion,
> By whose united friendship, this our state
> May be protected 'gainst all forrayne hate. (2)

We are back with Pocock, and an Anglo–Celtic alliance benefiting England. But are we any closer to decoding the politics of Shakespeare's play? Is it unionist, showing the effects of disunion, or anti-unionist, arguing that Albion must overcome Albany? Cyndia Susan Clegg appears to concur with Andrew Gurr's view of the play as loyalist/royalist: 'Even if Shakespeare did not write *Lear* at James I's behest, the play's position that a divided kingdom was a perilous thing, must have appealed to the Master of the Revels as he prepared the Christmas entertainments in 1606.'[79] Conversely, Philippa Berry sees *Lear* as 'dramatic antimasque', reacting against royalist panegyrics, and thus a Trojan horse at the heart of Britishness.[80]

John Draper was an early advocate of a reading of the play as preoccupied with union:

> The question of a divided, as opposed to a united, Britain is fundamental in the play. According to Holinshed, and obviously in Shakespeare, Lear is King of all Britain: the play refers to 'a British man', the 'British powers' as opposed to France, and the quarto of 1608 to the 'British party'. The dividing of Lear's realm is the first action depicted on the stage, and has every appearance of theatrical significance. At the very beginning of the initial scene, Kent and Gloucester are discussing this 'division'. After the old King has had his will and disinherited Cordelia, Kent objects, not only to this injustice, but to the whole 'hideous rashness', and, according to the folio text, cries out, 'Reserve thy state', and later, 'Revoke thy gift': apparently, this honest counsellor objects to the division as such, and will risk his head to warn his master.[81]

'Reserve thy state' (1.1.147) says Kent in the Folio, and at the close of the play he urges Albany/Edgar to 'the gored state sustain' (5.3.322), punning on 'gored' and 'stain'.

For Philip Schwyzer, 'The enduring habit of reading *King Lear* as a unionist work rests above all on the evident parallel between Lear's division of Britain between his three daughters and Brutus's division of the island between his three sons'. Schwyzer contends that *Lear* 'can be read as anti-unionist drama, subversively celebrating the division of Britain into England, Scotland, and Wales as a natural, inevitable, and irreversible historical process'.[82] Jonathan Gibson sees the play's strength in its balance between union and division:

> The figure of Lear is commonly glossed as an antitype of James, his dismemberment of his kingdom(s) signally contrasting with James's plans for union between England and Scotland. Many elements in the play, however, provide ammunition for the argument that *King Lear* was conceived as an implicit attack on James. In the final analysis, the play's relationship to King James seems uneasily balanced between panegyric and satire.[83]

According to Schwyzer, 'The word "British" occurs only three times in the Quarto text of *King Lear* (and just twice in the Folio), and the word "Britain" is never uttered at all'. When Schwyzer says, 'The world of *Lear* is not only ghostless, it is exorcized', the exorcized aspect is England initially, but Britain thereafter. Schwyzer insists that '*King Lear*'s negative program, its rebuttal of British nationalism through the systematic dismantling of its cherished tropes of survival and revival, runs to the very heart of the tragedy'.[84] What is exorcized in *King Lear*? Much has been made of Samuel Harsnett's *Declaration of Egregious Popish Impostures* (1603) as source-text.[85] Less noticed is Harsnett's *Discouery of fraudulent practises* (1599), which takes a sceptical view of Scotland and witches during a discussion of William Somers, who '*had named certain persons to be Witches*' as '*hath commonly hapned in Scotland*', concluding that 'those whom *Somers* had named for witches, no man could iustly blame'.[86] Likewise, in the *Declaration*, Ireland features as a threatening Other, 'a Furie from Hell', in whose bosom lurk those 'by terrifying of some, & peruerting of others, with strange reports of the strength, and preparation of the King of Spaine, and the Pope, ready to inuade this Land'.[87]

Frederick Flahiff, like Schwyzer, notes George Owen Harry's 1604 *Genealogy* of James I, tracing his lineage to Lear: 'according to Harry, the union of the English and Scottish lines in James was anticipated for the first time in the marriage of Lear's daughter Ragan to Henwyn, Duke of Cornwall'.[88] Lear's proposed division into three (which becomes two) echoes that of Brutus and Noah, 'reminding us that Britain's history began when, after a great flood, an old man, the world's *first Monarch*, called together his three children and divided the known world among them'.[89] As well as dipping into the deep past of myth and history, *Lear* contains a prophecy predicting a cloudy future for England:

Fool: Then shall the realm of Albion come to great confusion.
        Then comes the time, who lives to see't,

That going shall be used with feet.
This prophecy Merlin shall make, for I live before his time.
(3.2.91–94)

Andrew Hadfield draws our attention to the sense in which *Lear*, as a prophetic play, is riddled with historical ironies:

> Lear destroys Britain, while James was attempting – although unsuccessfully – to unite it. As if these parallels did not make the point obvious enough, James's two sons, Henry and Charles, had just been made duke of Cornwall and duke of Albany, the names of the suitors of Regan and Goneril. *King Lear* both reflects and inverts the contemporary political situation of James, representing a king who tears Britain apart in the mistaken belief that he is handing over a secure and well-ordered kingdom to the next generation. His plan may be to ensure a balance of power in Britain, but the result is a destructive civil war.[90]

As noted, with Henry's death, Charles became both Albany and Cornwall, and in his reign the three kingdoms would witness a destructive civil war.[91]

Albion and Albany remained in tension throughout the century. In Sir James Ware's edition of Edmund Spenser's *A View of the State of Ireland* (1633), under the heading 'Faults escaped', the following entry appears: 'pag. 27.lin.28. in some copies, for "Albany", read either "Albion" or "England".'[92] This refers to the crucial quote (in Ware's edition) casting doubt on the Brutus myth, where scepticism 'that there was ever any such *Brutus* of *England*' reads '*Brutus* of *Albany*' in some printings. Brutus of Albany would be Brutus of Scotland, and eager as he was to make the Irish Scots, Spenser had no wish to make the English Scots too. Fifty years after Ware's edition of Spenser's *View*, another writer grappled with relations between Albany and Albion:

> When Charles died suddenly in 1685 Dryden was writing an opera later to be called *Albion and Albanius*, including Charles (Albion) and also his successor James (Albanius) in the title. There can be little doubt that James's part was already prominent before his brother's death, though that event may have brought about a change of title. [. . .] Albion was the name given in the chronicles to the Britain ruled over by Brute after his flight from fallen Troy and more pertinently here was, as Spenser recorded (*Faerie Queene*, iv), the name of a mythical son of Neptune.[93]

Lear depicts a decisive moment of transition in Anglo–Scottish – or Albion-Albany – relations.

The Theatre of the Empire of Great Britain

James I presided over a union that threatened the loss of old names like 'England' and 'Scotland' – Albion and Albany – in favour of a new name with an old pedigree. In addition to 'division', critics use a variety of terms to describe Lear's break-up of Britain, from 'abdication'[94] to 'devolution' and 'divestment'.[95] *Lear* dramatizes homelessness in a new state, or statelessness in a new home. Peter Womack speaks of 'the extraordinary sense that *King Lear* belongs to beggars and outcasts, even though its *dramatis personae* are aristocrats and their servants'.[96] According to Womack,

> the new King's iconography made much of his uniting the crowns of England and Scotland, and this placed a premium on plays about 'Britain', the unified island which was supposed to have been ruled for generations before the coming of the Romans by the lineal descendants of the name-giving Trojan founder, Brutus.[97]

As John Kerrigan reminds us, King James warned Prince Henry of the danger of division in *Basilikon Doron* (1599):

> 'otherwayes by deuiding your Kingdomes, yee shall leaue the seede of diuisione and discorde among your posteritie'. A London edition of 1603 adds: 'as befell this Ile: by the diuision and assignement thereof, to the three sonnes of *Brutus*, *Locrine*, *Albanact*, and *Camber*'.[98]

Peter Holland surveys a series of British plays – including *Gorboduc*, *King Leir*, *Locrine*, *The Misfortunes of Arthur*, and *Thomas of Woodstock* – to which one might add John Fletcher's *Bonduca* – that can be read as part of Shakespeare's context for *King Lear*.[99] As Holland says, 'it may be that it is *King Lear* that should most properly have been called *The Theatre of the Empire of Great Britaine*', and not John Speed's cartographic enterprise of 1611.[100] Then again, perhaps its prominent division of the kingdom(s) makes the play stand equally today as a drama of devolution. If the new direction in Shakespeare studies that claims *Lear* as a British play, recalling a great thing of us forgot – the question of union and the constituent parts of an emerging state – leaves open the question of whether it is pro- or anti-British, or the kind of Britain it endorses or rejects, this need not be viewed as a failure of interpretation. S. H. Clark, in ' "Ancestral Englishness" in *King Lear*', views such vacillation as productive. Drawing on the work of Homi Bhabha, Clark suggests that 'dissidence within state ideology' and 'tragic epiphany' can be approached in ways that see the forgetting of Lear, in whom the fractured state is figured, and the forgetting of an ancestral Englishness – or ancient Britishness – as bound up together: 'the peculiar rupture of the final scene depends upon the co-presence of incompatible temporal frameworks, the tension between which is productive of a new mode of national self-determination'.[101] Where Kerrigan questioned the capacity of topicality to convey texture, Clark suggests historical and dramatic tensions are closely intertwined. Placing the play in a British context – or contexts – does not detract from the drama, but rather reveals from whence it draws some of its power. If the Folio backtracks on the Britishness of the Quarto, then the Quarto itself expresses anxiety about the loss of identity accompanying enlargement of the state.

How did the disappearance of 'England', an absence at the heart of *Lear* become the disappearance of Britain? In 'The Occasion of *King Lear*', John Draper, citing Arthur Wilson's *History of Great Britain, Being the Life and Reign of James I*, wrote:

> When King James in 1603 came down from Scotland to claim the thrones left vacant by the death of Queen Elizabeth, he had himself, as soon as possible, 'Proclaim'd King of Great Britain: England must be no more a Name; the Scotch coins are made current; and our Ships [so writes the chronicler] must have *St. George's* and *St. Andrew's* Crosses quartered together in their Flags, and all outward Ensigns of Amity'.[102]

Ironically, it was not England that was 'no more a Name' with the Act of Union, but Britain and Scotland. Conjuring Britain into being looked like it might entail exorcizing England. It transpired the reverse was true. 'Triumph my Britain' was Ben Jonson's cry, but it was Shakespeare and England that triumphed. On the eve of the Union of Parliaments Wilson's history was reprinted, ironically, as part of *A Complete History of England* (London, 1706). A writer with a great British name had been anglicized, and in some sense that's the story of *Lear* and of Shakespeare.

Notes

1 I am grateful to the editors, and also to Andrew Hadfield, John Kerrigan, Rob Maslen and Philip Schwyzer, for commenting on a draft of this chapter and making helpful suggestions.
2 Unless otherwise indicated, all references to *King Lear* are to, *King Lear*, ed. by Grace Ioppolo (New York: W. W. Norton, 2008). All references to Shakespeare's other plays are to *The Norton Shakespeare: Based on the Oxford Edition*, ed. by Stephen Greenblatt et al. (1997).

3   S. H. Clark, '"Ancestral Englishness" in *King Lear*', *Shakespeare Studies* (The Shakespeare Society of Japan), 31 (1996), 35–63 (pp. 53–54).

4   J. G. A. Pocock, 'British History: A Plea for a New Subject', *Journal of Modern History*, 47 (1975), 601–28 (pp. 605–6).

5   Gordon McMullan, 'The Colonization of Early Britain on the Jacobean Stage', in *Reading the Medieval in Early Modern England*, ed. by David Matthews and Gordon McMullan (Cambridge: Cambridge University Press, 2007), p. 137.

6   John Kerrigan, *Archipelagic English: Literature, History, and Politics 1603–1707* (Oxford: Oxford University Press, 2008), p. 14.

7   Kerrigan, *Archipelagic English*, p. 17.

8   Michael Warren, 'Quarto and Folio *King Lear* and the Interpretation of Albany and Edgar', in *Shakespeare: Pattern of Excelling Nature*, ed. by David Bevington and Jay L. Hallo (Newark: University of Delaware Press, 1978), pp. 95–107.

9   Kerrigan, *Archipelagic English*, p. 123.

10 John Kerrigan, 'Divided Kingdoms and the Local Epic: *Mercian Hymns* to *The King of Britain's Daughter*', *The Yale Journal of Criticism*, 13.1 (2000), 1–21 (p. 9).

11 Lyell Asher, 'Lateness in *King Lear*', *Yale Journal of Criticism*, 13.2 (2000), 209–28 (p. 216).

12 Kerrigan, *Archipelagic English*, p. 16.

13 J. W. Draper, 'The Occasion of *King Lear*', *Studies in Philology*, 34.2 (1937), p. 183.

14 Draper, 'The Occasion of *King Lear*', p. 184.

15 Philippa Berry, 'Cordelia's Bond and Britannia's Missing Middle: *King Lear* (c.1606)', in *Shakespeare's Feminine Endings: Disfiguring Death in the Tragedies* (London: Routledge, 1999), pp. 135–66 (p. 149).

16 Berry, 'Cordelia's Bond and Britannia's Missing Middle', p. 154.

17 Berry, 'Cordelia's Bond and Britannia's Missing Middle', p. 156.

18 Lisa Hopkins, 'The Edge: *King Lear*', in *Shakespeare on the Edge: Border-crossing in the Tragedies and the Henriad* (Aldershot: Ashgate, 2005), pp. 115–36 (p. 122).

19 Hopkins, 'The Edge: *King Lear*', p. 126.

20 Marion Trousdale, 'A Trip Through the Divided Kingdoms', *Shakespeare Quarterly*, 37.2 (1986), 218–23 (p. 221).

21 Irving Ribner, 'Shakespeare and Legendary History: *Lear* and *Cymbeline*', *Shakespeare Quarterly*, 7.1 (1956), 47–52 (p. 51).

22 *King Lear*, ed. by Grace Ioppolo (New York: W. W. Norton, 2008), p. 171.

23 J. E. Berg, '*Gorboduc* as a Tragic Discovery of "Feudalism"', *Studies in English Literature*, 40.2 (2000), 199–226 (p. 202).

24 Berg, '*Gorboduc* as a Tragic Discovery of "Feudalism"', p. 204.

25 Christopher Wortham, 'Shakespeare, James I and the Matter of Britain', *English*, 45.182 (1996), 97–122 (p. 111).

26 Andrew Hadfield, 'The Power and Rights of the Crown in *Hamlet* and *King Lear*: "The King – The King's to Blame"', *Review of English Studies*, n.s. 54.217 (2003), 566–86 (p. 578).

27 Lilian Winstanley, '*Macbeth*', '*King Lear*' and Contemporary History (Cambridge: Cambridge University Press, 1922), pp. 153–54.

28 Draper, 'The Occasion of *King Lear*', p. 182.

29 Wortham, 'Shakespeare, James I and the Matter of Britain', p. 112.

30 Draper, 'The Occasion of *King Lear*', p. 177.

31 Kerrigan, 'Divided Kingdoms and the Local Epic', p. 13.

32 Anon., *The True Chronicle History of King Leir* (1605), p. 4.

33 Andrew Hadfield, '"Hitherto she ne're could fancy him": Shakespeare's "British" plays and the exclusion of Ireland', in *Shakespeare and Ireland: History, Politics,*

Culture, ed. by Mark Thornton Burnett and Ramona Wray (London: Macmillan, 1997), pp. 47–67 (p. 53).

34   Andrew Hadfield, 'Briton and Scythian: Tudor Representations of Irish Origins', *Irish Historical Studies*, 28.112 (1993), 390–408.

35   Graham Holderness and Naomi Carter, 'The King's Two Bodies: Text and Genre in *King Lear*', *English*, 45.181 (1996), 1–31 (p. 4).

36   Scott Paul Gordon, 'Reading Patriot Art: James Barry's *King Lear*', *Eighteenth-Century Studies*, 36.4 (2003), 491–509 (p. 493).

37   Gordon, 'Reading Patriot Art: James Barry's *King Lear*', p. 495.

38   Cited in *King Lear*, ed. by Ioppolo, p. 208.

39   Christy Desmet, 'Some *Lears* of Private Life, from Tate to Shaw', in *'King Lear': New Critical Essays*, ed. by Jeffrey Kahan (New York: Routledge, 2008), pp. 326–50 (p. 344).

40   Holderness and Carter, 'The King's Two Bodies: Text and Genre in *King Lear*', p. 3.

41   John Milton, *The History of Britain: A facsimile edition with a critical Introduction*, ed. by Graham Parry (Stamford: Watkins, 1991), p. 60.

42   Dan Brayton, 'Angling in the Lake of Darkness: Possession, Dispossession, and the Politics of Discovery in *King Lear*', *English Literary History*, 70.2 (Summer 2003), 399–426 (p. 405).

43   Kerrigan, *Archipelagic English*, p. 17.

44   Donna Hamilton, '*King Lear* and the Historical Edgars', in *Renaissance Papers, 1982*, ed. by A. L. Deneef and M. T. Hester (Raleigh: The South-eastern Renaissance Conference, 1983), pp. 35–42 (p. 38); Trousdale, 'A Trip Through the Divided Kingdoms', p. 222.

45   Hamilton, '*King Lear* and the Historical Edgars', pp. 40–41.

46   Meredith Skura, 'Dragon Fathers and Unnatural Children: Warring Generations in *King Lear* and Its Sources', *Comparative Drama*, 42.2 (Summer 2008), 121–48 (p. 142).

47   *King Lear*, ed. by Ioppolo, p. 65.

48   Linda Colley, *Britons: Forging the Nation, 1707–1837* (New Haven: Yale University Press, 1992), p. 3.

49   Keechang Kima, '*Calvin's Case* (1608) and the Law of Alien Status', *The Journal of Legal History*, 17.2 (1996), 155–71.

50   C. B. Hardman, ' "Our Drooping Country Now Erects Her Head": Nahum Tate's *History of King Lear*', *Modern Language Review*, 95.4 (2000), 913–23 (p. 919).

51   W. W. Greg, 'Time, Place, and Politics in *King Lear*', *Modern Language Review*, 35.4 (1940), 431–46 (p. 440).

52   I am grateful to my colleague Rob Maslen for this point.

53   Derek Cohen, 'The Malignant Scapegoats of *King Lear*', *Studies in English Literature*, 49.2 (2009), 371–89 (p. 380).

54   Cohen, 'The Malignant Scapegoats of *King Lear*', pp. 380–81.

55   Greg, 'Time, Place, and Politics in *King Lear*', p. 440; Hamilton, '*King Lear* and the Historical Edgars', p. 42.

56   Stephen Greenblatt, 'Shakespeare and the Exorcists', in *Shakespeare and the Question of Theory*, ed. by Patricia Parker and Geoffrey Hartman (New York: Methuen), pp. 163–87.

57   Philip Schwyzer, 'The Jacobean Union Controversy and *King Lear*', in *Accession of James I: Historical and Cultural Consequences*, ed. by Glenn Burgess, Roland Wymer and Jason Lawrence (London: Palgrave, 2006), pp. 34–47 (p. 40).

58   Gavin Hollis, ' "Give me the map there": *King Lear* and Cartographic Literacy in Early Modern England', *The Portolan*, 68 (2007), 8–25 (p. 8).

59   Brayton, 'Angling in the Lake of Darkness', p. 421.

60   John Gillies, 'The Scene of Cartography in *King Lear*', in *Literature, Mapping, and the Politics of Space in Early Modern Britain*, ed. by Andrew Gordon and Bernhard Klein (Cambridge: Cambridge University Press, 2001), pp. 109–37.

61   Terence Hawkes, 'Lear's Maps', in *Meaning by Shakespeare* (London: Routledge, 1992), pp. 121–40 (p. 123).

62   Valerie Traub, 'The Nature of Norms in Early Modern England: Anatomy, Cartography, *King Lear*', *South Central Review*, 26.1&2 (2009), 42–81 (p. 43).

63   Greg, 'Time, Place, and Politics in *King Lear*', p. 28.

64   Traub, 'The Nature of Norms in Early Modern England', p. 47.

65   F. T. Flahiff, 'Lear's Map', *Cahiers elisabethains*, 30 (1986), 17–30 (p. 20).

66   Greg, 'Time, Place, and Politics in *King Lear*', p. 28.

67   Brayton, 'Angling in the Lake of Darkness', p. 402.

68   Flahiff, 'Lear's Map', p. 19.

69   Hollis, ' "Give me the map there" ', p. 21.

70   Ralph Berry, 'Lear's System', *Shakespeare Quarterly*, 35.4 (1984), 421–29 (p. 425).

71   I owe this point about the Englishness of *Lear* to John Kerrigan. See also Clark, ' "Ancestral Englishness" in *King Lear*'.

72   Nicholas Visser, 'Shakespeare and Hanekom, *King Lear* and Land: A South African Perspective', in *Post-Colonial Shakespeares*, ed. by Ania Loomba and Martin Orkin (London: Routledge, 1998), pp. 205–17 (p. 209).

73   Hopkins, 'The Edge: *King Lear*', p. 116.

74   Nina Taunton and Valerie Hart, '*King Lear*, King James and the Gunpowder Treason of 1605', *Renaissance Studies*, 17.4 (2003), 695–715 (p. 715).

75   Taunton and Hart, '*King Lear*, King James and the Gunpowder Treason of 1605', p. 713.

76   Mark Stoyle, 'Cornish Rebellions, 1497–1648', *History Today*, 47.5 (1997), 22–28 (p. 26); Mark Stoyle, ' "Knowest Thou My Brood?": Locating the Cornish in Tudor and Stuart England', in *West Britons: Cornish Identities and the Early Modern British State* (Exeter: University of Exeter Press, 2002), pp. 29–49.

77   Ronald W. Cooley, 'Kent and Primogeniture in *King Lear*', *Studies in English Literature*, 48.2 (2008), 327–48 (p. 327). See also Terry Reilly, '*King Lear*: The Kentish Forest and the Problem of Thirds', *Oklahoma City University Law Review*, 26.1 (2001), 379–401.

78   I owe this point to my colleague Rob Maslen.

79   Cyndia Susan Clegg, '*King Lear* and Early Seventeenth-Century Print Culture', in *'King Lear': New Critical Essays*, ed. by Jeffrey Kahan (New York: Routledge, 2008), pp. 155–83 (p. 172).

80   Berry, 'Cordelia's Bond and Britannia's Missing Middle', p. 149.

81   Draper, 'The Occasion of *King Lear*', p. 180.

82   Schwyzer, 'The Jacobean Union Controversy and *King Lear*', p. 39.

83   Jonathan Gibson, '*King Lear* and the Patronage System', *The Seventeenth Century*, 14.2 (1999), 95–114 (p. 107).

84   Philip Schwyzer, ' "Is this the promised end?" James I, *King Lear*, and the Strange Death of Tudor Britain', in *Literature, Nationalism and Memory in Early Modern England and Wales* (Cambridge: Cambridge University Press, 2004), p. 164.

85   Greenblatt, 'Shakespeare and the Exorcists'.

86   Samuel Harsnett, *A Discouery of the Fraudulent Practises of Iohn Darrel Bacheler of Artes* (London, 1599), pp. 138, 142.

87   Samuel Harsnett, *A Declaration of Egregious Popish Impostures* (London, 1603), pp. 5, 170.

88   Flahiff, 'Lear's Map', p. 24.

89   Flahiff, 'Lear's Map', p. 25.

90   Hadfield, 'The Power and Rights of the Crown in *Hamlet* and *King Lear*', p. 578.

91   Kiernan Ryan, '*King Lear*', in *A Companion to Shakespeare's Works*, Volume I, *The Tragedies*, ed. by Richard Dutton and Jean E. Howard (Oxford: Blackwell, 2003), pp. 375–92 (p. 383).

92   James Ware, ed., *Two Histories of Ireland* (Dublin, 1633), p. 20.

93   Hardman, ' "Our Drooping Country Now Erects Her Head" ', pp. 920–21.

94   Sonia Massai, 'Nahum Tate's Revision of Shakespeare's *King Lears*', *Studies in English Literature*, 40.3 (2000), 435–50 (p. 440).

95   Brayton, 'Angling in the Lake of Darkness', pp. 403, 422.

96   Peter Womack, 'Nobody, Somebody, and *King Lear*', *New Theatre Quarterly*, 23 (2007), 195–207 (p. 206).

97   Womack, 'Nobody, Somebody, and *King Lear*', p. 196.

98   Cited Kerrigan, *Archipelagic English*, p. 17.

99   Peter Holland, 'Mapping Shakespeare's Britain', in *Shakespeare's Histories and Counter-Histories*, ed. by Dermot Cavanagh, Stuart Hampton-Reeves and Stephen Longstaffe (Manchester: Manchester University Press, 2006), pp. 198–218 (p. 203).

100 Holland, 'Mapping Shakespeare's Britain', p. 215.

101 Clark, ' "Ancestral Englishness" in *King Lear*', p. 60.

102 Draper, 'The Occasion of *King Lear*', p. 176.

CHAPTER EIGHT

King Lear: Resources

Peter Sillitoe

Introduction

This chapter views Shakespeare's *King Lear* as a text for the university classroom and for individual study and research. As such, the section primarily approaches the play in terms of pedagogic strategies that might be usefully employed by the university classroom practitioner, both in terms of his or her development as an effective conveyer of early modern literature and as a facilitator of learning for students in higher education at all levels. Owing to this approach, the chapter explores various strategies for teaching this key text in terms of both generic expectations of tragedy, performance related investigation, and critical and theoretical approaches to the play, while always maintaining the importance of the work as a theatrical document for performance and as a literary text for close reading and critical investigation. A central concern of the chapter is to suggest approaches to the play that will enthuse students and facilitate a deeper understanding of the play by undergraduates at degree level, whether at first-, second-, or third-year level. Similarly, the chapter seeks to develop strategies for teaching the play in terms of new histories of the book, particularly in light of modern work on early modern print culture, and so the controversies over the two texts of *Lear* (Q1 and the Folio edition) are to be considered in terms of how best to articulate this to a student audience in a suitable, engaging manner. Equally importantly, this chapter makes reference to visual resources for the play, primarily in terms of online opportunities for viewing the different texts, *Early English Books Online* being an obvious example. Indeed, such resources should prove to be vital tools for the university teacher, allowing strategic access to the considerable visual literacy of the modern student audience. Firstly, however, we begin with a survey of the various published editions of the play that are still the most widely used resources for teachers and students alike.

Survey of Editions

One of the editions most frequently used for classroom exploration is the new, third series Arden version of *King Lear*, edited by R. A. Foakes (Walton-on-Thames: Thomas Nelson, 1997). In his edition, Foakes presents an excellent and particularly readable introduction (pp. 1–151) that understandably stresses the centrality of the play to the entire Shakespeare canon and the cultural reputation of the bard. There are useful notes about how the play may have been staged as well as accompanying detail about the Jacobean contexts of the work. Familiar but crucial themes are handled expertly, as Foakes delivers impressive discussion of theatrical productions, including many photographs from fairly recent performances in the 1990s, as well as a detailed overview of the play's critical history in the twentieth century. A further section on the inception of the play allows the editor to offer an overview on influences and source material, and the introduction presents a very informative narrative history in terms of the two texts (pp. 110–46). Indeed, this may well be the best edition for students to learn about the play's textual confusions, as Foakes is clear and lucid throughout on both versions of the play. Importantly, his edition gives sufficient space to discussion of how issues of characterization may be altered according to editorial decisions over Q1 and F, and so the debates about the two texts are conveyed clearly. As with all Arden editions, the textual notes are detailed and immensely readable throughout, and Foakes also includes an appendix on textual problems. In terms of editorial decisions over these textual issues, Foakes presents one text that is acutely aware of the differences between the Quarto and Folio versions, with very helpful notes directly addressing questions of textual selections.

The Norton Shakespeare: Based on the Oxford Edition (New York and London: W. W. Norton and Company, 1997), edited by Stephen Greenblatt, Walter Cohen, Jean E. Howard and Katharine Eisaman Maus, follows the decisions of the Oxford editors, and so we are presented with an extremely detailed selection of *texts*, rather than a single version. The superb introduction by Greenblatt is vital reading for all students of the play at any level (pp. 2307–14) and an additional textual note glosses the main issues surrounding the differing texts of the play. Following the Oxford editors, two distinct versions of the play are printed side-by-side offering readers a detailed view of both Quarto and Folio texts, but the *Norton* edition also provides a conflated text. Owing to this, the *Norton* is clearly an ideal classroom edition: for a very reasonable sum, students will have access to the complete works of Shakespeare in a version that includes three different versions of *Lear*.

In the edition prepared by Jay L. Halio, *The Tragedy of King Lear* (updated edition, Cambridge: Cambridge University Press, 1992; 2005) we have the version of the play that, along with the Arden edition, is probably the most widely used standalone text of the play. Like all entries in 'The New Cambridge Shakespeare' series, this edition is particularly good on textual history and performative concerns. The recent 2005 republication means that further work on staging and productions has been added, while retaining the student-friendly approach to the complex textual history as featured in the original. There is a detailed section on sources for Shakespeare's tragedy as well as the possible dating of it, and the introduction breaks down the play into useful scenic fragments for study and debate. Discussion of recent productions utilises various visual images from stage and screen, and the Q / F controversy is discussed at some length. Various textual alterations are examined in the subsequent appendix in a clear and insightful style; there is further discussion of textual issues, and a very detailed reading list for students and scholars alike is supplied at the end of the edition, making this version one of the most useful texts for the study of *Lear* as 'one' play (rather than two, or even three, after conflation).

Halio has also prepared a separate edition entitled *The First Quarto of King Lear* (Cambridge: Cambridge University Press, 1994). As the title suggests, this edition, like the previous one edited by Halio from Cambridge University Press, offers researchers, teachers and students the chance to see the earliest version of the play, Q1, without the need for online resources and digitized images, while still granting readers the pleasure of a full scholarly edition in terms of modern approaches to editing Renaissance texts. Indeed, this edition of *Lear* is actually part of a series from Cambridge University Press on 'The Early Quartos', and, as such, it is obvious that the series lends itself well to any teacher interested in encouraging their students to access the early Quartos in a modern, accessible form. Halio stresses that

> This edition of *King Lear* has been designed as a complementary text to the Folio-based edition published in the New Cambridge Shakespeare (1992). As such, it modernises spelling and punctuation, provides a collation of all significant variants, and includes Folio-only passages in an Appendix. (p. ix)

Clearly this edition of the First Quarto will be of primary benefit to researchers looking into the textual history of the play and / or modern editorial practices. However, the text could also be a significant resource in the university classroom for the discussion of Shakespearean authorship and the controversies about supposedly 'good' and 'bad' Quarto versions of the play. Similarly, a university module on modern editorial principles and the role of the editor would make excellent use of this valuable text. Furthermore, Halio's splendid introduction enables students to understand clearly the complicated nature of the two differing texts of the play, as his accessible discussion expertly relates the First Quarto to the later Q2 (1619) and, of course, the 1623 Folio version.

The central argument for the actual need for such an edition should be read alongside the Norton's introduction to the Oxford texts, as Halio explains that his work 'accepts the two-text hypothesis; indeed, that hypothesis is the main justification for bringing it to print' (p. ix). Indeed, Halio goes on, in his introduction (pp. 1–26), to trace the history of the two-text debate back to the 1970s, and rehearses the evolution of Q1 as a printing text at the start of the seventeenth century. A separate section looks at Q1's relation to Q2 (p. 21) giving the context of the 1619 copy from William Jaggard – interestingly, Halio underlines that Jaggard was less-than-honest in his use of the original title page. Similarly, there is a full and detailed section relating Q1 to the later Folio text, before Halio offers the original text in its entirety. Textual notes are collated at the end of the edition and an appendix prints passages that only appear in the Folio version of *Lear*.

Next we come to an edition prepared by Nick de Somogyi. His *King Lear: The Tragedie of King Lear* (London: Nick Horn Books, 2004) is similar to the Quarto edition prepared by Halio, as this version of the play is part of a full series entitled 'The Shakespeare Folios', in which the reader is offered the Folio versions of Shakespeare's plays alongside a parallel edited text, and offers 'easy access directly to the First Folio by presenting the text *in modern type* but otherwise unchanged'. This series also provides a modern, edited version side-by-side as we move through the play. Clearly, this edition may prove to be useful to teachers and students on a course that analyses the early modern notion of authorship, and might productively be read alongside the Halio Quarto text discussed above. Indeed, de Somogyi presents a student-friendly 'Possible Genealogy of the Text' (p. xxvi) as well as a useful section in his introduction on 'Re-reading *King Lear*' in which he traces facsimile Shakespeare editions back to the one published by E. and J. Wright in 1807. In addition, the reader is given a useful overview of the process from the entry in the Stationers' Register in 1607 through to Q1, Q2, and the Heminges and Condell Folio of 1623. There is a detailed summary of textual variants between Q and F, as well as a survey of critical and editorial approaches to the two texts, including the issues of textual conflation and parallel editions. The texts themselves are presented clearly and accurately, and should certainly be of interest in the university classroom in terms of editorial practice as well as a theoretically informed study of 'Shakespeare' as an appropriated authorial presence in literary criticism. Finally, at pp. 248–71 this edition presents the text of the 300 plus lines missing from the Folio version but present in Q1.

Students and critics might also wish to consult *King Lear: A Parallel Text Edition*, ed. by René Weis (London and New York: Longman, 1993). As the title suggests, in this edition Weis runs Q1 and F on opposite pages in modern, standardized texts. The introduction goes through the textual variations that will be familiar to students who have already examined other editions, but this version does contain a particularly detailed and thorough bibliography that should enrich student understanding on all of the major themes and issues that surround, and feature within, this key tragedy.

In terms of a text of *King Lear* in a complete edition of the Bard's plays, there is *William Shakespeare: The Complete Works*, 2nd edn, ed. by Stanley Wells, Gary Taylor, John Jowett, and William Montgomery (Oxford: Oxford University Press, 2005). This collection offers an updated version of the controversial Oxford edition from the 1980s, which famously treated the two versions of *Lear* as two very distinct texts. As such, this edition presents both Quarto and Folio versions of the play, but, unlike Greenblatt's *Norton* version, there is no conflated text from the Oxford editors. There is also the stand-alone edition of *Lear* edited by Stanley Wells and based on the Gary Taylor text (*The History of King Lear*, Oxford World's Classics, 2000), which contains the Quarto version of the play as well as a very detailed introduction and an additional literary context in the form of 'The Ballad of King Lear' from the Jacobean period.

By way of conclusion to this section, the anonymous source play, *The True Chronicle History of King Leir* may also be of interest. Though clearly harder to find than modern editions of the Shakespeare work, students and scholars wishing to see the earlier text might wish to consult an edition prepared by Sidney Lee entitled *The Chronicle History of King Leir: The Original of Shakespeare's 'King Lear'* (London: Chatto and Windus, 1909). This edition contains an introduction and the full text of the play, together with reasonably thorough notes at the end. More recently, there is an edition of *King Leir* edited by Tiffany Stern from the Globe Quartos series (London: Nick Horn Books, 2002). The unedited text is, of course, also available via the electronic resource *Early English Books Online*.

Online Resources

The British Library Website
www.bl.uk/treasures/shakespeare/kinglear.html
This enormously valuable resource enables teachers and students to see many of the British Library's Shakespeare Quartos in digitized form online, including *Lear* from 1608.

Early English Books Online (EEBO)
http://eebo.chadwyck.com/home
Access to this indispensable resource will allow students the chance to view the Shakespeare Quartos (including the two of *Lear*) along with the First Folio in its entirety.

The Furness Collection
http://dewey.library.upenn.edu/sceti/furness/
The site contains a complete online copy of the 1623 First Folio.

Teaching Strategies

1. King Lear *and Using Early English Books Online*
http://eebo.chadwyck.com/home

Resources required for this seminar activity: access to EEBO via university subscription; a web-linked computer and projector; reproductions of title pages via handouts.

As mentioned previously in the 'Online Resources' section, *EEBO* allows teachers and students alike the opportunity to view both Quartos of *King Lear* as well as the First Folio version from 1623. Because these can be viewed either online (perhaps using a projector in the classroom) or printed as handouts, parts of the original printed texts can be utilized in seminars and tutorials. Furthermore, the title pages, in particular, can be used to strengthen the considerable visual literacy of students today. For instance, a group activity that involves students viewing the title page of Q1 would enable discussion of early modern approaches to authorship, the modern 'birth' of the author, as well as early modern print and recent work on the materiality of the text and new histories of the book.

Possible activities and discussions relating to the Q1 title page:

- What might we infer from the positioning of Shakespeare's actual name on the front of Q1? Do you know if this is commonplace or unusual, and why might this be the case?

- What can we learn from the title page in terms of Shakespeare's approach to genre and / or the expectations of the potential reader in the period?
- What can we learn from this cultural document in terms of the play's original performance history?
- Similarly, students might be given digitized images from the Second Quarto and the Folio text in order to make useful links along similar lines. The two endings of the play in Q and F could be seen in their original form so as to highlight editorial decision-making and to problematize the concept of the author in early modern England. Additionally, selections from Shakespeare's sources might be used in this way, including extracts from Spenser's *Faerie Queene* and Sidney's *Arcadia*.

2. Violence and Spectacle in the Play

This approach to the tragedy in the university classroom might be used in order to engage with issues relating to performance, spectacle and the rendering of onstage violence in early modern London. There are several possible approaches to this:

In groups, remind yourselves of the blinding of Gloucester (at the end of the third act). In light of this scene, consider the following:

- How might this have been staged for an early modern audience?
- How could this scene be staged in a modern theatrical production?
- How might this scene consolidate or disrupt our understandings of genre in the period?
- Does anything in this scene alter our expectations of gender in early modern theatre and / or society?
- Are there any cultural events from Shakespeare's London that might be read alongside this particular spectacle?

3. A Contextual Approach to the Play

King Lear has often been discussed as a play that deals with the key issue of hierarchy, both in terms of modern critical discourse and in the university classroom. One way to access this theme in seminars and tutorials is to encourage students to read the play contextually alongside related material from the period. For instance, students could be given the following extract from the Elizabethan period:

Almighty God hath created and appointed all things in heaven, earth and waters in a most excellent and perfect order. In heaven he hath appointed distinct or several orders and states of archangels and angels. In earth he has assigned and appointed kings, princes, with other governors under them, all in good and necessary order. [. . .] Every degree of people, in their vocation, calling and office, hath appointed to them their duty and order. Some are in high degree, some in low; some kings and princes; some inferiors and subjects.[1]

In light of this contextual extract students should be asked to analyse this material alongside the play in terms of the following questions:

- To what extent does an understanding of this document alter or confirm our perception of hierarchy in the play?
- Try to find at least one scene that can be read alongside this document productively. Does this scene challenge or confirm the view of early modern society outlined in the extract?
- Which characters best fit this model of social stratification?
- Which characters disrupt the understanding of social rank and standing as is foregrounded in the document?
- In light of this material, do you think that we should see *Lear* as a radical or conservative play?
- How does the play present the concept of kingship and divine monarchical power and authority?

4. Close Textual Analysis

As is familiar to university teachers, all good student essays should contain detailed close reading and thorough textual analysis, even in contextual, historical and political approaches. Taking this into account, study of 'the words on the page' is still a vital activity in the classroom, and so any scene, soliloquy or verbal exchange between characters might be studied in pairs or groups. For instance, one example might focus upon the start of the play:

Remind yourselves of the opening scene of the tragedy, and, in your groups, consider the language used in some detail. You may wish to consider the register and tone used by the various characters and how Shakespeare employs language to establish key expectations about this dramatic world from the very beginning. Can we trace anything in the scene that might reveal something about the play's genre? Indeed, is there anything 'generic' about this opening scene?

5. Teaching the Play Through a Performance-Related Approach

Although all approaches to the play outlined here take into account the fact that *King Lear* is primarily a play for performance, it is perhaps worth highlighting this point when teaching the play. Because of this, suggestions for pedagogic strategies might usefully foreground the play as a theatrical spectacle. Some useful approaches are detailed below:

- Students could be shown images of various productions of the play from film and theatre and then asked to comment on the dress and visual presentation of the actors in those roles.
- A further progression would be to show the same actors performing the roles on film as this would feed into discussion of their self-presentation.
- Students could be asked to choose a key scene for their group to focus upon in light of performance and then be required to suggest two strongly contrasting approaches to playing the scene based upon their reading of the script.
- This approach could also be employed in terms of the onstage presentation of character, with students using textual evidence to support their own 'version' of the character in a theatrical performance.
- In terms of the formal onstage presentation, students could be asked to suggest ways in which they would physically stage the play and how they would render the world of the text visually for an audience. This should facilitate discussion of costume, props, staging and possible audience expectations of the tragedy in performance.
- Another possibility for performance-related study could include a focus upon gender and the idea of the manipulation of the audience. Students could be asked to think about how a stage version of the play might prioritize gender in the production. This could include, for instance, a discussion of Goneril and Regan and how the audience is meant to react to their presentation. Thus, how could the actors disrupt audience expectations of the two female characters?

6. Teaching the Play Through Textual and Thematic Comparison
It can be productive for the university teacher to engage his or her student audience by addressing the central themes through comparison with another Shakespearean work. In the following example, *King Lear* is compared with *Hamlet* and the idea of the court:

- Both plays are based at a royal court. How are these realms similar and in what ways are they very different as social and cultural settings?
- Compare the two central protagonists from both plays. How might both be seen as tragic?

7. Teaching the Play Through Student Debate

- In this scenario, the students could be split into two camps and each section would have to argue for a particular cause in a roundtable discussion. In this example, students on one side would have to argue for the literary merits of the text as a work primarily intended to be read, while the other section of the class would need to gather evidence that supports a case for *Lear* as, primarily, a theatrical text to be seen and heard.
- Another possibility is to follow a similar approach but to prioritize characterization. One camp could argue, for example, that Lear is a victim, whereas the other side could foreground his potential to be played as a tyrant. There could be a for and against debate regarding the actions of Goneril and Regan, or the honesty of Cordelia's speech at the beginning of the text.

8. Potential Essay Questions

- Consider the play in light of early modern expectations of tragedy.
- To what extent does *King Lear* demonstrate the breakdown of one social order and the emergence of another type of society?
- How do issues relating to gender and genre combine in the play?
- Is it possible to offer a Christian reading of the play?
- How would you account for the profound cultural impact of *King Lear*?
- How does your knowledge of the complicated textual history of this play alter your perception of the play as a unified, organic whole?
- Is *King Lear* a play about feudalism, capitalism or both?
- Is this a play about violence, spectacle or both?
- How and why is *King Lear* tragic?
- Is the play a tragedy, a history play or both?

Annotated Bibliography

Suggested Reading in Single-Authored Books and Edited Collections

Boose, Lynda E., and Richard Burt, eds, *Shakespeare the Movie: Popularizing the Plays on Film, TV, and Video* (London and New York: Routledge, 1997). See Chapter 8 by Tony Howard, 'When Peter Met Orson: The 1953 CBS *King Lear*' (pp. 121–34), as well as chapter 9 by Kenneth S. Rothwell, 'In Search of Nothing: Mapping *King Lear*' (pp. 135–47). The first *Lear* chapter deals with the Peter Brook production, while the second chapter looks at various stage and screen performances of the play, including work on Peter Brook, Grigori Kozintsev and Jean-Luc Godard.

Braunmuller, A. R., and Michael Hattaway, eds, *The Cambridge Companion to English Renaissance Drama*, 2nd edn (Cambridge: Cambridge University Press, 2003). A very fine collection of essays for the study of Shakespeare and his contemporaries, but see, in particular, the chapter on tragedy by Robert N. Watson (pp. 292–343).

Brown, Richard Danson, and David Johnson, eds, *A Shakespeare Reader: Sources and Criticism* (Basingstoke: Macmillan, 2000). Editors Richard Danson Brown and David Johnson present a section on the sources for *Lear*. More specifically, the volume offers extracts from Sir Philip Sidney's 1590 *Arcadia* and Edmund Spenser's *The Faerie Queene* that deal with the *Lear* source material, including the sub-plot of Gloucester and his sons. Furthermore, the later section in this book on critical discourse offers useful, thought-provoking material from Arnold Kettle on 'From *Hamlet* to *Lear*', Coppélia Kahn on 'The Absent Mother in *King Lear*', and Alexander Leggatt's excellent discussion of the 1971 film version of the play by Grigori Kozinstev.

Bruce, Susan, ed., *William Shakespeare: King Lear* (New York: Columbia University Press, 1998). An interesting attempt to explore the play in five quite distinct chapters, focusing on neo-classicism, Nahum Tate's adaptation and David Garrick as Lear, a discussion of the Romantics on the play (including Keats and Lamb), a section on realism, including Dickens, A. C. Bradley and pre-1960s criticism, and a fourth chapter on the years 1904–1960, including a look at the views of L. C. Knights and new critical theory, Freud, William Empson, Jan Knott and the 1962 Peter Brook production. The book concludes with a chapter on contemporary critical discourse, such as the new historicism of Jonathan Goldberg and Stephen Greenblatt and the recent work of Lisa Jardine.

Buchanan, Judith, *Shakespeare on Film* (Harlow: Pearson Longman, 2005). See the book in its entirety for a detailed overview of Shakespearean cinema, with work on productions of *King Lear* appearing throughout the book, including discussions of early silent American films (productions of the play by the Vitagraph Company and the Thanhouser Corporation). Furthermore, an entire chapter is devoted to the work of Akira Kurosawa, including his *Ran* from 1985, and there is also a section on Kristian Levring's *The King is Alive* from 2000 (pp. 220–22).

Callaghan, Dympna, *Woman and Gender in Renaissance Tragedy: A Study of King Lear, Othello, The Duchess of Malfi and The White Devil* (New York and London: Harvester Wheatsheaf, 1989). An excellent overview of key themes arising from a discussion of early modern tragedy and gender, this vital feminist study underlines the importance of gender to the study of Shakespeare and his contemporary John Webster. All four plays are discussed alongside the other, owing to the sensible decision from the author to explore and analyse the texts according to thematic links, such as family and church, genre and power, and the tragic hero. The monograph should be essential reading for students interested in an exploration of gendered approaches to Shakespeare's play. Indeed, the book is particularly intelligent in terms of generic subject matter as *Lear* is positioned as a key moment in the dramatic form of tragedy.

Cartelli, Thomas, and Katherine Rowe, *New Wave Shakespeare on Screen* (Cambridge: Polity, 2007). See 'Surviving Shakespeare: Kristian Levring's *The King is Alive*' (pp. 142–64).

Dillon, Janette, *The Cambridge Introduction to Shakespeare's Tragedies* (Cambridge: Cambridge University Press, 2007). See chapter 8 on *Lear* for detailed discussion of the play. The book as a whole offers an engaging and lively account of Shakespeare's tragedies as a generic category.

Dollimore, Jonathan, *Radical Tragedy: Religion, Ideology and Power in the Drama of Shakespeare and his Contemporaries*, 2nd edn (London: Harvester Wheatsheaf, 1989). This monograph should prove to be of great value to undergraduates wishing to explore cultural materialist strategies for understanding the play and early modern tragedy in general. For work exclusively on *Lear*, see pp. 189–203 of this landmark study.

Dollimore, Jonathan, and Alan Sinfield, eds, *Political Shakespeare: Essays in Cultural Materialism*, 2nd edn (Manchester: Manchester University Press, 1994). This collection of new historicist and cultural materialist essays on Shakespearean theatre does not actually contain specific work on *Lear*, but should be read as a useful introduction to political criticism on Shakespeare and the drama of his time.

Drakakis, John, ed., *Shakespearean Tragedy* (Harlow: Longman, 1992). A particularly good and wide-ranging collection of essays on Shakespeare and the generic expectations of tragedy. See, in particular, the excellent introduction by the editor (pp. 1–44), as well as Alessandro Serpieri on semiotics in 'The Breakdown of Medieval Hierarchy in *King Lear*' (pp. 84–95), Jonathan Dollimore on the play and 'Essentialist Humanism' (pp. 194–207; also available in his own *Radical Tragedy*, see above), and Marilyn French on 'The Late Tragedies' (pp. 227–79; discussion of *Lear* is at pp. 244–63). Furthermore, see the chapter by Malcolm Evans on poststructuralism and Shakespearean tragedy (pp. 374–88), and, finally, Terry Eagleton's work on several tragedies including *Lear* (pp. 388–99).

Dutton, Richard, and Jean E. Howard, eds, *A Companion to Shakespeare's Works: The Tragedies* (Oxford: Blackwell, 2003). A volume containing many important essays on Shakespearean tragedy. See particularly the chapter on *King Lear* by Kiernan Ryan, at pp. 375–92, in which the author reviews previous critical studies of the play and gives suggestions for detailed further reading.

Foakes, R. A., *Hamlet Versus Lear: Cultural Politics and Shakespeare's Art* (Cambridge: Cambridge University Press, 1993). An interesting study that reads the two 'great' tragedies together, including work on the texts of *Lear* and an impressive overview of previous critical studies.

Greenblatt, Stephen, *Shakespearean Negotiations: The Circulation of Social Energy in Renaissance England* (Oxford: Clarendon Press, 1988). See chapter 4, 'Shakespeare and the Exorcists', pp. 94–128. A key new historicist reading of Shakespearean theatre, including an examination of *King Lear* together with a contemporary printed tract entitled 'A Declaration of Egregious Popish Impostures' by Samuel Harsnett from 1603. This is a potentially difficult, but rewarding, piece for undergraduates, and would be particularly suitable for third-year level students who have some understanding of new historicism and its accompanying theoretical contexts.

Griggs, Yvonne, *Screen Adaptations: Shakespeare's King Lear, The Relationship Between Text and Film* (London: Methuen Drama, 2009). An excellent and very recent resource on Shakespeare's play in terms of cinematic adaptations. First, the monograph usefully presents a timeline of major adaptations of the play, from the 1909 Vitagraph production directed by William V. Ranous right through to the most recent 2001 *My Kingdom* directed by Don Boyd. Secondly, the opening section of the main part of the book looks at 'Literary Contexts', including discussion of 'origins and new directions', 'recycled narratives', performative issues, and an interesting section on 'the adaptation debate'. Part 2 on 'Production Contexts' offers an overview of the different film versions of the play, including the early silent films, the 'canonised' (p. 26) versions by Grigori Kozintsev, Peter Brook, and Akira Kurosawa, *The Dresser* by Peter Yates (1983), the 1987 Jean-Luc Godard production, and Kristian Levring's *The King is Alive*. This overview section also looks at what the author terms 'genre reworkings' (p. 28), including Francis Ford Coppola's *Godfather* trilogy, Jocelyn Moorhouse's 1997 *A Thousand Acres*, and *My Kingdom* from Don Boyd. Part 3 of the book offers 'Readings of Key Versions', including detailed, scholarly discussion of the major productions by Brook, Kozintsev, Kurosawa, as well as work on 'genre cinema', including *House of Strangers* (1949), *Broken Lance* (1954), *My Kingdom*, and *The Godfather* films. Of particular note in terms of new work on recent productions is the section on Boyd's gangster film that 'employ[s] *King Lear* as subtext' (p. 133). This chapter devotes a section to *A Thousand Acres* as well as a separate discussion of art house productions (including Godard's version and Levring's *The King is Alive*). Lastly, Part 4 of the book examines 'The Afterlife' of the play's relationship with modern film, as Griggs looks forward to future productions that are either planned or actually commissioned. In conclusion, it has to be said that this new monograph will certainly prove to be vital reading for all scholars and students of the play, but, particularly, for those working on the play and film adaptations this is surely the key resource on the topic in modern criticism.

Hadfield, Andrew, *Shakespeare and Renaissance Politics* (London: Thomson Learning, 2004). As the title makes clear, this single-authored monograph deals with Shakespeare and the cultural and political climate of his world. Students could approach this as an engaging and accessible account of the dominant themes, and Hadfield offers various references to *Lear* throughout the work.

Hadfield, Andrew, *Shakespeare, Spenser and the Matter of Britain* (Basingstoke: Palgrave Macmillan, 2004). See, in particular, pp. 156–60 for *Lear* in relation to the 'matter of Britain' and the potential Jacobean union of the kingdoms.

Hawkes, Terence, *William Shakespeare's King Lear* (Plymouth: Northcote House, 1995). An engaging and vibrant approach to the play that should prove to be encouraging for student and teacher alike. The book is organized into separate chapters on key themes and issues, including work on 'Using History', 'Masterless Men', and 'A Right Bastard', a section that explores the characterization of Edmund throughout the play.

Henderson, Diana E., ed., *A Concise Companion to Shakespeare on Screen* (Oxford: Blackwell, 2006). For Kurosawa's *Ran* in particular, see chapter 8 by Anthony Dawson entitled 'Cross-Cultural Interpretation: Reading Kurosawa Reading Shakespeare', pp. 155–75.

Hiscock, Andrew, and Lisa Hopkins, eds, *Teaching Shakespeare and Early Modern Dramatists* (Basingstoke: Palgrave Macmillan, 2007). See, in particular, the chapter by Hiscock on Shakespeare's tragedies.

Jackson, Russell, ed., *The Cambridge Companion to Shakespeare on Film* (Cambridge: Cambridge University Press, 2000). See particularly Chapter 7 by J. Lawrence Guntner entitled '*Hamlet*, *Macbeth* and *King Lear* on Film' (pp. 117–34; pp. 128–32 for *Lear*). The chapter includes discussion of Grigori Kozintsev's 1971 film, plus the 1971 Peter Brook production and Akira Kurosawa's *Ran* from 1985.

Jess-Cooke, Carolyn, *Shakespeare on Film: Such Things as Dreams are Made Of* (London and New York: Wallflower, 2007). Although this monograph does not feature a complete chapter on *Lear* or tragedy, it might be consulted for discussion of several related film versions, including *The King is Alive* and *Ran*.

Jorgens, Jack J., *Shakespeare on Film* (New York and London: University Press of America, 1991). See chapter 16 on '*King Lear*: Peter Brook and Grigori Kozintsev', pp. 235–51.

Kahan, Jeffrey, ed., *King Lear: New Critical Essays* (New York and London: Routledge, 2008). A very up-to-date collection that includes a particularly lengthy introduction by the editor (pp. 1–103) which surveys many of the most important issues around the play, including detailed work on sources, the two texts, and the play's full theatrical history. See, in particular, pp. 92–103 for a very detailed and thorough bibliography. The collection as a whole contains excellent new work by a number of distinguished critics, including R. A. Foakes, Richard Knowles, Stanley Stewart and Christy Desmet.

Leggatt, Alexander, *King Lear, Shakespeare in Performance*, 2nd edn (Manchester: Manchester University Press, 1991; 2004). A superb example of performance-related criticism, as the author explores various theatrical productions of the play. As part of the publisher's 'Shakespeare in Performance' series, detailed discussion is given to various productions, including Peter Brook's film version from 1971, Grigori Kozinstev's film version, Adrian Noble's 1982 version for the Royal Shakespeare Company, the 1982 BBC Shakespeare Series production, the 1983 Olivier version for Granada Television, and the more recent film *Ran* by Akira Kurosawa. Owing to this, this book engages most fully performance-related issues and theatrical history and should be of immense help to both teachers and students who are engaged in performative study of Shakespeare's tragedy.

Maguire, Laurie E., *Studying Shakespeare: A Guide to the Plays* (Oxford: Blackwell, 2004). This contains a section on *King Lear* in the chapter entitled 'Private Life: Shakespeare and Selfhood' (pp. 40–45) and also examines the play in an interesting discussion of 'Real Life: Shakespeare and Suffering' (pp. 184–85). Here Maguire looks at the text as 'a play of excess; it is as if Shakespeare thought of every painful thing that one human being could do to another. The play depicts injustice, ingratitude, misjudgement, misunderstanding, gratuitous violence. The play is an endurance test of our emotions'. The text also features in a discussion of familial relationships, including Lear as the patriarchal father (pp. 199–203). The resulting analysis offers a neat approach to teaching the play in terms of thematic devices such as suffering and violence, ideal material for a play as all-encompassing as *Lear*.

Marsh, Nicholas, *Shakespeare: The Tragedies* (Basingstoke: Macmillan, 1998). This single-authored study looks at various Shakespearean tragedies, and so *Lear* features in such sections as 'Openings', 'Endings',

'The Hero', 'The Heroines', 'Society in the Tragedies', 'Humour in the Tragedies', and 'Imagery and the Tragic Universe'. (See the last section on imagery for a sustained reading of 1.4.52–156.)

Mousley, Andy, *Renaissance Drama and Contemporary Literary Theory* (Basingstoke: Macmillan, 2000) (for *Lear* and structuralism, see pp. 52–57).

Patterson, Annabel, *Shakespeare and the Popular Voice* (Oxford: Blackwell, 1989). See chapter 5 for ' "What Matter Who's Speaking?" *Hamlet* and *King Lear*', (pp. 93–119) where Patterson reads Shakespeare's two 'great' tragedies alongside each other in terms of a 'popular' understanding of Shakespearean theatre (the discussion of *Lear* is at pp. 106–19). Patterson examines the play together with contextual work on James I and argues against a traditional reading that might see the play as a move from feudalism to capitalism. Significantly, this book is written in particularly lucid prose and should be able to introduce students to some difficult themes in an understandable and enthusiastic fashion.

Peck, John, and Martin Coyle, *How to Study a Shakespeare Play*, 2nd edn (Basingstoke: Macmillan, 1985; 1995). *King Lear* is featured at pp. 68–75 in a study that may be a little simplistic for more advanced students, but that would serve as an excellent resource and primer for beginners at first-year level study.

Ryan, Kiernan, ed., *Shakespeare: Texts and Contexts* (Basingstoke: Macmillan, 2000). This wide-ranging book tenders an entire chapter on *Lear* by Graham Martin and Stephen Regan (pp. 241–76) in which the authors read the play alongside an overview of early modern political and social contexts. However, this predominantly historicist reading is also given with useful details about performance and the play's relationship to a modern audience. The section surveys the Jacobean division of the kingdom context and also foregrounds the play's performance before King James and the court at Whitehall Palace, Christmas 1606. Furthermore, the chapter touches upon the history of the two texts, and, more usefully, goes into considerable detail when surveying the play's critical history in the twentieth century. This introductory source should prove especially useful for students who are new to the play and early modern theatre, and the section breaks down into smaller divisions on Cordelia, plot, character, theme, the double plot, the Fool, the use of minor characters, commentary on the action, historical actualities and Lear's own madness. As such, this chapter is well organized in terms of key issues that students might tackle and should therefore serve as an excellent resource for teachers looking for introductory pedagogic strategies. Indeed, the two authors suggest a number of key passages and themes for students to analyse either in essays or in the classroom, including possible explanations for Cordelia's speech in the first scene of the play (p. 244), as well as posing questions such as 'Why do you think there are two distinct "stories" – the story of Lear and the story of Gloucester?' (p. 250). This leads on to discussion of the Fool and Lear's madness, before moving on to an important section on 'Interpretations' (pp. 260–76), which breaks down into thematic explorations of *Lear* as a potentially religious play, of nature and history, and of power and morality. Further brief topic surveys include gender and performance, including material on *Lear's Daughters* from the Women's Theatre Group, 1987–88, as well as Grigori Kozintsev's 1971 film.

Ryan, Kiernan, ed., *King Lear*, New Casebooks Series (Basingstoke: Macmillan, 1993). A fine collection of essays on the play, though some of these are perhaps showing their age a little. Still, the collection should suffice for a detailed introduction to the major critical themes in and around the play. See, in particular, the discussions by Kate McLuskie, Leonard Tennenhouse, Coppélia Kahn and Leah Marcus. [Note: All of the chapters in this collection had been published as separate, non-related studies].

Smith, Emma, *The Cambridge Introduction to Shakespeare* (Cambridge: Cambridge University Press, 2007). Emma Smith organizes her study according to seven chapters on 'Character', 'Performance', 'Texts', 'Language', 'Structure', 'Sources' and 'History'. In doing so, she has produced a critical introduction that should be vital reading for all undergraduates who are new to Shakespeare studies in the university classroom. In terms of *King Lear* particularly, Shakespeare's tragedy appears in the 'Texts' section (pp. 61–64) as Smith uses the play as a case study for 'The Job of the Editor: The Example of *King Lear*'. In this important section, Smith employs a clear, articulate critical voice in order to talk students through the various debates about the Quarto and Folio versions of the play. This is an engaging and lucid explanation, offered in an accessible manner for students who will be new to the textual controversy entirely. For instance, key critical terminology such as 'Conflated' is explained alongside the possible editorial reasons for parallel texts. Usefully, Smith offers a selection of the best online resources for study of the play, including the Furness Collection at the University of Pennsylvania, which reproduces a copy of the First Folio and various early Quartos. (See earlier for further discussion of 'Online Resources'). Furthermore, Smith's book opens up a space for classroom discussion and student study of the play in terms of Shakespeare's dramatic and non-dramatic sources for the basic plots and characters (pp. 127–31), as she notes that

> since *King Lear* is unusual among Shakespeare's plays in having a previous play, rather than prose or poetry, as a substantial source,

we might be able to assume that at least some members of the audience were familiar with that play, the anonymous *The True Chronicle of Historie of King Leir and his Three Daughters* published in 1605. (p. 127)

Indeed, such resources are explored further here in the 'Teaching Strategies' section of this chapter, but for now it suffices to say that students might be asked to compare the title page of this text to the Shakespearean Quartos, or study extracts from the source play alongside the more famous work. Indeed, Smith's impressive book presents textual quotations from the 1605 text that might prove to be fruitful for classroom discussion. Moreover, there is an examination of Shakespeare's tragedy alongside *Macbeth* with reference to questions of Jacobean patronage (pp. 142–44). Thus, this study serves as a useful introduction for students to the key context of James's potential union of the kingdoms of England and Scotland.

Starks, Lisa S., and Courtney Lehmann, eds, *The Reel Shakespeare: Alternative Cinema and Theory* (London: Associated University Presses, 2002). See Alan Walworth's chapter 'Cinema *Hysterica Passio*: Voice and Gaze in Jean-Luc Godard's *King Lear*', pp. 59–94.

Taylor, Gary, and Michael Warren, eds, *The Division of the Kingdoms: Shakespeare's Two Versions of King Lear* (Oxford: Oxford University Press, 1983). A crucial study for students and scholars interested in the details of the two-text issues surrounding the play.

Womack, Peter, *English Renaissance Drama* (Oxford: Blackwell, 2006). This is a potentially useful book for the study of early modern theatre and Shakespeare. See pp. 174–8 for discussion of *Lear* as a key text in the Renaissance canon.

Zimmerman, Susan, ed., *Shakespeare's Tragedies* (New York: St Martin's Press, 1998). This collection contains a valuable essay by Jonathan Goldberg, entitled 'Perspectives: Dover Cliff and the Conditions of Representation' (pp. 155–66). Also in this book, see the essay by Margreta de Grazia, 'The Ideology of Superfluous Things: *King Lear* as Period Piece' (pp. 255–84).

Journal Articles

Brooks, Douglas A., '*King Lear* (1608) and the Typography of Literary Ambition', *Renaissance Drama*, 30 (1999–2001), 133–59. The article seeks to shed new light on the authorial strategies behind the printing of the first text in 1608 (Q1). This will be of particular benefit to study of early modern title pages as Brooks analyses the text alongside Ben Jonson's authorial presentation of himself in various plays and entertainments in print.

Dodd, William, 'Impossible Worlds: What Happens in *King Lear*, Act 1, Scene 1', *Shakespeare Quarterly*, 50.4 (1999), 476–507. See this article for a detailed discussion of the love test between Lear and his daughters, the character of Cordelia, and also Kent.

Hadfield, Andrew, 'The Power and Rights of the Crown in *Hamlet* and *King Lear*: "The King – The King's to Blame"', *Review of English Studies*, 54.217 (2003), 566–86. An outstanding example of historicist work that gives readers a clear sense of the political contexts of Jacobean England and monarchical power.

Holahan, Michael, '"Look, her lips": Softness of Voice, Construction of Character in *King Lear*', *Shakespeare Quarterly*, 48.4 (1997), 406–31. Of particular interest to students wishing to explore 'character' in the play, particularly of Cordelia.

Kelly, Philippa, 'See What Breeds about her Heart: *King Lear*, Feminism, and Performance', *Renaissance Drama*, 33 (2004), 137–57. A gendered and performative approach to the play, asking what happens when we foreground the female characters in modern performances.

Li, Ruru, '"Who is it that can tell me who I am?" / "Lear's shadow": A Taiwanese Actor's Personal Response to *King Lear*', *Shakespeare Quarterly*, 57.2 (2006), 195–215. An article examining the response of actor Wu Hsing-Kuo after his performances in Paris 2000.

Saunders, J. G., '"Apparent Perversities": Text and Subtext in the Construction of the Role of Edgar in Brook's Film of *King Lear*', *Review of English Studies*, 47.187 (1996), 317–30. Saunders offers a defence of some of the changes made to the play text by Brook for his film version of the play, particularly in terms of the alteration of the character of Edgar in this version.

Shannon, Laurie, 'Poor, Bare, Forked: Animal Sovereignty, Human Negative Exceptionalism, and the Natural History of *King Lear*', *Shakespeare Quarterly*, 60.2 (2009), 168–96. The article presents a 'zoographic' reading of the play.

Spotswood, Jerald W., 'Maintaining Hierarchy in *The Tragedie of King Lear*', *Studies in English Literature*, 38 (1998), 265–80. An excellent study of the play and class expectations in early modern England which is particularly sensitive to the differences between the two main texts of *King Lear*.

Taunton, Nina, and Valerie Hart, '*King Lear*, King James and the Gunpowder Treason of 1605', *Renaissance Studies*, 17.4 (2003), 695–715. A particularly insightful essay that historicizes the play alongside one of the key contexts of the period.

Turner, Henry S., '*King Lear* Without the Heath', *Renaissance Drama*, 28 (1997), 161–93. A place-specific article that features the valuable observation that neither Q1 nor the Folio versions of the play actually name the Heath as a geographical location. Owing to this, the study should be of use to those interested in the history of Shakespearean editing back into the eighteenth century.

Website for Further Study

www.thelastlearmovie.com/ The official website for the recent film entitled *The Last Lear*, directed by Rituparno Ghosh in 2007.

Note

1   'An Exhortation Concerning Good Order and Obedience', in *The English Renaissance: An Anthology of Sources and Documents*, ed. by Kate Aughterson (London: Routledge, 1998), pp. 92–95 (p. 93). Text from 1559.

Bibliography

Adelman, Janet, *Suffocating Mothers: Fantasies of Maternal Origin in Shakespeare's Plays, 'Hamlet' to 'The Tempest'* (New York. Routledge, 1992)

Anon, 'Exhortation Concerning Good Order and Obedience', in *The English Renaissance: An Anthology of Sources and Documents*, ed. by Kate Aughterson (London: Routledge, 1998), pp. 92–95

Aquinas, Thomas, *The Catholic Encyclopedia*, www.newadvent.org/cathen/index.html [accessed 13 October 2006]

Asher, Lyell, 'Lateness in *King Lear*', *Yale Journal of Criticism*, 13.2 (2000), 209–28

Aughterson, Kate, ed., *The English Renaissance: An Anthology of Sources and Documents* (London: Routledge, 1998)

Bacon, Francis, *Novum Organum*, ed. and trans. by Graham Rees and Maria Wakely, The Oxford Francis Bacon (Oxford: Clarendon Press, 2004), XI

Bate, Jonathan, ed., *The Romantics on Shakespeare*, New Penguin Shakespeare Library (London: Penguin, 1992)

Bate, Jonathan, *The Song of the Earth* (London: Picador, 2000)

Beauregard, David N., 'Human Malevolence and Providence in *King Lear*', *Renascence: essays on values in literature*, 60.3 (Spring 2008), 199–224

Belsey, Catherine, 'Psychoanalytic Speculations on the Pain and Joy of Tragedy: The Case of King Lear', in *Reconstructing Pain and Joy: Linguistic, Literary and Cultural Perspectives*, ed. and intro. by Chryssoula Lascaratou, Anna Despotopoulou, and Elly Ifantidou (Newcastle upon Tyne: Cambridge Scholars, 2008), pp. 339–55

Berg, J. E., '*Gorboduc* as a Tragic Discovery of "Feudalism"', *Studies in English Literature*, 40.2 (2000), 199–226

Berry, Philippa, 'Cordelia's Bond and Britannia's Missing Middle: *King Lear* (c.1606)', in *Shakespeare's Feminine Endings: Disfiguring Death in the Tragedies* (London: Routledge, 1999), pp. 135–66

Berry, Ralph, 'Lear's System', *Shakespeare Quarterly*, 35.4 (1984), 421–29

Bickersteth, Geoffrey L., *The Golden World of 'King Lear'*, Annual Shakespeare Lecture (London: Geoffrey Cumberlege, 1946)

Bloom, Harold, *Shakespeare: The Invention of the Human* (New York: Riverhead Books, 1998)

Boose, Lynda E., and Richard Burt, eds, *Shakespeare the Movie: Popularizing the Plays on Film, TV, and Video* (London and New York: Routledge, 1997)

Booth, Stephen, 'On the Greatness of King Lear', in *Twentieth Century Interpretations of King Lear*, ed. by Janet Adelman (Englewood Cliffs, NJ: Prentice Hall, 1978), pp. 98–113

Bradbrook, M. C., *Elizabethan Stage Conditions: A Study of Their Place in the Interpretation of Shakespeare's Plays* (Cambridge: Cambridge University Press, 1968)

Bradley, A. C., *Shakespearean Tragedy: Lectures on 'Hamlet', 'Othello', 'King Lear', 'Macbeth'* (London: Macmillan, 1904)

Bradshaw, Graham, *Misrepresentations: Shakespeare and the Materialists* (Ithaca: Cornell University Press, 1993)

Braunmuller, A. R., and Michael Hattaway, eds, *The Cambridge Companion to English Renaissance Drama*, 2nd edn (Cambridge: Cambridge University Press, 2003)

Brayton, Dan, 'Angling in the Lake of Darkness: Possession, Dispossession, and the Politics of Discovery in *King Lear*', *English Literary History*, 70.2 (Summer 2003), 399–426

Brontë, Emily, *Wuthering Heights* (London: Everyman, 1975)

Brooks, Douglas A., '*King Lear* (1608) and the Typography of Literary Ambition', *Renaissance Drama*, 30 (1999–2001), 133–59

Brown, John Russell, '*King Lear': A Guide to the Text and the Play in Performance* (Basingstoke: Palgrave, 2009)

Brown, Richard Danson, and David Johnson, eds, *A Shakespeare Reader: Sources and Criticism* (Basingstoke: Macmillan, 2000)

Brownlow, Frank, 'Richard Topcliffe: Elizabeth's Enforcer and the Representation of Power in *King Lear*', in *Theatre and Religion: Lancastrian Shakespeare*, ed. by Richard Dutton, Alison Findlay, and Richard Wilson (Manchester and New York: Manchester University Press, 2003), pp. 161–78

Bruce, Susan, ed., *William Shakespeare: King Lear* (New York: Columbia University Press, 1998)

Buchanan, Judith, *Shakespeare on Film* (Harlow: Pearson, 2005)

Budden, Julian, *Verdi* (New York: Oxford University Press, 2008)

Buechner, Frederick, *Speak What We Feel* (New York: HarperCollins, 2001)

Bullough, Geoffrey, ed., *Narrative and Dramatic Sources of Shakespeare*, 8 vols (London: Routledge and Kegan Paul, 1957–75)

Bullough, Geoffrey, ed., *Narrative and Dramatic Sources of Shakespeare* (New York: Columbia University Press, 1978)

Burnett, Mark Thornton, *Filming Shakespeare in the Global Marketplace* (Basingstoke: Palgrave, 2007)

Burnett, Mark Thornton, 'King Lear, Service and the Deconstruction of Protestant Idealism', in *The Shakespearean International Yearbook, Volume 5: Special Section, Shakespeare and the Bonds of Service*, ed. by Michael Neill (Aldershot: Ashgate Press, 2005), pp. 66–85

Cakebread, Catherine, 'Remembering *King Lear* in Jane Smiley's *A Thousand Acres*', in *Shakespeare and Appropriation*, ed. by Christy Desmet and Robert Sawyer (London and New York: Routledge, 1999)

Callaghan, Dympna, *Shakespeare Without Women: Performing Race and Gender on the Renaissance Stage* (London and New York: Routledge, 2000)

Calvin, John, *Institutes of the Christian Religion*, ed. by John T. McNeill, trans. by Ford Lewis Battles (Louisville: Westminster John Knox Press, 1960)

Campbell, Lily B., *Shakespeare's Tragic Heroes: Slaves of Passion* (London: Methuen, 1961)

Cantor, Paul, 'The Cause of Thunder: Nature and Justice in King Lear', in *King Lear: New Critical Essays*, ed. and intro. by Jeffrey Kahan (New York: Routledge, 2008), pp. 231–52

Cartelli, Thomas, and Katherine Rowe, *New Wave Shakespeare: Shakespeare on Screen* (Oxford: Polity, 2007)

Chamberlain, Stephanie, 'She Is Herself a Dowry': *King Lear* and the Problem of Female Entitlement in Early Modern England', in *Domestic Arrangements in Early Modern England*, ed. and intro. by Kari McBride (Pittsburgh: Duquesne University Press, 2002), pp. 169–87

Champion, Larry, *Shakespeare's Tragic Perspective* (Athens: University of Georgia Press, 1976)

Clark, S. H., '"Ancestral Englishness" in *King Lear*', *Shakespeare Studies* (The Shakespeare Society of Japan), 31 (1996), 35–63

Clegg, Cyndia Susan, '*King Lear* and Early Seventeenth-Century Print Culture', in '*King Lear*': *New Critical Essays*, ed. by Jeffrey Kahan (New York: Routledge, 2008), pp. 155–83

Clemen, Wolfgang H., *The Development of Shakespeare's Imagery* (London: Methuen, 1951)

Cohen, Derek, 'The Malignant Scapegoats of *King Lear*', *Studies in English Literature*, 49.2 (2009), 371–89

Coleridge, Samuel Taylor, *Coleridge on Shakespeare: A Selection of the Essays, Notes and Lectures of Samuel Taylor Coleridge on the Poems and Plays of Shakespeare*, ed. by Terence Hawkes (Harmondsworth: Penguin., 1969)

Colie, Rosalie, *Paradoxia Epidemica: The Renaissance Tradition of Paradox* (Princeton: Princeton University Press, 1966)

Colley, Linda, *Britons: Forging the Nation, 1707–1837* (New Haven: Yale University Press, 1992)

Collick, John, *Shakespeare, Cinema and Society* (Manchester and New York: Manchester University Press, 1989)

Cook, Ann Jennalie, *Making a Match: Courtship in Shakespeare and His Society* (New Jersey: Princeton University Press, 1991)

Cooley, Ronald W., 'Kent and Primogeniture in *King Lear*', *Studies in English Literature*, 48.2 (2008), 327–48

Craig, Harold Leon, *Of Philosophers and Kings: Political Philosophy in Shakespeare's Macbeth and King Lear* (Toronto: University of Toronto Press, 2001)

Crowl, Samuel, *Shakespeare and Film: A Norton Guide* (New York and London: Norton, 2008)

Crowl, Samuel, *Shakespeare Observed: Studies in Performance on Stage and Screen* (Athens: Ohio University Press, 1992)

Cummings, Brian, *The Literary Culture of the Reformation: Grammar and Grace* (Oxford: Oxford University Press, 2002)

Danby, John F., *Shakespeare's Doctrine of Nature: A Study of 'King Lear'* (London: Faber and Faber, 1949)

Daugherty, Diane, 'The Pendulum of Intercultural Performance: Kathakali *King Lear* at Shakespeare's Globe', *Asian Theater Journal*, 22.1 (Spring 2005), 52–72

Desmet, Christy, 'Some *Lears* of Private Life, from Tate to Shaw', in *'King Lear': New Critical Essays*, ed. by Jeffrey Kahan (New York: Routledge, 2008), pp. 326–50

Diehl, Huston, 'Religion and Shakespearean Tragedy', in *The Cambridge Companion to Shakespearean Tragedy*, ed. by Claire McEachern (Cambridge: Cambridge University Press, 2002), pp. 86–102

Dillon, Janette, *The Cambridge Introduction to Shakespeare's Tragedies* (Cambridge: Cambridge University Press, 2007)

Diniz, Thaïs Flores Nogueira, 'Godard: A Contemporary *King Lear*', in *Foreign Accents: Brazilian Readings of Shakespeare*, ed. by Aimara de Cunha Resende (Newark, NJ: Delaware University Press, 2002), pp. 198–206

Dodd, William, 'Impossible Worlds: What Happens in *King Lear*, Act 1, Scene 1', *Shakespeare Quarterly*, 50.4 (1999), 476–507

Dollimore, Jonathan, *Radical Tragedy: Religion, Ideology and Power in the Drama of Shakespeare and His Contemporaries* (Brighton: Harvester, 1984)

Dollimore, Jonathan, *Radical Tragedy: Religion, Ideology and Power in the Drama of Shakespeare and His Contemporaries*, 2nd edn (London: Harvester Wheatsheaf, 1989)

Dollimore, Jonathan, and Alan Sinfield, eds, *Political Shakespeare: Essays in Cultural Materialism*, 2nd edn (Manchester: Manchester University Press, 1994)

Donaldson, Peter, *Shakespearean Films/Shakespearean Directors* (Boston: Unwin Hyman, 1990)

Donne, John, *An Anatomy of the World: The First Anniversary* (London, 1611)

Donne, John, *John Donne: The Complete English Poems*, ed. by A. J. Smith (London: Penguin Classics, 1986)

Doran, Madeleine, *The Text of King Lear* (Stanford, CA: Stanford University Press; London: Oxford University Press, 1931)

Dowden, Edward, *Shakespere: A Critical Study of His Mind and Art* (London: Henry S. King, 1875)

Drakakis, John, ed., *Shakespearean Tragedy* (Harlow: Longman, 1992)

Draper, J. W., 'The Occasion of *King Lear*', *Studies in Philology*, 34.2 (1937)

Dryden, John, *John Dryden: Selected Criticism*, ed. by James Kinsley and George Parfitt, Oxford Paperback English Texts (Oxford: Clarendon Press, 1970)

Dubrow, Heather, ' "They Took from Me the Use of Mine Own House": Land Law in Shakespeare's *Lear* and Shakespeare's Culture', in *Solon and Thespis: Law and Theater in the English Renaissance*, ed. by Dennis Kezar (Notre Dame, IN: Notre Dame University Press, 2007), pp. 81–98

Dusinberre, Juliet, 'Third Preface', *Shakespeare and the Nature of Women* (New York: Palgrave Macmillan, 2003)

Dusinberre, Juliet, *Shakespeare and the Nature of Women*, 2nd edn (New York: St Martin's Press, 1996)

Dutton, Richard, and Jean E. Howard, eds, *A Companion to Shakespeare's Works: The Tragedies* (Oxford: Blackwell, 2003)

Edwards, Michael, '*King Lear* and Christendom', *Christianity & Literature*, 50.1 (Autumn 2000), 15–29

Efalu, Paul A., 'Rethinking the Discourse of Colonialism in Economic Terms: Shakespeare's *The Tempest*, Captain John Smith's Virginia Narratives, and the English Response to Vagrancy', *Shakespeare Studies*, 28 (2000), 85–119

Egan, Gabriel, *Green Shakespeare: From Ecopolitics to Ecocriticism, Accents on Shakespeare* (London: Routledge, 2006)

Elton, William R., '*King Lear' and the Gods* (San Marino: Huntington Library, 1966)

Erne, Lukas, 'Editing the Real *Lear*', in L. Erne, *Shakespeare's Modern Collaborators* (London: Continuum, 2008), pp. 87–102

Erne, Lukas, *Shakespeare as Literary Dramatist* (Cambridge: Cambridge University Press, 2003)

Estok, Simon C., 'Shakespeare and Ecocriticism: An Analysis of "Home" and "Power" in *King Lear*', *AUMLA: Journal of the Australasian Universities Modern Language Association*, 103 (May 2005), 15–32

Everett, Barbara, 'The New *King Lear*', *Critical Quarterly*, 2 (1960), 325–39

Everett, Barbara, 'The New *King Lear*', in *Shakespeare, 'King Lear': A Casebook*, rev. ed. by Frank Kermode, Casebook Series (Basingstoke: Macmillan, 1992), pp. 159–76

Fernie, Ewan, *Shame in Shakespeare* (London and New York: Routledge, 2002)

Ferrell, Lori Anne, 'Method as Knowledge: Scribal Theology, Protestantism, and the Re-invention of Shorthand in Sixteenth Century England', in *Knowledge and Its Making in Early Modern Europe*, ed. by Pamela Smith and Benjamin Schmidt (Chicago: University of Chicago Press, 2008), pp. 163–77

Ferrell, Lori Anne, 'The Sacred, the Profane, and the Union', in *Politics, Religion, and Popularity in Early Stuart Britain: Essays in Honour of Conrad Russell*, ed. by T. Cogswell, R. Cust and P. Lake (Cambridge: Cambridge University Press, 2002), pp. 45–64

Ferrell, Lori Anne, 'William Perkins and Protestant Aesthetics', in *John Foxe and His World*, ed. by Chris Highley and John N. King (London: Ashgate, 1998), pp. 160–79

Fischlin, Daniel, and Mark Fortier, eds, *Adaptations of Shakespeare: A Critical Anthology of Plays from the Seventeenth Century to the Present* (New York: Routledge, 2000)

Flahiff, F. T., 'Lear's Map', *Cahiers Elisabéthains*, 30 (1986), 17–30

Foakes, R. A., *Hamlet Versus Lear: Cultural Politics and Shakespeare's Art* (Cambridge: Cambridge University Press, 1993)

Foakes, R. A., 'The Reshaping of *King Lear*', in *King Lear: New Critical Essays*, ed. and intro. by Jeffrey Kahan (New York: Routledge, 2008), pp. 104–23

Gibson, Jonathan, 'King Lear and the Patronage System', The Seventeenth Century, 14.2 (1999), 95–114

Gillies, John, 'The Scene of Cartography in King Lear', in Literature, Mapping, and the Politics of Space in Early Modern Britain, ed. by Andrew Gordon and Bernhard Klein (Cambridge: Cambridge University Press, 2001), pp. 109–37

Goodland, Katharine, 'Inverting the Pietà in Shakespeare's King Lear', in Marian Moments in Early Modern British Drama, ed. by Regina Buccola and Lisa Hopkins (Aldershot: Ashgate, 2007), pp. 47–74

Goodman, Elspeth, 'Women's Alternative Shakespeares and Women's Alternatives to Shakespeare in Contemporary British Theatre', in Shakespeare, Feminism and Gender, ed. by Kate Chedgzoy, New Casebooks (London: Palgrave, 2001), pp. 70–92

Goodman, Godfrey, The Fall of Man (London, 1616)

Gordon, Scott Paul, 'Reading Patriot Art: James Barry's King Lear', Eighteenth-Century Studies, 36.4 (2003), 491–509

Granville-Barker, Harley, 'King Lear', in Shakespeare Criticism 1919–35, ed. by Anne Ridler (London: Oxford University Press, 1936)

Granville-Barker, Harley, Prefaces to Shakespeare, vol. 1 (London: Batsford, 1930)

Granville-Barker, Harley, Prefaces to Shakespeare, vol. 1: Hamlet, King Lear, The Merchant of Venice, Antony and Cleopatra, Cymbeline, 2 vols (London: Batsford, 1958)

Greenblatt, Stephen, 'Invisible Bullets', in Political Shakespeare: New Essays in Cultural Materialism, ed. by Jonathan Dollimore and Alan Sinfield (Manchester: Manchester University Press, 1985)

Greenblatt, Stephen, 'Shakespeare and the Exorcists', in Critical Essays on Shakespeare's King Lear, ed. by Jay L. Halio (New York: G. K. Hall, 1996), pp. 88–121

Greenblatt, Stephen, 'Shakespeare and the Exorcists', in Shakespeare and the Question of Theory, ed. by Patricia Parker and Geoffrey Hartman (New York: Methuen), pp. 163–87

Greenblatt, Stephen, Shakespearean Negotiations: The Circulation of Social Energy in Renaissance England (Oxford: Clarendon Press, 1988)

Greg, W. W., 'Time, Place, and Politics in King Lear', Modern Language Review, 35.4 (1940), 431–46

Greg, W. W., The Variants in the First Quarto of 'King Lear': A Bibliographical and Critical Inquiry (London: Bibliographical Society, 1940)

Grene, Nicholas, Shakespeare's Serial History Plays (Cambridge: Cambridge University Press, 2002)

Griggs, Yvonne, ' "All Our Lives We'd Looked Out for Each Other the Way That Motherless Children Tend to Do": King Lear as Melodrama', Literature/Film Quarterly, 35.2 (2007), 101–7

Griggs, Yvonne, 'King Lear as Western Elegy', Literature/Film Quarterly, 35.2 (2007), 92–100

Griggs, Yvonne, Screen Adaptations: Shakespeare's 'King Lear': The Relationship Between Text and Film (London: A. & C. Black, 2009)

Grove, Richard H., *Green Imperialism: Colonial Expansion . . . and the origins of environmentalism, 1600–1860* (Cambridge: Cambridge University Press, 1995)

Gurr, Andrew, 'Headgear as a Paralinguistic Signifier in *King Lear*', *Shakespeare Survey*, 55 (2002), 43–52

Hadfield, Andrew, 'Briton and Scythian: Tudor Representations of Irish Origins', *Irish Historical Studies*, 28.112 (1993), 390–408

Hadfield, Andrew, '"Hitherto she ne're could fancy him": Shakespeare's "British" plays and the exclusion of Ireland', in *Shakespeare and Ireland: History, Politics, Culture*, ed. by Mark Thornton Burnett and Ramona Wray (London: Macmillan, 1997), pp. 47–67

Hadfield, Andrew, 'The Power and Rights of the Crown in *Hamlet* and *King Lear*: "The King – The King's to Blame"', *Review of English Studies*, n.s. 54.217 (2003), 566–86

Hadfield, Andrew, *Shakespeare and Renaissance Politics* (London: Thomson Learning, 2004)

Hadfield, Andrew, *Shakespeare, Spenser and the Matter of Britain* (Basingstoke: Palgrave Macmillan, 2004)

Halio, Jay L., 'The Study of Shakespearean Playbooks', in *Acts of Criticism: Performance matters in Shakespeare and his contemporaries: essays in honor of James P. Lusardi*, ed. by Paul Nelsen and June Schlueter (Madison, NJ: Fairleigh Dickinson University Press, 2006)

Halio, Jay L., *The Tragedy of King Lear* (Cambridge: Cambridge University Press, 1992)

Hallet, Charles, '*King Lear*, Act 3: Storming the Stage', in *Acts of Criticism: Performance Matters in Shakespeare and his Contemporaries: Essays in Honor of James P. Lusardi*, ed. by Paul Nelsen and June Schlueter (Madison, NJ: Fairleigh Dickinson University Press, 2006), pp. 126–43

Hamilton, Donna '*King Lear* and the Historical Edgars', in *Renaissance Papers, 1982*, ed. by A. L. Deneef and M. T. Hester (Raleigh: The South-eastern Renaissance Conference, 1983), pp. 35–42

Hardman, C. B., '"Our Drooping Country Now Erects Her Head": Nahum Tate's *History of King Lear*', *Modern Language Review*, 95.4 (2000), 913–23

Harris, Victor, *All Coherence Gone* (Chicago: Chicago University Press, 1949)

Harsnett, Samuel, *A Declaration of Egregious Popish Impostures* (London, 1603)

Harsnett, Samuel, *A Discouery of the Fraudulent Practises of Iohn Darrel Bacheler of Artes* (London, 1599)

Hawkes, Terence, 'Lear's Maps', in *Meaning by Shakespeare* (London: Routledge, 1992), pp. 121–40

Hawkes, Terence, *William Shakespeare's King Lear* (Plymouth: Northcote House, 1995)

Haydn, Hiram, *The Counter-Renaissance* (New York: Charles Scribner's Sons, 1950)

Hazlitt, William, *Characters of Shakespeare's Plays*, intro. by Sir Arthur Quiller-Couch, World's classics (Oxford: Oxford University Press, 1916)

Heinemann, Margot, 'Demystifying the Mystery of State: *King Lear* and the World Upside Down', in *Shakespeare and Politics*, ed. by Catherine Alexander and intro. by John Joughin (Cambridge: Cambridge University Press, 2004), pp. 155–68

Henderson, Diana E., ed., *A Concise Companion to Shakespeare on Screen* (Oxford: Blackwell, 2006)

Hibbard, G. R., '*King Lear*: A retrospect, 1939–79', *Shakespeare Survey*, 30 (1980), 1–12

Hiscock, Andrew, and Lisa Hopkins, eds, *Teaching Shakespeare and Early Modern Dramatists* (Basingstoke: Palgrave Macmillan, 2007)

Holahan, Michael, '"Look, her lips": Softness of Voice, Construction of Character in *King Lear*', *Shakespeare Quarterly*, 48.4 (1997), 406–31

Holderness, Graham, and Naomi Carter, 'The King's Two Bodies: Text and Genre in *King Lear*', *English*, 45.181 (1996), 1–31

Holinshed, R., *The Second Booke of the Historie of England* (London, 1587)

Holland, Peter, 'Mapping Shakespeare's Britain', in *Shakespeare's Histories and Counter-Histories*, ed. by Dermot Cavanagh, Stuart Hampton-Reeves and Stephen Longstaffe (Manchester: Manchester University Press, 2006), pp. 198–218

Hollis, Gavin, '"Give me the map there": *King Lear* and Cartographic Literacy in Early Modern England', *The Portolan*, 68 (2007), 8–25

Hooker, Richard, *The Works of Richard Hooker*, ed. by John Keble, 3 vols (Oxford: Clarendon Press, 1888)

Hopkins, Lisa, 'The Edge: *King Lear*', in *Shakespeare on the Edge: Border-crossing in the Tragedies and the Henriad* (Aldershot: Ashgate, 2005), 115–36

Hopkins, Lisa, 'Lear's Castle', *Cahiers Elisabéthains: Late Medieval and Renaissance Studies*, 62 (October 2002, xi), 25–32

Hopkins, Lisa, 'Reading between the Sheets: Letters in Shakespearean Tragedy', *Critical Survey*, 14.3 (2002), 5–13

Hopkinson, A. F., ed., *The True Chronicle History of King Leir*, Old English Plays (London: Sims, 1895)

Howlett, Kathy, *Framing Shakespeare on Film* (Athens: Ohio University Press, 2000)

Huang, Alexander C. Y., *Chinese Shakespeares: Two Centuries of Cultural Exchange* (New York: Columbia University Press, 2009)

Hughes, Alan, *Henry Irving, Shakespearean* (Cambridge: Cambridge University Press, 1981)

Hughes, John, 'The Politics of Forgiveness: A Theological Exploration of *King Lear*', *Modern Theology*, 17.3 (July 2001), 261–87

Hutchings, Mark, 'The End of II *Tamburlaine* and the Beginning of *King Lear*', *Notes and Queries: For Readers and Writers, Collectors and Librarians*, 47.1 (March 2000), 82–86

Hyman, Stanley Edgar, *The Armed Vision: A Study in the Methods of Modern Literary Criticism* (New York: Alfred A. Knopf, 1948)

Ioppolo, Grace, *A Routledge Literary Sourcebook on William Shakespeare's King Lear* (London: Routledge, 2003)

Jackson, Russell, ed., *The Cambridge Companion to Shakespeare on Film* (Cambridge: Cambridge University Press, 2000)

James I, *The Letters of James VI and I*, ed. by G. P. V. Akrigg (Berkeley and London: University of California Press, 1984)

James I, *King James VI and I: Political Writings*, ed. by Johann P. Sommerville (Cambridge: Cambridge University Press, 1994)

James, Henry, *The Scenic Art: Notes on Acting and the Drama, 1872–1901*, ed. by Allan Wade (London. R. Hart-Davis, 1949)

Jardine, Lisa, 'Boy Actors, Female Roles, and Elizabethan Eroticism', in *Staging the Renaissance: Reinterpretation of Elizabethan and Jacobean Drama*, ed. by David Scott Kastan and Peter Stallybrass (London and New York: Routledge, 1991), pp. 57–67

Jenkins, Gary W., 'Smith, Henry (c.1560–1591)', in *Oxford Dictionary of National Biography* (Oxford: Oxford University Press), www.oxforddnb.com/index/25/101025811/ [accessed 12 September 2004]

Jess-Cooke, Carolyn, '"The Promised End of Cinema": Portraits of Cinematic Apocalypse in Twenty-First-Century Shakespearean Cinema', *Literature/Film Quarterly*, 34.2 (2006), 161–68

Jess-Cooke, Carolyn, *Shakespeare on Film: Such Things as Dreams are Made Of* (London and New York: Wallflower, 2007)

Johnson, Samuel, 'Preface to the Edition of Shakespeare's Plays (1765)', in *Samuel Johnson on Shakespeare*, ed. by H. R. Woudhuysen (London: Penguin, 1989)

Jones, R. F., *Ancients and Moderns* (St Louis: Washington University Studies, 1961)

Jorgens, Jack J., *Shakespeare on Film* (New York and London: University Press of America, 1991)

Kahan, Jeffrey, ed., *King Lear: New Critical Essays* (New York and London: Routledge, 2008)

Kahn, Coppélia, 'The Absent Mother in *King Lear*', in *Rewriting the Renaissance: The Discourses of Sexual Difference in Early Modern Europe*, ed. by Margaret W. Ferguson, Maureen Quilligan and Nancy J. Vickers (Chicago: University of Chicago Press, 1986), pp. 33–49

Kahn, Coppélia, 'Magic of Bounty: *Timon of Athens*, Jacobean Patronage, and Maternal Power', in *Shakespearean Tragedy and Gender*, ed. by Shirley Nelson Garner and Madelon Sprengnether (Bloomington: Indiana University Press, 1996), pp. 135–67

Kahn, Paul W., *Law and Love: The Trials of King Lear* (New Haven: Yale University Press, 2000)

Keats, John, *Letters of John Keats: A New Selection*, ed. by Robert Gittings (London and Oxford: Oxford University Press, 1975)

Keats, John, *The Poems of John Keats*, ed. Miriam Allott (London: Longman, 1970)

Keats, John, *John Keats: Selected Poems*, ed. by John Barnard (London: Penguin, 1988)

Kelly, Philippa, *The Bell Shakespeare 'King Lear'* (Sydney: Halstead Press, 2002)

Kelly, Philippa, 'See What Breeds about her Heart: *King Lear*, Feminism, and Performance', *Renaissance Drama*, 33 (2004), 137–57

Kennedy, Dennis, *Looking at Shakespeare: A Visual History of Twentieth-Century Performance* (Cambridge: Cambridge University Press, 1993)

Kermode, Frank, ed., *Shakespeare: King Lear: A Casebook* (London: Macmillan, [1969] 1973; rev. edn, 1992)

Kermode, Frank, *Shakespeare's Language* (London: Allen Lane, 2000)

Kerrigan, John, *Archipelagic English: Literature, History, and Politics 1603–1707* (Oxford: Oxford University Press, 2008)

Kerrigan, John, 'Divided Kingdoms and the Local Epic: *Mercian Hymns* to *The King of Britain's Daughter*', *The Yale Journal of Criticism*, 13.1 (2000), 1–21

Kima, Keechang, 'Calvin's Case (1608) and the Law of Alien Status', *The Journal of Legal History*, 17.2 (1996), 155–71

Kishlansky, Mark, *A Monarchy Transformed: The Penguin History of England, 1603–1688* (London and New York: Penguin, 1997)

Klein, Bernhard, *Maps and the Writing of Space* (Basingstoke: Palgrave, 2001)

Knight, G. Wilson, *The Wheel of Fire: Interpretations of Shakespearean Tragedy* (London: Methuen, 1954)

Knights, L. C., *How Many Children Had Lady Macbeth? An Essay in the Theory and Practice of Shakespeare Criticism* (Cambridge: Minority Press, 1933)

Knowles, Richard, 'The Evolution of the Texts of *King Lear*', in *King Lear: New Critical Essays*, ed. and intro. by Jeffrey Kahan (London: Routledge, 2008), pp. 124–54

Kostis, Nicholas, and Claudine Herrmann, 'The Dramatic Motive of Incest in *King Lear*', *Shakespeare Studies* (Tokyo, Japan), 39 (2001), 22–58

Kott, Jan, *Shakespeare Our Contemporary*, trans. by Boleslaw Taborski (London: Methuen, 1964)

Kott, Jan, *Shakespeare Our Contemporary*, 2nd rev. edn (London: Methuen, 1967)

Kozintsev, Grigori, *'King Lear:' The Space of Tragedy: The Diary of a Film Director*, trans. from the Russian by Mary Mackintosh, intro. by Peter Brook (London and Berkeley: Heinemann Educational, California University Press, 1977)

Kronenfeld, Judy, *King Lear and the Naked Truth: Rethinking the Language of Religion and Resistance* (Durham and London: Duke University Press, 1998)

Lamb, Charles, 'On the Tragedies of Shakespeare', *The Reflector* (1810–11)

Lamb, Charles, 'On the Tragedies of Shakespeare' (1810), in *The Works of Charles Lamb in Two Volumes* (London, 1818), vol. 2, pp. 25–26

Lamb, Charles, *Charles Lamb on Shakespeare*, ed. by Joan Coldwell (Gerrards Cross: Smythe, 1978)

Lamb, Charles, and Mary Lamb, *Tales from Shakespeare* (Washington, DC: Folger Shakespeare Library, 1979)

Lawrence, Seán, 'The Difficulty of Dying in *King Lear*', *English Studies in Canada*, 31.4 (December 2005), 35–52

Lawrence, Seán, 'Gods That We Adore': The Divine in *King Lear*', *Renascence: Essays on Values in Literature*, 56.3 (Spring 2004), 143–59

Leech, Clifford, *Shakespeare's Tragedies: And Other Studies in Seventeenth Century Drama* (London: Chatto and Windus, 1950)

Leggatt, Alexander, *King Lear, Shakespeare in Performance* (Manchester: Manchester University Press, 1991; 2nd edn, 2004)

Lehmann, Courtney, 'The Postnostalgic Renaissance: The "Place" of Liverpool in Don Boyd's *My Kingdom*', in *Screening Shakespeare in the Twenty-First Century*, ed. by Mark Thornton Burnett and Ramona Wray (Edinburgh: Edinburgh University Press, 2006), pp. 72–89

Li, Ruru, '"Who Is It That Can Tell Me Who I Am? / Lear's Shadow": A Taiwanese Actor's Personal Response to *King Lear*', *Shakespeare Quarterly*, 57.2 (Summer 2006), 195–215

Linton, Joan Pong, 'Kurosawa's *Ran* (1985) and *King Lear*: Towards a Conversation on Historical Responsibility', *Quarterly Review of Film and Video*, 23.4 (August 2006), 341–51

Luther, Martin, *Luther's Works*, ed. by Hilton C. Oswald (Saint Louis: Concordia Publishing, 1972)

Luther, Martin, *Tischreden*, III (Weimar: Bohlau, 1983)

Lyons, Anthony, 'Visible Spirits: Kozintsev's Cinematic Art in *Koral Lier/King Lear*', *Use of English*, 55.1 (Autumn 2003), 27–36

MacDonald, Michael, and Terence R. Murphy, *Sleepless Souls: Suicide in Early Modern England* (Oxford: Clarendon Press, 1990)

Maerz, Jessica M., 'Godard's *King Lear*: Referents Provided Upon Request', *Literature/Film Quarterly*, 32.2 (2004), 108–14

Maguire, Laurie E., *Studying Shakespeare: A Guide to the Plays* (Oxford: Blackwell, 2004)

Manvell, Roger, *Shakespeare and the Film* (London: Dent, 1971)

Margolies, David, '*King Lear*: Kozintsev's Social Translation', in *Shifting the Scene: Shakespeare in European Culture*, ed. and intro. by Ladina Bezzola Lambert and Balz Engler (Newark, NJ: University of Delaware Press, 2004), pp. 230–38

Marsden, Jean I., *The Re-imagined Text: Shakespeare, Adaptation, and Eighteenth-century Literary Theory* (Lexington: University Press of Kentucky, 1995)

Marsden, Jean, 'Shakespeare and Sympathy', in *Shakespeare and the Eighteenth Century*, ed. by Peter Sabor and Paul Yachnin (Aldershot: Ashgate, 2008), pp. 29–41

Marsh, Nicholas, *Shakespeare: The Tragedies* (Basingstoke: Macmillan, 1998)

Massai, Sonia, 'Nahum Tate's Revision of Shakespeare's *King Lears*', *Studies in English Literature*, 40.3 (2000), 435–50

McLuskie, Kathleen, 'The Patriarchal Bard: Feminist Criticism and Shakespeare: *King Lear* and *Measure for Measure*', in *Political Shakespeare: New Essays in Cultural Materialism*, ed. by Jonathan Dollimore and Alan Sinfield (Manchester: Manchester University Press, 1985), pp. 88–108

McMullan, Gordon, 'The Colonization of Early Britain on the Jacobean Stage', in *Reading the Medieval in Early Modern England*, ed. by David Matthews and Gordon McMullan (Cambridge: Cambridge University Press, 2007)

Milton, John, *The History of Britain: A facsimile edition with a critical Introduction*, ed. by Graham Parry (Stamford: Watkins, 1991)

Miola, Robert, 'Jesuit Drama in Early Modern England', in *Theatre and Religion: Lancastrian Shakespeare*, ed. by Richard Dutton, Alison Findlay and Richard Wilson (Manchester: Manchester University Press, 2003), pp. 71–86

Montaigne, M. de, 'Of Phisiognomy', in *The Essays of Montaigne* (London: David Nutt, 1892), III

Mousley, Andy, *Renaissance Drama and Contemporary Literary Theory* (Basingstoke: Macmillan, 2000)

Murphy, Andrew, *Shakespeare in Print: A History and Chronology of Shakespeare Publishing* (Cambridge: Cambridge University Press, 2003)

Murry, John Middleton, *Shakespeare* (Jonathan Cape: London, 1956)

Myrick, Kenneth, 'Christian Pessimism in King Lear', in *Shakespeare 1564–1964*, ed. by Edward A. Bloom (Providence: Brown University Press, 1964), pp. 56–70

Nevo, Ruth, *Tragic Form in Shakespeare* (Princeton, NJ: Princeton University Press, 1972)

Newman, Neville F., 'Shakespeare's *King Lear*', *The Explicator*, 60.4 (Summer 2002), 191–93

Norden, John, *The Surveyors Dialogue* (1607)

Norden, John, *Vicissitudo Rerum* (1600)

Orwell, George, *Collected Essays*, 2nd edn (London: Secker and Warburg, 1961)

Orwell, George, *The Collected Essays, Journalism and Letters of George Orwell: 'My country right or left', 1940–1943*, II, ed. by Sonia Orwell and Ian Angus (New York: Harcourt, Brace & World, 1968)

Orwell, George, 'Lear, Tolstoy and the Fool', in *Shakespeare: King Lear: A Casebook*, ed. by Frank Kermode (London: Macmillan, [1969] 1973; rev. edn, 1992)

The Oxford English Dictionary, 2nd edn (Oxford: Clarendon Press, 1989)

Palfrey, Simon, *Doing Shakespeare* (London: Arden Shakespeare, 2005)

Palfrey, Simon, with Tiffany Stern, *Shakespeare in Parts* (Oxford: Oxford University Press, 2007)

Patterson, Annabel, *Shakespeare and the Popular Voice* (Oxford: Blackwell, 1989)

Peck, John, and Martin Coyle, *How to Study a Shakespeare Play*, 2nd edn (Basingstoke: Macmillan, 1985; 1995)

Peterson, Kaara L., 'Historica Passio: Early Modern Medicine, *King Lear*, and Editorial Practice', *Shakespeare Quarterly*, 57.1 (Spring 2006), 1–23

Planinc, Zdravko, ' . . . This Scattered Kingdom: A Study of *King Lear*', *Interpretation: A Journal of Political Philosophy*, 29.2 (2001/2), 171–85

Pocock, J. G. A., 'British History: A Plea for a New Subject', *Journal of Modern History*, 47 (1975), 601–28

Poole, Adrian, 'The Shadow of Lear's "Houseless" in Dickens', *Shakespeare Survey*, 53 (2000), 103–13

Poole, Adrian, *Shakespeare and the Victorians*, Arden Critical Companions (London: Arden Shakespeare, 2004)

Proudfoot, Richard, 'Some Lears', *Shakespeare Survey: An Annual Survey of Shakespeare Studies and Production*, 55 (2002), 139–52

Rackin, Phyllis, 'Misogyny Is Everywhere', in *A Feminist Companion to Shakespeare*, ed. by Dympna Callaghan (Oxford: Blackwell, 2000), pp. 42–56

Regan, Stephen, and Graham Martin, 'King Lear', in *Shakespeare: Texts and Contexts*, ed. by Kiernan Ryan (London: Macmillan, 2000), pp. 241–76

Reilly, Terry, '*King Lear*: The Kentish Forest and the Problem of Thirds', *Oklahoma City University Law Review*, 26.1 (2001), 379–401

Ribner, Irving, 'Shakespeare and Legendary History: *Lear* and *Cymbeline*', *Shakespeare Quarterly*, 7.1 (1956), 47–52

Rosen, Alan, '*King Lear* Without End: Shakespeare, Dramatic Theory, and the Role of Catastrophe', in *Dislocating the End: Climax, Closure and the Invention of Genre* (New York: Peter Lang, 2001), pp. 6–26

Rossiter, A. P., *Angel with Horns* (London: Longman, 1957)

Rothwell, Kenneth S., *A History of Shakespeare on Screen*, 2nd edn (Cambridge: Cambridge University Press, 2004)

Rubinstein, Frankie, 'Speculating on Mysteries: Religion and Politics in *King Lear*', *Journal of the Society for Renaissance Studies*, 16.2 (June 2002), 234–62

Rutter, Carol, *Enter the Body: Women and Representation on Shakespeare's Stage* (London and New York: Routledge, 2001)

Ryan, Kiernan, '*King Lear*', in *A Companion to Shakespeare's Works*, Volume I, *The Tragedies*, ed. by Richard Dutton and Jean E. Howard (Oxford: Blackwell, 2003), pp. 375–92

Ryan, Kiernan, '*King Lear*: A Retrospect, 1980–2000', in *Shakespeare Survey*, 55 (Cambridge: Cambridge University Press, 2002)

Ryan, Kiernan, ed., *Shakespeare: Texts and Contexts* (Basingstoke: Macmillan, 2000)

Ryle, Simon J., 'Filming Non-Space: The Vanishing Point and the Face in Brook's *King Lear*', *Literature/Film Quarterly*, 35.2 (2007), 140–47

Rymer, Thomas, *The Critical Works of Thomas Rymer*, ed. by Curt A. Zimansky (Westport, CT: Greenwood, 1971)

Salgādo, Gāmini, *Eyewitnesses of Shakespeare: First Hand Accounts of Performances, 1590–1890* (London: Chatto and Windus (for) Sussex University Press, 1975)

Sanders, Wilbur, *The Dramatist and the Received Idea: Studies in the Plays of Marlowe and Shakespeare* (Cambridge: Cambridge University Press, 1968)

Saunders, J. G., '"Apparent Perversities": Text and Subtext in the Construction of the Role of Edgar in Brook's Film of *King Lear*', *Review of English Studies*, 47.187 (1996), 317–330

Schafer, Elizabeth, *MsDirecting Shakespeare* (London: Women's Press, 1998)

Schiff, James, 'Contemporary Retellings: *A Thousand Acres* as the Latest *Lear*', *Studies in Contemporary Fiction*, 39.4 (1998), 367–81

Schleiner, Winfried, 'Justifying the Unjustifiable: The Dover Cliff Scene in *King Lear*', *Shakespeare Quarterly*, 36.3 (Autumn 1985), 337–43

Schneider, Ben Ross, Jr, 'King Lear in Its Own Time: The Difference that Death Makes', *Early Modern Literary Studies*, 1.1 (1995), 3.1–49

Schwyzer, Philip, '"Is this the promised end?" James I, *King Lear*, and the Strange Death of Tudor Britain', in *Literature, Nationalism and Memory in Early Modern England and Wales* (Cambridge: Cambridge University Press, 2004), pp. 151–74

Schwyzer, Philip, 'The Jacobean Union Controversy and *King Lear*', in *Accession of James I: Historical and Cultural Consequences*, ed. by Glenn Burgess, Roland Wymer and Jason Lawrence (London: Palgrave, 2006), pp. 34–47

Scott, William O., 'Contracts of Love and Affection: Lear, Old Age, and Kingship', *Shakespeare Survey*, 55 (2002), 36–42

Scott-Douglass, Amy, 'Theatre', in *Shakespeares after Shakespeare: An Encyclopedia of the Bard in Mass Media and Popular Culture*, ed. by Richard A. Burt, 2 vols (Westport and London: Greenwood, 2007), II, pp. 733–812

Seaver, Paul, 'Suicide and the Vicar General in Early Modern England', in *From Sin to Insanity: Suicide in Early Modern Europe*, ed. by Jeffrey Watt (Ithaca, NY: Cornell University Press, 2004), pp. 25–47, 195–99

Segal, Lore, '*King Lear*, Several Little Boys, and an Old Crazy Woman in My Mother's Nursing Home', *Parnassus*, 26.2 (2002), 29–30

Shakespeare, William, *The Chronicle History of King Leir: The Original of Shakespeare's 'King Lear*, ed. by Sidney Lee (London: Chatto and Windus, 1909)

Shakespeare, William, *The Complete Works*, prepared by William Montgomery and Lou Burnard, Oxford Electronic Publishing (Oxford: Oxford University Press, 1989).

Shakespeare, William, *The Family Shakespeare, in Ten Volumes*, ed. by Thomas Bowdler (London: Longman, 1855)

Shakespeare, William, *The First Quarto of King Lear*, ed. by Jay L. Halio, New Cambridge Shakespeare (Cambridge: Cambridge University Press, 1994)

Shakespeare, William, *The History of King Lear*, ed. by Stanley Wells, The Oxford Shakespeare (Oxford: Oxford University Press, 2000)

Shakespeare, William, *[King Lear] M. William Shak-speare: His True Chronicle Historie of the Life and Death of King Lear and His Three Daughters* (London [Nicholas Okes] for Nathaniel Butter, 1608). STC 22292 BEPD 265a (Q1)

Shakespeare, William, *King Lear*, ed. by J. S. Bratton, Theatre History Edition (Bristol: Bristol Classical Press, 1982)

Shakespeare, William, *King Lear*, ed. by Raffel Burton, with an essay by Harold Bloom (New Haven, CT: Yale University Press, 2007)

Shakespeare, William, *King Lear*, ed. by R. A. Foakes, The Arden Shakespeare, Third Series (Walton-on-Thames: Thomas Nelson, 1997)

Shakespeare, William, *King Lear*, ed. by Russell Fraser (New York: Signet, 1998)

Shakespeare, William, *King Lear*, ed. by Kenneth Muir, The Arden Shakespeare (London: Methuen, 1952)

Shakespeare, William, *King Lear*, ed. by Kiernan Ryan, New Casebooks Series (Basingstoke: Macmillan, 1993)

Shakespeare, William, *King Lear: A Norton Critical Edition*, ed. by Grace Ioppolo (New York: Norton, 2008)

Shakespeare, William, *King Lear: A Parallel Text Edition*, ed. by René Weis (London and New York: Longman, 1993; 2nd edn, 2010)

Shakespeare, William, *King Lear: The Tragedie of King Lear*, ed. by Nick de Somogyi (London: Nick Horn Books, 2004)

Shakespeare, William, *King Leir*, facsimile of the 1605 edition (London: Oxford University Press for the Malone Society, 1908)

Shakespeare, William, *King Leir*, ed. by Tiffany Stern, Globe Quartos Series (London: Nick Horn Books, 2002)

Shakespeare, William, *A New Variorum Edition of Shakespeare: King Lear*, ed. by Horace Howard Furness (Philadelphia: Lippincott, 1880)

Shakespeare, William, *The Norton Shakespeare: Based on the Oxford Edition*, ed. by Stephen Greenblatt, Walter Cohen, Jean E. Howard and Katharine Eisaman Maus (New York and London: Norton, 1997)

Shakespeare, William, *The Plays of William Shakespeare in Eight Volumes*, ed. by Samuel Johnson (London: J. and R. Tonson et al., 1765)

Shakespeare, William, *Richard III*, ed. by Antony Hammond, The Arden Shakespeare (London: Methuen, 1981)

Shakespeare, William, *The Riverside Shakespeare*, ed. by G. Blakemore Evans et al. (Boston, MA: Houghton Mifflin, 1974)

Shakespeare, William, *The Tragedy of King Lear*, ed. by Jay L. Halio, New Cambridge Shakespeare, rev. edn (Cambridge and New York: Cambridge University Press, 2005)

Shakespeare, William, *The Tragedy of King Lear*, ed. by Claire McEachern (London; New York: Pearson Longman, 2005)

Shakespeare, William, *William Shakespeare: The Complete Works*, ed. by Stanley Wells, Gary Taylor, John Jowett, and William Montgomery, 2nd edn (Oxford: Oxford University Press, 2005)

Shakespeare, William, *Works*, ed. by Stephen Greenblatt et al. (New York: Norton, 1997)

Shakespeare, William, *The Works of Shakespeare*, ed. by Lewis Theobald (London: A. Bettesworth and C. Hitch, [and] J. Tonson [etc.], 1733)

Shannon, Laurie, 'Poor, Bare, Forked: Animal Sovereignty, Human Negative Exceptionalism, and the Natural History of *King Lear*', *Shakespeare Quarterly*, 60.2 (2009), 168–96

Shaw, George Bernard, *Pen Portraits and Reviews* (London: Constable, 1932)

Shell, Alison, *Catholicism, Controversy and the English Literary Imagination: 1558–1660* (Cambridge: Cambridge University Press, 1999)

Shrimpton, Nicholas, 'Shakespeare Performances in Stratford-upon-Avon and London, 1981–2', *Shakespeare Survey*, 36 (1983), 149–55

Shurgot, Michael W., '"The Thing Itself": Staging Male Sexual Vulnerability in *King Lear*', *Shakespeare and Renaissance Association of West Virginia Selected Papers*, 22 (1999) (www.marshall.edu/engsr/SR1999.html#A20)

Sidney, Philip, *The Countess of Pembroke's Arcadia* (1590), Book II (reprinted in *Narrative and Dramatic Sources*, ed. by Geoffrey Bullough (New York: Columbia University Press, 1978), pp. 402–8

Skura, Meredith, 'Dragon Fathers and Unnatural Children: Warring Generations in *King Lear* and Its Sources', *Comparative Drama*, 42.2 (Summer 2008), 121–48

Smith, Bruce, 'Speaking What We Feel about *King Lear*', in *Shakespeare, Memory and Performance*, ed. by Peter Holland (Cambridge; New York: Cambridge University Press, 2006), pp. 23–42

Smith, Emma, *The Cambridge Introduction to Shakespeare* (Cambridge: Cambridge University Press, 2007)

Sokolyansky, Mark, 'Grigori Kozintsev's Hamlet and King Lear', in *Shakespeare on Film*, ed. and intro. by Russell Jackson (Cambridge: Cambridge University Press, 2000), pp. 199–211

Spotswood, Jerald W., 'Maintaining Hierarchy in *The Tragedie of King Lear*', *Studies in English Literature*, 38 (1998), 265–80

Sprott, S. E., *The English Debate on Suicide from Donne to Hume* (LaSalle, IL: Open Court, 1961)

Spurgeon, Caroline, *Shakespeare's Imagery: And What It Tells Us* (Cambridge: Cambridge University Press, 1935)

Starks, Lisa S., and Courtney Lehmann, eds, *The Reel Shakespeare: Alternative Cinema and Theory* (London: Associated University Presses, 2002)

Stetner, S. C. V., and O. B. Goodman, 'Lear's Darker Purpose', *Literature and Psychology*, 18 (1968), 82–90

Stoyle, Mark, 'Cornish Rebellions, 1497–1648', *History Today*, 47.5 (1997), 22–28

Stoyle, Mark, ' "Knowest Thou My Brood?": Locating the Cornish in Tudor and Stuart England', in *West Britons: Cornish Identities and the Early Modern British State* (Exeter: University of Exeter Press, 2002), pp. 29–49

Swinburne, Algernon Charles, *A Study of Shakespeare* (London: Chatto and Windus, 1880)

Takakuwa, Yoko, '(En) Gendering Desire in Performance: *King Lear*, Akira Kurosawa's *Ran*, Tadashi Suzuki's *The Tale of Lear*', in *Shakespeare and His Contemporaries in Performance*, ed. and preface by Edward J. Esche, intro. by Dennis Kennedy (Aldershot: Ashgate, 2000), pp. 35–49

Targoff, Ramie, *Common Prayer: The Language of Prayer in Early Modern England* (Chicago: University of Chicago Press, 2001)

Tate, Nahum, *The History of King Lear. Acted at the Duke's Theatre. Reviv'd with Alterations* (London, 1681). Wing S2918

Taunton, Nina, and Valerie Hart, '*King Lear*, King James and the Gunpowder Treason of 1605', *Renaissance Studies*, 17.4 (2003), 695–715

Taylor, Gary, and Michael Warren, eds, *The Division of the Kingdoms: Shakespeare's Two Versions of King Lear*, Oxford Shakespeare (Oxford: Oxford University Press, 1983)

Teimist, David, ' "Fortune, That Arrant Whore, Ne'er Turns the Key to th' Poor": Vagrancy, Old Age and the Theatre in Shakespeare's *King Lear*', *Cahiers Elisabéthains*, 71 (Spring 2007), 37–47

Teixeira, Antonio João, 'The Construction of National Identity in Shakespeare's *King Lear* and Its Filmic Adaptation by Peter Brook', *Ilha do Desterro: A Journal of Language and Literature*, 51 (July-December 2006), 283–99

Thomas, Keith, *Man and the Natural World: Changing Attitudes in England, 1500–1800* (London: Allen Lane, 1983)

Thompson, Ann, 'Who Sees Double in the Double Plot', in *Stratford-Upon-Avon Studies 20: Shakespearian Tragedy*, ed. by David Palmer and Malcolm Bradbury (New York: Holmes and Meier, 1984), pp. 47–75

Tillyard, E. M. W., *Shakespeare's History Plays* (London: Chatto & Windus, 1974)

Tink, James, ' "Expose Thyself to What [*sic*] Wretches Feel": The Figure of Bare Life in *King Lear* and *Timon of Athens*', *Shakespeare Studies* (Shakespeare Society of Japan), 43 (2005), 37–61

Tolstoy, Leo, *Tolstoy on Art*, ed. Aylmer Maude (London. Oxford University Press, 1924)

Traub, Valerie, 'Jewels, Statues and Corpses: Containment of Female Erotic Power in Shakespeare's Plays', in *Shakespeare and Gender: A History*, ed. by Deborah Parker and Ivo Kamps (London: Verso, 1995), pp. 120–41

Traub, Valerie, 'The Nature of Norms in Early Modern England: Anatomy, Cartography, *King Lear*', *South Central Review*, 26.1&2 (2009), 42–81

Trivedi, Poonam, *Shakespeare in India: 'King Lear'*: A Multimedia CD-ROM (2006). Available from poonamtrivedi2004@yahoo.com

Tromly, Fred B., 'Grief, Authority and the Resistance to Consolation in Shakespeare', in *Speaking Grief in English Literary Culture: Shakespeare to Milton*, ed. by Margo Swiss and David A. Kent (Pittsburgh: Duquesne University Press, 2002), pp. 20–41

Trousdale, Marion, 'A Trip Through the Divided Kingdoms', *Shakespeare Quarterly*, 37.2 (1986), 218–23

Turner, Henry S., '*King Lear* Without the Heath', *Renaissance Drama*, 28 (1997), 161–93

Vickers, Brian, *Shakespeare: The Critical Heritage: Vol. 4: 1753–1765*, The Critical Heritage (London. Routledge and Kegan Paul, 1976)

Visser, Nicholas, 'Shakespeare and Hanekom, *King Lear* and Land: A South African Perspective', in *Post-Colonial Shakespeares*, ed. by Ania Loomba and Martin Orkin (London: Routledge, 1998), pp. 205–17

Walworth, Alan, 'Cinema *hysterica passio*: Voice and Gaze in Jean-Luc Godard's *King Lear*', in *The Reel Shakespeare: Alternative Cinema and Theory*, ed. by Lisa S. Starks and Courtney Lehmann (Madison, NJ: Fairleigh Dickinson University Press; London: Assoc. University Presses, 2002), pp. 59–94

Ware, James, ed., *Two Histories of Ireland* (Dublin, 1633)

Warner, David, '*King Lear*', in *Performing Shakespeare's Tragedies Today: The Actor's Perspective*, ed. and intro. by Michael Dobson (Cambridge: Cambridge University Press, 2006), pp. 131–42

Warren, Michael, 'Quarto and Folio *King Lear* and the Interpretation of Albany and Edgar', in *Shakespeare: Pattern of Excelling Nature*, ed. by David Bevington and Jay L. Hallo (Newark: University of Delaware Press, 1978), pp. 95–107

Watson, Robert N., *Back to Nature: The Green and the Real in the Late Renaissance* (Philadelphia: University of Pennsylvania Press, 2006)

Watt, Jeffrey R., 'The Impact of the Reformation and Counter-Reformation', in *Family Life in Early Modern Times, 1500–1789*, ed. by D. I. Kertzer and Marzio Barbagli (New Haven: Yale University Press, 2001), pp. 125–54

Watt, Jeffrey R., 'Suicide, Gender, and Religion: The Case of Geneva', in *From Sin to Insanity: Suicide in Early Modern Europe*, ed. by Jeffrey Watt (Ithaca, NY: Cornell University Press, 2004), pp. 138–57

Weis, René, *King Lear: A Parallel Text Edition*, Longman Annotated Texts (London and New York: Longman, 1993; 2nd rev. edn, 2010)

Wells, Stanley, *Shakespeare in the Theatre: An Anthology of Criticism* (Oxford: Clarendon Press, 1997)

Wells, Stanley, Gary Taylor, John Jowett and William Montgomery, *William Shakespeare: A Textual Companion* (Oxford. Clarendon Press, 1987)

Werner, Sarah, *Shakespeare and Feminist Performance*, Accents on Shakespeare Series (London and New York: Routledge, 2001)

White, Robert, 'King Lear and Film Genres', in *Renaissance Poetry and Drama in Context: Essays for Christopher Wortham*, ed. by Andrew Lynch and Anne M. Scott (Newcastle: Cambridge Scholars Publishing, 2008), pp. 317–32

Williams, George Walton, 'Invocations to the Gods in *King Lear*: A Second Opinion', *Shakespeare Newsletter*, 251 (Winter 2001–2)

Wilson, Richard, *Secret Shakespeare: Studies in Theatre, Religion, and Resistance* (Manchester: Manchester University Press, 2004)

Wingate, Edmund, *Justice Revived: Being the Whole Office of a Justice of the Peace* (London, 1661)

Winstanley, Lilian, '*Macbeth*', '*King Lear*' *and Contemporary History* (Cambridge: Cambridge University Press, 1922)

Womack, Peter, *English Renaissance Drama* (Oxford: Blackwell, 2006)

Womack, Peter, 'Nobody, Somebody, and *King Lear*', *New Theatre Quarterly*, 23 (2007), 195–207

Woodbridge, Linda, *Vagrancy, Homelessness, and English Renaissance Literature* (Urbana and Chicago: University of Illinois Press, 2001)

Wortham, Christopher, 'Shakespeare, James I and the Matter of Britain', *English*, 45.182 (1996), 97–122

Wymer, Rowland, *Suicide and Despair in the Jacobean Drama* (Brighton: Harvester Press, 1986)

Yeats, W. B., *Michael Robartes and the Dancer* (Dundrum: Cuala Press, 1921)

Yong, Li Lan, 'Shakespeare and the Fiction of the Intercultural', in *A Companion to Shakespeare and Performance*, ed. by Barbara Hodgdon and W. B. Worthen (Oxford: Blackwell, 2005), pp. 527–49

Young, Bruce W., 'King Lear and the Calamity of Fatherhood', in *In the Company of Shakespeare: Essays on English Renaissance Literature in Honor of G. Blakemore Evans*, ed. and intro. by Thomas Moisan and Douglas Bruster, appendix by William H. Bond (Madison: Fairleigh Dickinson University Press, 2002), pp. 43–64

Zimmerman, Susan, ed., *Shakespeare's Tragedies* (New York: St Martin's Press, 1998)

Notes on Contributors

Lori Anne Ferrell is Professor of Early Modern Literature and History in the School of Arts and Humanities at Claremont Graduate University in California. She is the author, most recently, of *The Bible and the People* (Yale University Press, 2009) and is currently editing the St Paul's sermons of John Donne for *The Oxford Edition of the Sermons of John Donne* (Oxford University Press).

Joan Fitzpatrick is Lecturer in English at Loughborough University. Her third monograph *Food in Shakespeare*, was published by Ashgate in 2007 and her fourth, a dictionary entitled *Shakespeare and the Language of Food*, was published by Continuum in 2010. She is currently preparing an edition of three early modern dietaries for the Revels Companion Library Series published by Manchester University Press. She also writes the Sidney and Spenser section of *The Year's Work in English Studies* for Oxford University Press.

Andrew Hiscock is Professor of English at Bangor University, Wales. He has published widely on early modern literature, including the monographs *Authority and Desire: Crises of Interpretation in Shakespeare and Racine* (1996) and *The Uses of this World: Thinking Space in Shakespeare, Marlowe, Cary and Jonson* (2004). He has edited critical collections which include the 2008 *Yearbook of English Studies* devoted to Tudor literature, *Middleton: Women Beware Women* (2011), and co-edited *Teaching Shakespeare and Early Modern Dramatists* (2007) with Lisa Hopkins. He is co-editor of the journal *English* (Oxford University Press) and becomes the editor (English & American literature) for *Modern Language Review* (MHRA) in 2011. His forthcoming monograph is entitled *Reading Memory in Early Modern Literature* (Cambridge University Press).

Lisa Hopkins is Professor of English and Head of the Graduate School at Sheffield Hallam University and co-editor of *Shakespeare*, the journal of the British Shakespeare Association. Her most recent publications include *Christopher Marlowe, Dramatist* (Edinburgh University Press, 2008) and *The Cultural Uses of the Caesars on the English Renaissance Stage* (Ashgate, 2008). She has just completed an edition of Ford's *The Lady's Trial* for the Revels series and her forthcoming monograph is *Drama and the Succession to the Crown, 1561–1633* (Ashgate).

Philippa Kelly has published widely in Shakespeare studies and on the subject of individuality in sixteenth- and seventeenth-century England. Her latest book, *The King and I* was published by Continuum in the *Shakespeare Now! Series* in 2011. Philippa grew up in Australia and now lives in Berkeley, California, with her husband and son. She works as resident dramaturg for the California Shakespeare Theater, is a Visiting Fellow at the University of New South Wales, serves as a panel chair for Australia's Endeavour Foundation, teaches part-time for the University of California Osher Lifelong Learning program, and travels to Saudi Arabia to teach accreditation to university women.

Willy Maley is Professor of Renaissance Studies at Glasgow University and is author of *A Spenser Chronology* (1994), *Salvaging Spenser: Colonialism, Culture and Identity* (1997), and *Nation, State and Empire in English Renaissance Literature: Shakespeare to Milton* (2003), and editor, with Andrew Hadfield, of *A View of the Present State of Ireland* (1997). He has edited eight essay collections: with Brendan Bradshaw and Andrew Hadfield, *Representing Ireland: Literature and the Origins of Conflict, 1534–1660* (1993); with Bart Moore-Gilbert and Gareth Stanton, *Postcolonial Criticism* (1997); with David Baker, *British Identities and English Renaissance Literature* (2002); with Andrew Murphy, *Shakespeare and Scotland* (2004); with Alex Benchimol, *Spheres of Influence: Intellectual and Cultural Publics from Shakespeare to Habermas* (2007), with Philip Schwyzer, *Shakespeare and Wales: From the Marches to the Assembly* (2010), with Margaret Tudeau-Clayton, *This England, That Shakespeare: New Angles on Englishness and the Bard* (2010), and with Michael Gardiner, *The Edinburgh Companion to Muriel Spark* (2010).

John J. Norton is Associate Professor of English at Concordia University Irvine, California. Over the past several years he has served Concordia

University in a variety of roles, from international studies mentor to graduate supervisor to varsity tennis coach. He graduated in Applied Communication from Point Loma Nazarene University, San Diego, and subsequently trained for ministry at Talbot Theological Seminary. He earned a master's degree in English from California State University, Fullerton, and a PhD in English from Sheffield Hallam University, United Kingdom. He has published articles on literature and religion. He has also acted as a reader for the peer-reviewed journal *Early Modern Literary Studies*. He currently serves on the board of directors of Boy with a Ball, a non-profit mentoring organization that works with at-risk youth.

Anthony Parr is Professor of English at the University of the Western Cape in Cape Town, South Africa. He has edited a wide range of Renaissance drama, including plays by Ben Jonson for the Revels Plays and the forthcoming *Complete Works of Ben Jonson* (Cambridge), and by Shakespeare, Dekker and Middleton, as well as a collection of *Three Renaissance Travel Plays* (Manchester University Press, 1995). He has written several essays on travel writing, and is currently completing a book entitled *Renaissance Mad Voyages*, a study of the way in which the ancient trope of the fantastic voyage is activated in English travel and related enterprises as well as in literary uses of the voyage motif during the early modern period.

Peter Sillitoe studied English Literature at Bangor University, Wales, before completing a PhD on Renaissance drama and elite space at the University of Sheffield. He has taught at the universities of Sheffield, De Montfort and Wolverhampton, and is now a Marie Curie Research Fellow on his project at University College Cork. He has published several articles, including a study of civil war royalist nostalgia for Whitehall Palace in *The Seventeenth Century* journal, and is finishing a monograph entitled *Performing Spaces*.

René Weis is Professor of English at UCL where he has taught since 1980. He has edited a parallel Quarto / Folio text of *King Lear* for Longman Annotated Texts, 1993 (2nd revised edn 2010), *Henry IV Part 2* for the Oxford Shakespeare, and *The Duchess of Malfi and Other Plays of John Webster* for Oxford World's Classics. He is the author of a biography of Shakespeare published as *Shakespeare Revealed* (London: John Murray, 2007) and as *Shakespeare Unbound* (New York: Henry Holt, 2008). His book *The Yellow Cross* (Viking, Penguin, Knopf, 2000) has been widely translated. His new edition of *Romeo and Juliet* for the Arden Shakespeare will appear in 2011. In 2009 he was awarded a three-year Major Leverhulme Research Fellowship 2010–2013 for a book on the genesis of Verdi's opera *La Traviata*.

Ramona Wray is Senior Lecturer at the Queen's University of Belfast. She is the author of *Women Writers in the Seventeenth Century* (Northcote House, 2004) and the co-editor of *Screening Shakespeare in the Twenty-First Century* (Edinburgh University Press, 2006), *Reconceiving the Renaissance: A Critical Reader* (Oxford University Press, 2004), *Shakespeare, Film, Fin de Siècle* (Macmillan, 2000) and *Shakespeare and Ireland: History, Politics, Culture* (Macmillan, 1997). She is currently editing Elizabeth Cary's *The Tragedy of Mariam* for the Arden Early Modern Drama Series.

Index